PRAIS ERVICES

This book is definitely required reading for any head of development or advancement, or anyone in an advancement leadership role. The technical and regulatory environments are changing at a blistering pace, and with that, the importance of advancement services areas is growing exponentially. Any effective leader needs to have a grasp of the issues and practices of the field to be able to plan for—and lead—his or her organization, and this is just the ticket.

—Christina Pulawski, Principal, Christina Pulawski Consulting

John Taylor has clearly established himself as the point guard for the advancement services discipline. There isn't a veteran in our area who doesn't have John's name on their short list of people to go to for quick, good answers. In this book, John taps seasoned professionals in the advancement services industry to present a well-rounded resource—a must-read for the novice but also a solid refresher for those of us who have been around for years.

—Michael A. Reopell, Director, Advancement Information Systems, Williams College

CASE and John Taylor have put it all together in one easy-to-read "A to Z" on advancement services. The information is current, comprehensive, and well-researched. This book raises the bar on advancement services practices and challenges us to implement best practices.

—Anne Garvey, Senior Director, Development Administration & Operations, Development and Alumni Affairs, Wake Forest University Baptist Medical Center

Council For Advancement and Support of Education
1307 New York Avenue, NW
Suite 1000
Washington, DC 20005-4701
www.case.org

CASE Europe
Entrance A, Tavistock House North
Tavistock Square
London WC1H 9HX
United Kingdom

ISBN 10: 0-89964-408-2
ISBN 13: 978-0-89964-408-0
Printed in United States of America

Council for Advancement and Support of Education (CASE) is the professional organization for advancement professionals at all levels who work in alumni relations, communications, development and advancement services.

CASE offers high-quality training, information resources, and a wide variety of books and publications for advancement professionals.

For more information on CASE or a copy of our books catalog, visit *www.case.org*, or call (202) 328-5900.

Book design: TFW Design Inc.
Art Director: Angela Carpenter Gildner
Assistant Art Director: William A. Hayden
Editor: Theodore Fischer
Editorial Director: Lori A. Woehrle

2nd Edition

Advancement
SERVICES

A Foundation for Fundraising

John H. Taylor, Editor

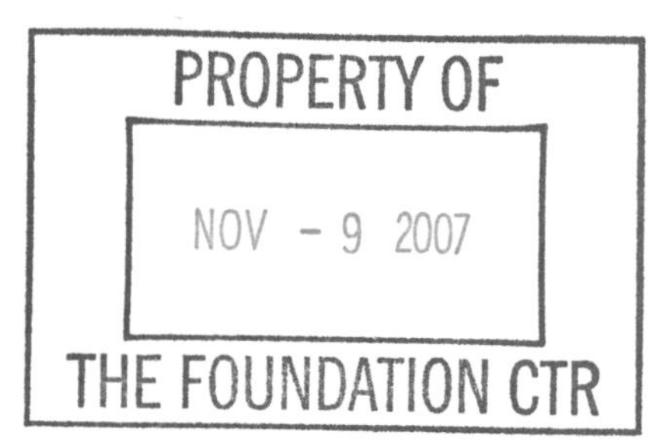

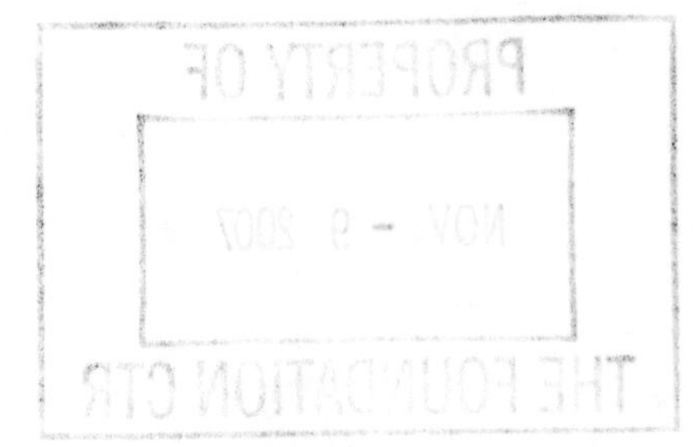

TABLE OF CONTENTS

The Changing Face of Advancement

In 2004 we saw a return to the "good old days" before September 11, 2001, when the economy was generally strong and people generally optimistic. To be sure, 9/11 had a devastating effect in many international arenas. Of particular note was its impact on philanthropy in the United States, where—for the first time in memory—charitable giving declined in most sectors.

Thankfully, the education community was largely spared the economic woes of the majority of the nonprofit community. For whatever reasons (although most likely related to alumni affinity), individual giving to education remained, at worst, flat during the two years after 9/11. In 2003 we began to see an upward curve, a trend that continued throughout 2004 and in 2005. Surveys indicated that 2005 would be a very good year, even in the wake of many natural disasters. A review of submissions for the CASE Circle of Excellence fund-raising awards for 2003-04 provided evidence that the sluggishness of the previous two years had diminished.

Yet those working in nonprofit management face challenges of a more structural and organizational nature than ever before. Certainly the economy continues to rank as the number one concern of fundraisers. When it slows or completely slumps, we all suffer. And the omnipresent, increasingly prominent issue of competition remains significant for nonprofits. In the past few years, the number of nonprofit organizations in the United States has grown by 25 percent, from approximately 1.2 million to 1.5 million. Disposable income, however, certainly has not increased at a similar pace. Nonprofit organizations that are substantially more worthy and viable than ever before are asking for funding from a comparatively static pool of available resources. And as our population becomes more highly educated, those working at educational institutions find themselves competing more and more fiercely with other organizations in the academic community, as well as with the increasing number of other nonprofit entities. "My" undergraduate degree holder may be "your" graduate degree holder, who may also be "someone else's" Ph.D. recipient. To compete, we have to become smarter in the areas of branding, marketing, public relations, etc. But this is not a surprising new development; it is just far more prevalent than it was 10 years ago.

At the heart of the changing context of advancement is the general public's undeniable lack of confidence in charitable organizations. Clearly, accounting fiascos in the for-profit sector have soured public opinion toward those institutions and directed their attention in a similar way toward nonprofit organizations. In the meantime, new laws and regulations are being enacted to address substantive issues in the for-profit sector. Many of these regulations are spilling over and in some cases directly affecting the nonprofit sector. The advancement community needs to be much more aware of these increasingly demanding and legalese-ridden directives. In this area, the advancement services community is taking the lead in pursing understanding of—and compliance with—the continually growing number of government regulations.

It has taken the nonprofit community more than three decades to understand the implications of the Family Education Rights and Privacy Act of 1974 (FERPA) on educational fundraising programs. More recently, the Health Insurance Portability and Accountability Act of 1996 (HIPAA) has directly influenced our activities, though it was written to protect individuals' health-related information. In 1999, the Graham-Leach-Bliley Act (GLB) was passed in an effort to place additional "controls" on financial institutions. Since then we have learned that nonprofit organizations are not exempt from many of these new regulations. Most recently, the Sarbanes Oxley Act (SOX), evolving out of widely publicized accounting scandals, was meant to affect for-profit organizations and their release of financial and accounting information, as well as to protect whistle-blowers who suspect misrepresentation of that data. Now we see in many states a variety of legislation and a spectrum of interpretation of SOX being applied to the nonprofit community. Additionally, the USA PATRIOT Act suggests "voluntary" best practices for charities with regard to governance, disclosure, financial accountability, and antiterrorist financing procedures.

In addition to these regulations, the IRS has been taking a much harder look at the nonprofit organizations' activities related to acceptance and receipting of charitable contributions. As a result of frequent filing of erroneous tax returns by individuals either claiming exaggerated gift amounts or reporting donations that did not comply with the law, the IRS has determined that the nonprofit sector must be held to higher accountability standards in accepting donations and reporting their value. Should we violate these new rules, much stiffer penalties are to be imposed. In the past year the IRS has issued new and burdensome regulations that directly affect how—and in some circumstances whether—nonprofits accept certain types of gifts.

We cannot control the imposition of many new rules and regulations that have an immediate impact on our fundraising activities. Significantly greater resources must be allocated to comply with these rules in tandem with our overall fundraising programs. Significantly greater respect for and understanding of the role of the advancement services community is critical at this changing time. There are signs that this is occurring; the most recent CASE compensation survey showed that those responsible for fundraising continue to be the most highly compensated, but advancement services personnel no longer lag behind the alumni relations or communications and marketing professions.

This publication is dedicated to all who work diligently for their organization behind the scenes. The various chapters should help us become better at what we do. I also hope, however, that those in other areas of advancement will have occasion to review these carefully scripted thoughts and ideas and gain a greater measure of understanding, and appreciation of what the advancement services professional does for the organization. We are all in this together—as equal partners.

—By John H. Taylor, Principal, Advancement Solutions

Advancement
SERVICES

Section I: Management

CHAPTER 1

Ethics of Advancement and Advancement Services

By Lynne D. Becker | Senior Counsel | Advancement Solutions

We hear that the world is becoming more complex, with a profusion of information that influences our decision making by informing or confusing it. In actuality, we face the same ethical dilemmas earlier generations faced. Is it ever right to lie? Have you ever decided not to tell the absolute truth? What kinds of guidelines are in place in your operation concerning ethical behavior, confidentiality, and reporting of conflicts? What do your present guidelines say? At what point do you begin discussing ethical behavior and confidentiality issues?

This chapter discusses three major ethical areas that concern all of us in the profession of fundraising and services: What guidelines work for personal behavior? I will look at the CASE Statement of Ethics. How do we handle our donors in an ethical manner? I will review the Association of Fundraising Professionals (AFP) Donor Bill of Rights. What are best ethical practices for organizations? I will examine the Independent Sector (IS) guidelines for responsible ethical behavior of organizations.

Ethical Guidelines for Fundraising Professionals

Have you ever considered not telling the absolute truth? When teaching about ethical issues, I always lead with this question and the following exercise. I ask everybody to turn to their neighbor and share their answer. Then I hear what they have to say. Each time the discussion breaks down into similar categories. There are the little white lies that are deemed unharmful and that preserve the social order. There are instances when the truth must be shared because another's welfare, respect, or personal relationship is at stake. And, finally, there are the situations in which legal issues come into play and laws determine an individual's actions.

I also hear during this exercise that we readily say public figures are bound by more stringent guidelines than are average citizens. So our adherence becomes introspective and circumstancial. These observations help explain why individuals who rise to prominent positions of leadership and power in our organizations have such a difficult time weighing in on ethical questions. Recently, countless violations of accounting principles by large corporations have brought home this realization. Hostile work environments, prosecutions for insider trading, and unethical gift acceptance are only a few examples of declining adherence to ethical principles.

Philosophers throughout history have debated these paradigms, and it is our responsibility to know exactly where we stand in these circumstances. Knowing ourselves enables us to be more ready to commit to ethical values in times of stress, unexpected developments, and expected dilemmas. Being prepared by having examined guidelines for personal behavior beforehand eliminates unsure footing and avoids costly mistakes.

Knowing ourselves enables us to be more ready to commit to ethical values in times of stress, unexpected developments, and expected dilemmas.

Review this statement of ethics from the standpoint of personal behavior, and remember the tenets as you conduct your daily work in the field of advancement:

CASE Statement of Ethics

Institutional advancement professionals, by virtue of their responsibilities within the academic community, represent their colleges, universities, and schools to the larger society. They have, therefore, a special duty to exemplify the best qualities of their institutions and to observe the highest standards of personal and professional conduct.

- In so doing, they promote the merits of their institutions and of education generally, without disparaging other colleges and schools.
- Their words and actions embody respect for truth, fairness, free inquiry, and the opinions of others.
- They respect all individuals without regard to race, color, sex, sexual orientation, marital status, creed, ethnic or national identity, handicap, or age.

- They uphold the professional reputation of other advancement officers and give credit for ideas, words, or images originated by others.
- They safeguard privacy rights and confidential information.
- They do not grant or accept favors for personal gain, nor do they solicit or accept favors for their institutions where a higher public interest would be violated.
- They avoid actual or apparent conflicts of interest and, if in doubt, seek guidance from appropriate authorities.
- They follow the letter and spirit of laws and regulations affecting institutional advancement.
- They observe these standards and others that apply to their professions and actively encourage colleagues to join them in supporting the highest standards of conduct.

The CASE Board of Trustees adopted this statement of ethics to guide and reinforce professional conduct in all areas of institutional advancement. The statement is also intended to stimulate awareness and discussion of ethical issues that may arise in our professional activities. The board adopted the final text in Toronto on July 11, 1982, after a year of deliberation by national and district leaders and countless volunteers among the membership.

Ethical Guidelines for Relating to Donors

Foremost after our own ethical behavior guidelines are the rights of our donors. In November 1999, CASE, AFP, American Association for Healthcare Philanthropy, and American Association of Fund-Raising Counsel adopted ethical standards and principles for dealing with donors. They felt these were the foundation for maintaining public trust. They also have developed a self-governed process for addressing ethical concerns.

The CASE Web site *(www.case.org)* and the AFP Web site *(www.afpnet.org/ethics)* contain a plethora of information, including a code of ethics with guidelines and standards, the donor bill of rights and principles for the online donor, position papers on selected ethics issues, principles of practice and a significant discussion about the emerging issues in our fast-paced business, including donor involvement, fundraising costs, and more.

The Donor Bill of Rights

Philanthropy is based on voluntary action for the common good. It is a tradition of giving and sharing that is primary to the quality of life. To ensure that philanthropy merits the respect and trust of the general public, and that donors and prospective donors can have full confidence in the nonprofit organizations and causes they are asked to support, we declare that all donors have these rights:

1. To be informed of the organization's mission, of the way the organization intends to use donated resources, and of its capacity to use donations effectively for their intended purposes.
2. To be informed of the identity of those serving on the organization's governing board, and to expect the board to exercise prudent judgment in its stewardship responsibilities.
3. To have access to the organization's most recent financial statements.
4. To be assured their gifts will be used for the purposes for which they were given.
5. To receive appropriate acknowledgment and recognition.
6. To be assured that information about their donation is handled with respect and with confidentiality to the extent provided by law.
7. To expect that all relationships with individuals representing organizations of interest to the donor will be professional in nature.
8. To be informed whether those seeking donations are volunteers, employees of the organization, or hired solicitors.
9. To have the opportunity for their names to be deleted from mailing lists that an organization may intend to share.
10. To feel free to ask questions when making a donation and to receive prompt, truthful, and forthright answers.

The large increase in online giving since 9/11, five hurricanes in fall 2004, the tsunami of December 26, 2004, hurricanes Katrina and Rita, and the 2005 earthquake in Pakistan have all justified the creation of the E-Donor Bill of Rights. In a timely manner, it addresses the concerns and challenges arising from charitable giving via the internet. The principles involve what we owe the donors as well as the expectations donors should have of our organizations when making their gifts.

We must work not only with our philanthropic organizations, but also with our online service providers to ensure that online donors have greater confidence in the organizations and causes they are asked to support. Because the internet is a relatively new medium for giving, we have to be aggressively diligent in protecting donors.

Because the internet is a relatively new medium for giving, we have to be aggressively diligent in protecting donors.

Principles of the E-Donor Bill of Rights

Online donors should demand the following of their online solicitors:

- To be clearly and immediately informed of the organization's name, identity, nonprofit or for-profit status, its mission and purpose when first accessing the organization's Web site
- To have easy and clear access to alternative contact information other than through the Web site or e-mail
- To be assured that all third-party logos, trademarks, trust marks, and other identifying, sponsoring, and/or endorsing symbols displayed on the Web site are accurate, justified, up-to-date, and clearly explained
- To be informed of whether a contribution entitles the donor to a tax deduction and of all limits on such deduction based on applicable laws
- To be assured that all online transactions and contributions occur through a safe, private, and secure system that protects the donor's personal information
- To be clearly informed if a contribution goes directly to the intended charity, or is held by or transferred through a third party
- To have easy and clear access to an organization's privacy policy posted on its Web site and be clearly and unambiguously informed about what information an organization is gathering about the donor and how that information will be used
- To be clearly informed of opportunities to opt out of data lists that are sold, shared, rented, or transferred to other organizations

- To not receive unsolicited communications or solicitations unless the donor has "opted in" to receive such materials

Since nonprofits rely on voluntary donations to meet a portion of their budgets, donor trust is of paramount importance.

We also should focus on the numerous Web sites established to facilitate online donations as a service to our organizations and the transaction fees associated with this activity. Recent laws adopted by at least 38 states require that the entities maintaining these Web sites not ask for money because they are not tax-exempt. They are only providing administrative and related services. As a result, such Web sites retain either a negotiated percentage or a uniform percentage of each donation as an administrative fee, deducted from the donation before payment of the net to our organizations.

Whether these sponsored Web sites are within ethical guidelines in their fee structure is the dilemma. This debate cannot be resolved here. The issue concerns the proper characterization of the "fee" taken by Web site operators who facilitate donations to our organizations. They are to be distinguished from those maintained by our own personnel for the purpose of receiving direct donations. The goal, therefore, is to keep such transactions and related fees similar to charges for electronic fund transfers, credit card fees, and stock transfers by brokerage houses.

Ethical Guidelines for Nonprofits

Nonprofit organizations are integral to society. Their fundraising programs reach areas of social need and cultural enrichment that for-profit enterprises often cannot address. Since nonprofits rely on voluntary donations to meet a portion of their budgets, donor trust is of paramount importance. To earn and keep that trust, these organizations must act ethically in every aspect. Nowhere is ethical behavior more essential, nor its absence more damaging, than in fundraising.

An ethical organization must have characteristics that act as checks and balances as it conducts day-to-day business. Being mission-led is a solid beginning. In addition, nonprofits should not give wrong messages or stray from their 501(c)(3) IRS classifications.

Training volunteers and ensuring programs are volunteer-driven provide additional ethical safeguards. And nonprofits must see that their staff members are professionally supported in an environment free of improper motive, unreasonable reward, or personal aggrandizement. Nonprofit organizations must represent high standards and ethical principles to continue to encourage the public trust. The Independent Sector Web site *(www.IndependentSector.org)* displays the code of ethics for nonprofits, as well as many recommended practices of national, regional, and subsector groups—a definitive compendium of standards, codes, and principles.

Statement of Values

Any code of ethics is built on a foundation of widely shared values. The values of the independent sector include:

- Commitment to the public good
- Accountability to the public
- Commitment beyond the law
- Respect for the worth and dignity of individuals
- Inclusiveness and social justice
- Respect for pluralism and diversity
- Transparency, integrity, and honesty
- Responsible stewardship of resources
- Commitment to excellence and to maintaining the public trust

These values lead to the Independent Sector's Code of Ethics for Nonprofit and Philanthropic Organizations that follows. The values inform and guide the actions that organizations should take in developing their policies and informing their practices.

Personal and Professional Integrity. All staff, board members and volunteers of the organization act with honesty, integrity, and openness in all their dealings as representatives of the organization. The organization promotes a working environment that values respect, fairness, and integrity.

Mission. The organization has a clearly stated mission and purpose, approved by the board of directors, in pursuit of the public good. All of its programs support that mission and all who work for or on behalf of the organization understand and are loyal to that mission and purpose. The mission is responsive to the constituency and communities served by the organization and of value to the society at large.

Governance. The organization has an active governing body that is responsible for setting the mission and strategic direction of the organization and oversight of the finances, operations, and policies of the organization. The governing body:

- Ensures that its board members or trustees have the requisite skills and experience to carry out their duties and that all members understand and fulfill their governance duties, acting for the benefit of the organization and its public purpose
- Has a conflict-of-interest policy that ensures that any conflicts of interest or the appearance thereof are avoided or appropriately managed through disclosure, recusal, or other means
- Is responsible for the hiring, firing, and regular review of the performance of the chief executive officer, and ensures that the compensation of the chief executive officer is reasonable and appropriate
- Ensures that the CEO and appropriate staff provide the governing body with timely and comprehensive information so that the governing body can effectively carry out its duties
- Ensures that the organization conducts all transactions and dealings with integrity and honesty
- Ensures that the organization promotes working relationships with board members, staff, volunteers, and program beneficiaries that are based on mutual respect, fairness and openness
- Ensures that the organization is fair and inclusive in its hiring and promotion policies and practices for all board, staff, and volunteer positions
- Ensures that policies of the organization are in writing, clearly articulated, and officially adopted
- Ensures that the resources of the organization are responsibly and prudently managed
- Ensures that the organization has the capacity to carry out its programs effectively

Legal Compliance. The organization is knowledgeable of and complies with all laws, regulations and applicable international conventions.

Responsible Stewardship. The organization and its subsidiaries manage their funds responsibly and prudently. This should include the following considerations:

- It spends a reasonable percentage of its annual budget on programs in pursuance of its mission.
- It spends an adequate amount on administrative expenses to ensure effective accounting systems, internal controls, competent staff, and other expenditures critical to professional management.
- The organization compensates staff, and any others who may receive compensation, reasonably and appropriately.
- Organizations that solicit funds have reasonable fundraising costs, recognizing the variety of factors that affect fundraising costs.
- Organizations do not accumulate operating funds excessively.
- Organizations with endowments (both foundations and public charities) prudently draw from endowment funds consistent with donor intent and to support the public purpose of the organization.
- Organizations ensure that all spending practices and policies are fair, reasonable, and appropriate to fulfill the mission of the organization.
- All financial reports are factually accurate and complete in all material respects.

Openness and Disclosure. The organization provides comprehensive and timely information to the public, the media, and all stakeholders and is responsive in a timely manner to reasonable requests for information. All information about the organization will fully and honestly reflect the policies and practices of the organization. Basic informational data about the organization, such as the Form 990, reviews and compilations, and audited financial statements will be posted on the organization's Web site or otherwise available to the public. All solicitation materials accurately represent the organization's policies and practices and will reflect the dignity of program beneficiaries. All financial, organizational, and program reports will be complete and accurate in all material respects.

Program Evaluation. The organization regularly reviews program effectiveness and has mechanisms to incorporate lessons learned in future programs. The organization is committed to improving program and organizational effectiveness and develops mechanisms to promote learning from its activities and the field. The organization is responsive to changes in its field of activity and is responsive to the needs of its constituencies.

Organizations that raise funds from the public or from donor institutions are truthful in their solicitation materials.

Inclusiveness and Diversity. The organization has a policy of promoting inclusiveness and its staff, board, and volunteers reflect diversity in order to enrich its programmatic effectiveness. The organization takes meaningful steps to promote inclusiveness in its hiring, retention, promotion, board recruitment, and constituencies served.

Fundraising. Organizations that raise funds from the public or from donor institutions are truthful in their solicitation materials. Organizations respect the privacy concerns of individual donors and expend funds consistent with donor intent. Organizations disclose important and relevant information to potential donors. In raising funds from the public, organizations will respect the rights of donors, as follows:

- To be informed of the mission of the organization, the way the resources will be used, and their capacity to use donations effectively for their intended purposes
- To be informed of the identity of those serving on the organization's governing board and to expect the board to exercise prudent judgment in its stewardship responsibilities
- To have access to the organization's most recent financial reports
- To be assured their gifts will be used for the purposes for which they were given
- To receive appropriate acknowledgment and recognition
- To be assured that information about their donations is handled with respect and with confidentiality to the extent provided by the law
- To expect that all relationships with individuals representing organizations of interest to the donor will be professional in nature

- To be informed whether those seeking donations are volunteers, employees of the organizations, or hired solicitors
- To have the opportunity for their names to be deleted from mailing lists that an organization may intend to share
- To feel free to ask questions when making a donation and to receive prompt, truthful, and forthright answers

Grant-maker Guidelines. Organizations that are grant makers have particular responsibilities in carrying out their missions. These include the following:

- They will have constructive relations with grant seekers based on mutual respect and shared goals.
- They will communicate clearly and on a timely basis with potential grantees.
- They will treat grant seekers and grantees fairly and with respect.
- They will respect the expertise of grant seekers in their fields of knowledge.
- They will seek to understand and respect the organizational capacity and needs of grant-seeking organizations.
- They will respect the integrity of the mission of grant-seeking organizations.

Studying these guidelines each day keeps front and center the principles we need to conduct ourselves ethically, personally, with our donors, and within our organizations. Public display of the Donor Bill of Rights, banners reminding us that "Ethics is an Everyday Activity," and ongoing discussions of ethics as we conduct our daily business will ensure that we are diligent in protecting the public confidence in our profession and the effectiveness of our service to society.

CHAPTER 2

The Advancement Services Team and its Role in a Conversion

By Gail A. Ferris | Director, Development Systems | United States Holocaust Memorial Museum

Many factors both internal and external play critical roles in determining whether your advancement services operation meets its goals. These factors include budget, availability of skilled staff, leadership, your institution's fundraising efforts, organizational history, duties outside the advancement sphere, and others.

Nonetheless, your operation can either overcome its limitations or fall short of its potential on the basis of one thing: teamwork. An environment that encourages teamwork may be the strongest determinant of success. Creating a productive team is challenging yet rewarding. It is vital to understand the mechanics of setting up a team, the roles its members play, and the stages you may encounter along the way to meeting your objectives.

This chapter explores factors that contribute to the creation of productive advancement services teams and shows how they can affect this challenge: conversion of advancement information systems.

Forming the Team

A team exists when individuals work together toward a common goal.

From this short sentence, three crucial themes emerge. First, the team must work together as a unit. Second, the unit must have clear goals so its members can focus their efforts. Finally, every member must share the goals, for without universal acceptance it will be impossible for the team to achieve optimal results.

Teamwork produces benefits at many levels. The organization profits from better use of staff resources because a team produces much more together than individuals working separately. Likewise, individuals benefit from a greater sense that they are working toward a common goal.

Teams can exist on several levels. The simplest type comes together on an ad hoc basis to solve a particular problem or work on a project of relatively short duration, such as implementing volunteer screening or developing a new gift-acceptance policy. Different in nature, but still governed by the same rules, are teams created within work units in advancement services—the prospect research staff, for instance.

Intermediate types include cross-functional teams developed for large projects drawing on many areas of the advancement services department and beyond. This is the kind of team that would accomplish a system conversion.

Mechanics of Team Building

1. Defining the team's mission. It is vitally important for the leader of any advancement services team to plan before assembling the team for a major project such as a conversion. Thinking through the team's mission and purpose is an essential first step. The team needs to define its own mission, but the team leader must guide this exercise. Having team members define the mission will result in your group's developing a sense of ownership.

2. Choosing members. In the initial planning stage, the team leader must examine the team's composition. Understanding that the group might discover that someone important to the team's success was overlooked, the leader still must decide on its initial composition. Six to eight members are ideal, although teams as large as 20 or as small as three, depending on the size of the organization, can be very effective. By choosing people who already have a vested interest in the project's mission, you help ensure that the right information is available, that those not present don't have to revisit decisions, and that individuals actually affected by the outcomes have influence. If it becomes apparent after assembling the team that someone important was overlooked, the leader can add that person, preferably at an early stage of the project.

Examine the qualifications and background of all proposed members to ascertain special contributions they can make. Valuable attributes for team members include organizational skills; ability to summarize, synthesize, and see the bigger picture; attentiveness to detail; inclusiveness; and the ability to be an effective educator.

Understanding the makeup of your team is essential to facilitating its success. I will discuss how you can observe your members to discern some of these qualities—if you do not already know them—as part of the leader's role in group work.

Understanding the makeup of your team is essential to facilitating its success.

3. Establishing ground rules. These are the behavioral norms team members can expect from one another in their various interactions, especially team meetings. Such rules are a powerful determinant of the group's informal structure and will heavily influence its success.

Draw up the ground rules when the team is created, and see to it that everyone subscribes to them from the start, keeping in mind that they may need tuning later on. Usually a team facilitator is charged with monitoring how well team members are adhering to the rules. The facilitator's role will be spelled out in greater detail in the section on structural roles.

A set of ground rules might include:

- Mutual respect of all members on the team
- Civil behavior and good manners
- Openness to questions
- Investing in communication
- Being specific and using examples
- Dealing directly with other team members
- Understanding and valuing one another's differences
- Being committed to one another's success
- Listening to one another

Team members should be:

- Committed to the institution
- Trustworthy
- Collaborative
- Dedicated to distributed decision making
- Innovative and risk-taking
- Results-oriented

By stipulating that everyone is expected to adhere to the ground rules, you make sure no one person has to be the "bad guy" when team members need to be reined in. Thus ground rules guide the team's operation.

4. Define operating procedures. Meetings are perhaps the most important means of team communication. They provide a forum for everyone to hear the same message, air differences on matters of importance related to achieving goals, and reach consensus on actions the team will take. Establishing procedures early will reduce the time you need to identify who is responsible for what as the work begins. The team should start developing these operating procedures by looking at the following logistical issues that must be addressed at the outset:

- How often will the team meet?
- When will it meet?
- Where will it meet?
- How long will the meeting be?
- Who will be responsible for which tasks?

All teams must consider these basic logistics. The ideal meeting lasts an hour to an hour-and-a- half; busy team members usually find it impossible to set aside more time than that. Meetings that drag on encourage spotty attendance. Enforcing time limits let groups accomplish more in less time. Setting a standard meeting schedule is also critical. Whether the meeting is weekly, biweekly, or monthly, knowing that the team meets at a predetermined frequency ensures good attendance. Team members have other jobs, too. And while their role in this team should be high priority, the ability to schedule around these meetings will help them perform their other work as well.

The meeting room's physical layout is important. Consider:

- Table configuration that lets all members see one another
- Comfortable chairs
- Adequate lighting
- Appropriate room temperature

- Meeting supplies, including a flip chart, tape, and markers
- Laptop and LCD projector
- A clock

Understanding Team Roles and Concerns

The team as a whole must deal with some functions. Collective responsibilities include setting the agenda, obtaining information the group needs, taking minutes and recording other information, making decisions, and communicating with others outside the group about issues the team is addressing. Other functions, however, require people in specific roles to take responsibility.

Structural Roles

Team members in structural roles require particular knowledge of group process. The job of those who play structural roles is to keep the team on track and moving toward the goal. They provide guidance about the members' roles and how they carry out their responsibilities, or about how a team functions best.

The team leader's job is to guide the team in performing its duties.

1. Team leader. The team leader's job is to guide the team in performing its duties. In addition to ensuring that the team meets its goals, the leader acts as a content resource for the team and knows problem-solving techniques. The leader needs to be trained in group process, if possible, and must have strong knowledge of the team and organizational missions and goals.

When the team comes together, the leader needs to closely observe the membership's makeup. Who are the high and low participators? Who is most influential and, more important, how does he or she do the influencing? Are most of the members autocratic, telling others what must happen, or are they more democratic, letting others contribute their thoughts? Given the ground rules, what are the dynamics of decision making for the group?

In addition, the leader needs to encourage behavior that contributes to creating a team atmosphere, maintaining harmonious working relationships, and getting the job done. Understanding what hinders or helps is critical to the leader's most important function: ensuring that everyone focuses on the task at hand and meets the team's goals.

2. Facilitator. The team facilitator is a person who understands how to make groups work well. His or her background includes education in group process, role definition, conflict resolution, meeting management, leadership issues and styles, motivation theory, decision-making styles, and similar topics.

If you want to encourage risk-taking, trust is essential.

Often a facilitator will have a contract with the team. To be effective, this person must remain a neutral observer. At no time should the facilitator offer an opinion about substantive matters before the team. The facilitator's role is to see that team members stay within the ground rules and set operating procedures; to advise them and teach them tools and techniques that will enhance their functioning; and to consult with the team leader.

Functional and Behavioral Roles

These roles determine how team members carry out their responsibilities. The roles evolve naturally, depending on how the group processes information and solves problems. One person may assume different roles depending on the nature of the task, and the roles may shift mid-task. These shifts often occur informally as time goes by and the mission attains clarity.

1. Information resource members. Whenever people gather in a group, issues of trust inevitably arise. If you want to encourage risk-taking, trust is essential. So early in the life of the team, members should place their trust in certain members who might be thought of as "information resource members." Their role will be to obtain information for the team, clarify obscure points, and summarize their findings for the team. Trust in them is significant because in many ways they will be defining the reality in which the team functions by getting the information the team needs and helping the team coalesce.

2. Helpful members. Because the team naturally seeks stability, maintenance roles soon develop. Those in maintenance roles are "helpful members," who encourage, harmonize, effect compromise, and bring the team to consensus. These team members help the group concentrate on the bigger picture, eventually leaving worries about consensus building behind. Helpful members facilitate movement toward the goal.

3. Obstructionist members. Unfortunately, some team members inevitably assume blocking roles until everyone in the group feels secure. These "obstructionists" hold themselves up as experts on the team's business; they tend to dominate, attack, doubt, withdraw, and seek recognition. The team leader must deal with these negative, know-it-all members in due course to accomplish the team's goals. Although frustrating and seemingly unproductive, spending time dealing with the issues obstructionists raise is perfectly normal, especially at the beginning of the team's work. As the team matures, less and less time is required for dealing with the obstructionist.

Team Concerns

Just as it is common for team members to play several roles, the team will have to deal with several types of concerns. Three areas of concern are inclusion, control, and openness.

1. Concerns about inclusion. All team members naturally want to feel accepted, like insiders. They want to know they are working for a clear and worthwhile common purpose; they receive recognition and support; and they can draw from the backgrounds, skills, and talents of other team members. Completing activities as a team will foster this sense of inclusion. So will establishing ground rules, objectives, and operating procedures and tackling behavioral issues. Once team members become "we" rather than "you," emotional maturity develops and the team can move on to bigger concerns.

2. Concerns about control. These concerns usually arise while a team is getting organized. Individual team members may become overzealous to express their individuality or resist group formation. They may argue among themselves and become competitive or defensive. During this period, you can expect tension, disunity, discomfort, and even open hostility. You can also expect the group to make only a small amount of progress until it organizes itself.

3. Concerns about openness. Emotional reactions are neither bad nor good; they are simply to be expected. However, the team's ability to encourage openness, including emotional openness, is vital. The job of the facilitator and the leader is to channel this emotional openness into a constructive relationship for the benefit of the team. If all goes well, expressing feelings freely will clear obstacles between the team and its goals.

Remember that all the self-oriented behavior described above is normal and usual while any team is preparing to go in the right direction. In fact, this behavior is helpful in settling control and inclusion issues. This is why the team leader must be prepared to ride out the conflicts and resist imposing a solution. Such attempts probably would be fruitless, as initial conflict often contributes to eventual team success.

For example, those inclined to fight are often the initiators, the critics, and the evaluators, who thus make critical contributions to the team. These are countered by those inclined to gloss over troubles, reducing tension with humor, or help the group rise above petty personal issues. Each individual brings strengths to the group; the challenge is to maximize the contribution each team member's strength can make to the team.

Applying Team Dynamics to a System Conversion

An understanding of team dynamics generally is a considerable asset in organizing for a system conversion. Projects of this magnitude and duration require a great deal of consensus building, conflict resolution, and unwavering focus on the goal.

Assembling the Conversion Team

Getting the right players on the conversion team is one of the most important factors in ensuring a smooth system conversion. The leader needs to be suited to the role by personality, knowledge, and relationship to the other players. Frequently the leader ends up being the head of advancement services, but often leadership will come from the information technology area. The leader must have an adequate technology background, but choosing the leader from the advancement services area is more likely to result in functional needs being met and understood. However, especially where leadership is weak in advancement services, the information technology specialist with a solid understanding of advancement business requirements may be more effective in leading the team.

Having a facilitator for the team is critical. With the team leader providing functional support, he or she should not be in the position of dealing with the logistics of setting up meetings or vendor demonstrations and circulating materials; otherwise, the leader will not be able to perform the functions of that position, or not in a timely fashion, and the project will be damaged. A strong facilitator can keep this from happening.

Once the team's goal and mission have been defined as system selection and conversion, the leader's next critical task is selecting team members. Advancement services clearly will play a key role, along with representatives from biographic records, gift processing, prospect research and management, and donor relations. Information technology will need strong representation, within and outside advancement, depending on the organization's structure. Fundraising, alumni/constituent relations, accounting, and public relations probably also will need representation on the team.

The team's first task should be to determine whether conversion is necessary, desirable, and feasible.

To Convert or Not

Many conversion efforts make the mistake of starting from the position that conversion is a foregone conclusion. The team's first task should be to determine whether conversion is necessary, desirable, and feasible. Factors to be taken into account in determining whether to convert include:

- Age, efficiency, and cost of maintaining existing hardware
- Utility, cost, and compliance with standards of existing software
- User satisfaction with existing software, including an analysis of the users' "wish list" and "need list" and the level of "freelancing" occurring to work around software deficiencies
- Practical factors, such as response time, shoring, and adequacy of features
- Changes in business needs
- Changing customers, such as new users of the existing system since it was implemented, and potential new users of a new system
- New technology, such as Web interfaces and document imaging

Specifications and RFPs

Once the team has determined that a new system is needed, it proceeds to a determination of the system's requirements. A SWOT (strengths, weaknesses, opportunities, and threats) analysis is often an effective starting point for this part of the team's work.

The process should begin with a frank and thorough documentation of the strengths and weaknesses of the existing system, as well as the opportunities and threats presented by a conversion. In the team's meetings, all ideas and concerns should be recorded, with chart and easel being an effective medium for all team members to ensure that their thoughts are properly interpreted. This discussion also should confront institutional issues, such as limitations imposed by policy, politics, practicality, or budget.

From here the team should explore what a new system could do for the institution. The team's advancement services and information technology members should have a good idea of functionality available in products on the market, and they can work with other members to determine which might or might not be relevant to the institution. It is always a good idea at this stage to check with members' contacts at other institutions for information and ideas, to determine best practices that your institution can follow.

. . . ask other institutions that have developed a system RFP to share theirs . . .

After the team has determined the requirements of the new system, reduce them to a request for proposal (RFP). This document is necessary to send to vendors so they can make their proposals responsive to the institution's needs. It is a good practice to ask other institutions that have developed a system RFP to share theirs with you; this can save a great amount of time and effort for the team.

An RFP typically includes:

- Executive summary
- Functional description
- Output/outcomes
- Project timeline
- Standards: CASE, FASB/GASB, IRS, state
- Key contacts
- Implementation requirements
- Proposal requirements

Research on vendors to whom the institution plans to send the RFP should begin during RFP assembly. Again, team member contacts at other institutions and attendance at professional meetings can provide useful information. The RFP should circulate as widely as possible to potential vendors offering products that appear to meet the institution's needs, since many probably will not submit proposals. Considering whom to send the RFP may be part of institutional purchasing policies, which could eliminate some vendors—especially if the institution is using public money for the purchase. Be sure to send the RFP to a contact person, not simply a vendor address, and be sure to enclose a response card.

Managing Proposals

To keep the project on schedule, it is important for the team facilitator to take the lead in managing proposals. They should be logged in as they are received, and the facilitator should review them to ensure that they respond to the RFP. Proposals meeting RFP requirements should circulate among all team members, without exception, for review. Team members then will be in a position to determine which vendor proposals will advance to the reference and demonstration stage of the selection process.

Once the team has agreed on a short list of vendors, reference checking should begin. These checks may include not only the "official" references listed in the proposal but also "unofficial" references from team members with contacts at other institutions using the systems. Querying various listservs also can yield good reference candidates. For all reference checks, it is important that team members be professional and discreet.

After thinning the list through reference checking, team members gain additional exposure to the software through demonstration. The team needs to formulate a uniform agenda or script for all the vendor demonstrations to provide a level playing field on which to judge the systems most accurately. These agendas should be distributed to vendors before their arrival on site. Vendors that do not follow the agenda should be deemed unresponsive, as if their proposals had not corresponded to the points of the RFP.

When all vendor demonstrations are complete, site visits to other institutions to view the installed systems can begin. It is important for the team to formulate an agenda for the site visit to make sure it judges all systems by the same standards, and so it does not succumb to the temptation of touring the other institution's advancement services or information technology operations.

Now the team is ready to make its recommendation. At this point, the team leadership needs to hear everyone's opinions without allowing the decision-making process to grind to a halt. A parallel tension may exist between the need for team members to buy into a consensus decision and the proclivity of some team members to hold out for their favored system. Focusing the team on institutional goals should help mitigate the tendency toward putting smaller departmental goals first.

Implementing the System

Budgeting

. . . contingency costs of a system conversion typically run 10 percent to 15 percent beyond sticker price.

Even before signing the contract with the vendor, the administrator must confirm that institutional funding is available to pay for the implementation of the system as proposed. Most budgets cover the implementation's "sticker price," which usually includes hardware and software. However, frequently overlooked contingency costs of a system conversion typically run 10 percent to 15 percent beyond sticker price. Some "sneak" costs may include consultants, overtime, temporary help, copying, training, rework, and testing. To obtain the necessary contingency funding, team members should enumerate contingencies they can see from their areas. The team as a whole should ask for the necessary funding at the beginning of the conversion.

Planning the Conversion

The team needs to start conversion planning with a comprehensive appraisal of the skills needed at the various stages of the process. Although the team should have had representation from all affected areas of the institution from the outset, members from each area need to identify the amount of resources necessary for implementation. Key areas for additional resources include:

- Technology support
- Advancement staff from all areas
- Institutional leadership
- Finance and accounting
- Vendor support

Once the vendor has been selected, it becomes a de facto member of the conversion team, and adequate identification of vendor resources is crucial. The availability of resources will be the major factor in determining the project timeline. Establishing the timeline also requires a reality check on a number of fronts, including:

- Overall institutional preparedness
- Data integrity of the existing system
- Personnel skill sets
- Other institutional priorities
- Calendar considerations

Technology planning forms a special subset of the team's work. Considerations include whether the new system constitutes a major technological change for the institution, entailing retooling of current staff. Database administration probably will shift substantially in the course of a conversion. If retraining technical staff is necessary, this is the time to undertake it, not in the throes of the conversion.

Planning for conversion procedures will streamline the team's work as the conversion shifts into high gear. Many documents will result from the process, and it is critical that they be handled so they will be available when needed. Another area that can make or break a conversion is training. Team members should be polled on particular training needs for their areas since different types of training will be appropriate for disparate groups such as data-entry staff, end-users who primarily query the database, and technical staff.

Often, reporting is mistakenly left until the final stages. But with adequate planning, it should be addressed in tandem with conversion of the data to the new system. A subcommittee may form with key members representing their areas. It then prioritizes the reporting needs for the technical staff who will do the programming.

Completing the Conversion

Once the conversion plan is in place, in an ideal world everyone could focus all energies on the project. However, in the real world, this is seldom the case. The exigencies of everyday work still command much of the team's time. To navigate the resulting time conflicts and keep the conversion on schedule, the team needs to reach consensus on two critical questions:

- Who handles new efforts during the conversion period?
- What new initiatives will be supported, by whom, and with how much prior notice?

. . . as the checkpoints are successfully achieved, the team needs to announce and celebrate its successes.

Issues of life after conversion will begin to emerge on the team's agenda:

- What opportunities for different distribution of duties does the new system permit?
- If users are not all "onboard," what will be necessary to obtain their participation?

Communication becomes a critical function for all team members as the conversion shifts into high gear. It is important to establish reality checks on the conversion timeline; as the checkpoints are successfully achieved, the team needs to announce and celebrate its successes. On the other hand, if or when the unexpected happens, the team has to know its alternatives and keep its constituencies abreast of what is happening, since misinformation can be very damaging to the project at this stage.

As the conversion reaches its final stages, communication again is critical to seeing the goals of the conversion through to accomplishment. Letting end-users know how the new system will permit them to perform their jobs more effectively reduces anxiety while helping ensure that their transition is smooth. At this point, it is important to communicate the team's roles and responsibilities for the post-conversion period, explaining exactly how they will be available to support end-users during this stressful time. Finally, the team needs to establish formal communication mechanisms that will continue after the conversion, in the form of meetings, newsletters, or other forms of communication.

Molding an effective team can have a critical impact on institutional advancement projects great and small, whether based in one area of advancement services or spanning your institution. In a major project such as a system conversion, following the basic rules will help ensure that your team completes the project successfully and on time. By investing in educating staff in effective team dynamics, the institution will reap the maximum benefit from its human resources in pursuing critical institutional goals.

CHAPTER 3

Easy and Effective Campaign Reporting

By Scott Fendley | Director of Advancement Services | Wabash College

Reporting on any fundraising campaign, especially a comprehensive capital campaign, is absolutely critical. Knowing its status at any time during the campaign is vital for campaign management and for staff who need information to be timely, accurate, and relevant.

This can be daunting because you may have several masters. The president's staff may want one set of information, the campaign committee another, the comptroller or controller another, and so on.

Compounding the complications of fulfilling these requests are the idiosyncrasies of fundraising software. What may seem like a straightforward task may require hours to program and result in reports that may turn out to be incomplete or unusable.

In an effort to serve all the masters, staff sometimes create reports that have considerable information that may or not be relevant to other constituents. Because of software limitations, some reports may have hidden inaccuracies. Or if one tries to simplify reports too much, an inaccurate picture could result.

Campaign reporting may seem an intimidating task. But it need not be. It may not fulfill the textbook definition of "easy," but reporting can be simpler than it may seem at first.

Planning—The Key to Success

Effective campaign reporting depends on planning. Whether you have to design a set of reports from the onset of a campaign or have to start in the middle, planning your reporting strategy is most important for success. Planning can reduce and eliminate potential problems, such as:

- Rewriting reports to suit various offices' needs

. . . planning your reporting strategy is most important for success.

- Requests for minor variations in reports for one office's needs
- Duplication of reporting efforts among offices
- Reactive instead of proactive report requests
- Lack of clarity and focus in the reports
- Finding limitations in your software and reporting package after reports have been generated and distributed
- Lack of flexibility in accommodating new reporting needs
- Inability to compare reports from one reporting period to the next

While you may find it more difficult to solve these problems in the middle of a campaign, planning a new reporting strategy before implementing new and improved reports will make the problems surmountable.

What follows is advice on matters to remember in planning.

Know the Case for Support

The statement for support of any fundraising campaign is the one document that lists campaign priorities and the amount the institution hopes to raise to reach its goals. It is imperative that the overall fundraising reports refer to this statement, so you can measure how much each initiative must raise, what cash flow and pledge expectations are for these areas, how many planned gifts are due, and how much will have to come from unrestricted funds to make up the difference.

Each of the funds to which donors can give should be linked in your fundraising software to an overall area of support. It is critical to complete this task before the campaign begins. One should work with development, advancement, and the business office to make sure the funds are mapped correctly; otherwise, remapping funds will require changes to the reports and make comparative reports more difficult to produce.

Any new fund set up during the course of a campaign also should be mapped properly when entered in the software system. This should be done before any gifts or pledges are recorded to that fund, otherwise various reports might not tie together.

While this seems elementary, I have seen instances where campaign reports have been generated with individual funds not tied to a particular case for support, but rather to a broader area of support that encompassed several of the individual cases. In one example, funds under one case for support were split among several overall areas of support, leading to a logistical nightmare when staff realized that the campaign reports should be tied to the case for support.

Know the Database and Reporting Medium

Each development software package has its share of unique characteristics and challenges for reporting. Some packages make it fairly straightforward to report on pledges and cash flows, but not on contacts by major gift officers. Others capture a rich amount of data but are challenging when related to third-party payment reporting. Still others make it easy to report in Excel or Access, but difficult to extract the data for Web-based reporting.

Some questions to ask are:

- How does the database store and retrieve gift and pledge information?
- How does the database handle special pledge cases (pledges paid early, or designation changes for one payment of a pledge, or partially paid, written-off pledges)?
- Does the software have a built-in reporting tool?
- How can the data be extracted to the reporting tool of choice?
- How does the software handle planned or deferred gifts?
- How does the software store and retrieve contact information?
- How can we summarize this information to produce quantitative reports?
- What reports can we set up for end-users to execute independently, and what must be massaged further before distribution?

Be sure reports can be generated for CASE and Council for Aid to Education (CAE). Institutions may have different ways to report internally on yearly and long-term fundraising campaigns; however, it is imperative that reports be written to match the CASE Management and Reporting Standards, as both these organizations require.

If you have a large or complicated database, constructing a data warehouse may offer the best solution for reporting. This allows you to report as of the prior day's activities without bogging down the database. Then gift entry and other updates can be performed at maximum processing capacity.

By understanding the architecture of the software package, one can plan reports that will gather all the information from the database and present it in an appealing manner.

Know the Audience

What may appear to be an awesome report could fail if it does not reach the proper audience. Not everybody connected with a campaign needs to know every last detail of campaign activity. Everyone loves to know the campaign total, but some care only marginally about campaign cash flows; others may not care about the actual day-to-day increases in the campaign total.

Not everybody connected with a campaign needs to know every last detail of campaign activity.

Also, the audience may want the report in different formats. Some may want hard copy only, while others will want spreadsheets and tables so they can do their own analysis. Still others may want Web-based reports for portability.

The best way to tackle this is to do a reporting census. Meet with all the people who have a need for campaign reporting and find out what information they want, how they want it presented, and in what format they want the reports. Be sure to keep the limitations of your software and reporting tools in mind while performing this poll. One could take this opportunity to make a case for a software change or enhanced reporting tools.

Take the poll and construct reports that best suit the largest audience. The ideal situation would be to have these reports generated automatically and sent to the recipients via e-mail in a format such as Excel or a PDF file, or generated and reported on a secure Web site.

Certainly some reports will need to be written for a limited audience. Some may want information that pertains only to their operation. In those situations, construct the reports so that the end-user can run the report on an as-needed basis, if at all possible (based on your software limitations). But before constructing reports for limited audiences, be sure to ask how this information will be used and how often it is needed, so that the most accurate report can be delivered and does not have to be altered after its creation.

Periodically check with each department to see if the current reports are meeting its needs. Being proactive in reporting means less scrambling when it comes to report changes and enhancements and allows for discussion of why the change is needed. It also allows time to examine how that change will affect others' use of the information in the report. Also, continue to improve delivery of reports. Pushing more reports to be automatically delivered to the end-users and producing more Web-based reports permits more flexibility in creating new reports and enhancing existing reports.

Report Design—Keep It Simple

When designing campaign reports, keep them as simple and concise as possible. Do not try to mix several different types of information in one report, unless the report is a broad brush of all campaign activities. Even then the report should be as simple and concise as possible.

Use large, clear, and readable fonts in your reports. Include headers, footers, and dates to ensure readers know exactly what report they are looking at and when it was generated. Make sure tables and charts are clear and the key information is highlighted.

If possible, try to keep the information on one page (especially for summary reports). If you have reports that go into a great deal of detail on multiple pages, be sure to include page numbers, headers, footers, and dates on all the pages.

Graphs are an excellent way to present information. Keep them as simple as possible and use colors that will look distinguishable on both color and gray-scale printers. Complicated pie charts will lose effect if you cannot tell the differences in shading of the pieces.

Sample Reports

The following are sample campaign reports. There are many ways to measure the success and progress of a campaign effort, and it is easy to get bogged down in minutiae. Keep the formats simple, the data clear and easy to read, and the information relevant.

Overall Progress Report

This report is a good overview of campaign activity for the week. It shows pertinent fundraising information for both the campaign and the annual fund, the number of open proposals, and new contributors.

Campaign Report by Priority

This report is an overview of countable campaign gifts, cash received, and planned/deferred gifts received by the area of support spelled out in the campaign case statement.

A cash flow report is a companion report to this, spelling out the due dates for the open pledges for the next five years of the campaign.

The Campaign - Report by General Funding Area
6/30/2004

	Campaign Goal	Total Gifts and Pledges	Cash Collected	Open Pledges	Total Planned Gifts
Science	$33,000,000	$1,868,780	$763,129	$105,652	$1,000,000
Scholarships	$5,000,000	$18,799,547	$13,695,929	$1,250,468	$3,853,149
Professorships	$4,000,000	$4,437,872	$982,002	$729,834	$2,726,037
Innovation	$2,500,000	$2,064,087	$1,162,938	$160,176	$740,973
Student Institute	$2,000,000	$340,683	$246,240	$94,443	$0
Research	$10,750,000	$1,491,888	$1,342,656	$149,232	$0
Admissions Facility	$2,000,000	$2,064,470	$2,064,470	$0	$0
Athletic Center	$25,000,000	$3,281,789	$3,275,362	$6,427	$0
Residences	$18,000,000	$9,438,113	$2,926,009	$2,669,105	$3,842,999
Fund for the Future	$5,750,000	$1,284,984	$1,264,984	$20,000	$0
Annual Fund	$12,500,000	$20,268,835	$16,159,434	$3,930,276	$179,125
Philanthropy Fund	$12,000,000	$1,131,369	$1,006,374	$24,995	$100,000
Undesignated	$0	$69,649,565	$34,718,890	$8,311,055	$26,619,620
TOTALS	$132,500,000	$136,121,982	$79,608,416	$17,451,663	$39,061,903

Planned Giving Summaries

Planned giving is an important part of any campaign. It is vital that the planned giving office, the campaign cabinet, the treasurer, and the business office know the status of all of the planned gifts received during the campaign for planning and cash flow purposes.

Campaign Planned Giving Summary
6/30/2004

Estimated Maturation Date	Booked Pledges	Assets "Received"	Face Value	Present Value	Future Value
0-5 years	$5,055,520	$4,540,520	$5,055,520	$3,910,615	$5,055,520
5-10 years	$3,924,75	$2,277,323	$3,924,75	$3,814,934	$4,871,504
10-15 years	$15,395,663	$1,270,357	$16,871,688	$12,541,873	$27,208,770
15-20 years	$5,913,533	$1,048,719	$6,067,824	$4,721,001	$6,280,094
20-25 years	$3,110,225	$111,044	$4,817,146	$2,216,563	$7,891,556
25-30 years	$4,680,001	$21,037	$12,918,137	$5,226,608	$18,522,694
30-35 years	$766,875	$0	$3,587,500	$985,650	$5,159,303
35-40 years	$215,330	$0	$811,320	$661,080	$5,230,127
TOTALS	$39,061,903	$9,269,000	$54,053,892	$34,078,324	$80,219,569

By Vehicle	Booked Pledges	Assets "Received"	Face Value	Present Value	Future Value
Bequests	$19,157,990	$3,518,404	$30,507,784	$16,571,896	$44,855,988
CRTs	$12,497,069	$3,439,294	$14,501,373	$9,099,743	$17,663,807
IRA Bequest	$4,819,531	$0	$6,268,635	$6,061,116	$14,258,598
Annuities	$1,681,222	$1,405,211	$1,870,008	$1,439,477	$1,869,988
Real Property	$906,092	$906,092	$906,092	$906,092	$1,571,188
TOTALS	$39,061,903	$9,269,000	$54,053,892	$34,078,324	$80,219,569

Chart of Donations by Source

This graph illustrates the source of the contributions received for the campaign. This is important to measure, as many boards feel that although they have an obligation to give generously, they do not want to "foot the bill" for the campaign.

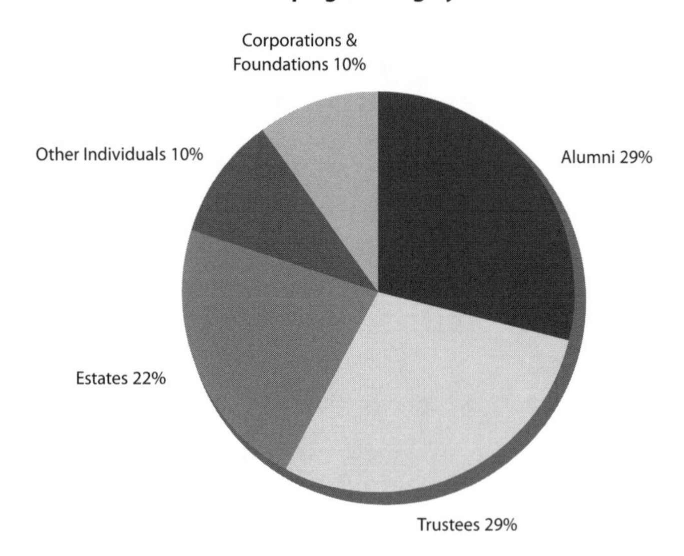

Personal Visits and Contacts by Year

Keeping track of visits and contacts by your development officers is crucial for staff development and to ensure that your officers are on the road seeing prospects, making solicitations, closing gifts, and exercising stewardship. A simple graph will tell you how the development staff is progressing on visits and signal that something may be changing in the dynamic of the campaign.

Personal Visits and Contacts

Contacts
Personal Visits
2500
2000
1500
1000
500
0
Contacts
1998 1999 2000 2001 2002 2003 2004
Year

Campaign reports need not be daunting. By planning in advance, knowing the software's limitations and restrictions, communicating with your audience regularly, and keeping the reports simple, clean, and direct, you will find that campaign reporting will be less of a headache for advancement services and more of a benefit to the end-users of the information and the institution's decision makers.

CHAPTER 4

Creating Comparative Reports:
Three Ways to Track Progress in Your Fundraising Performance

By Madelyn Miller | Director, Information Services | Case Western Reserve University

As an old adage goes, "You can't figure out where you are going until you see where you have been." That is why you should gather data, analyze it, and then prepare reports that give insights into both your institution's fundraising performance and that of other institutions. Such comparative reports are valuable in two main ways. They help with strategic planning by revealing your development office's strengths and weaknesses, and they form a statistical basis for setting private-support priorities and goals.

Comparative reports are a significant part of the strategy we use to develop fundraising objectives at Case Western Reserve University. They provide the context in which we judge areas of opportunities and national trends in philanthropy. They help us determine where we have been and provide a map to where we should be going.

Although your advancement office can use comparative reports to make your institution look good, at times they may uncover facts that make it look not so good. Don't worry. You still have not wasted your time. Reports that reveal weaknesses can show internal staff the areas that need more attention and help convince your administration to invest in areas that need shoring up.

There are three basic kinds of comparative private-support reporting:

1. Institutional internal reporting typically shows your institution's historical data on private support by source, by fund account, and by the schools or management centers on your campus. These reports highlight giving trends and the impact of your past fundraising efforts.

2. National ranking reporting compares data from your institution with data from other educational institutions nationally. These reports display comparison data from all national institutions or from subsets of institutions categorized by the Carnegie Classification of Institutions of Higher Education.

3. Peer group reporting displays data for 10 to 12 institutions similar to your own. You determine your peer group by examining similarities in student enrollment, size of alumni base, and size of endowment, among other things.

For the purposes of this chapter, we will assume that every month your advancement services office is already preparing at least a cumulative private-support report by source, fund account, and school, if your institution has more than one management center. We also will assume that you use the CASE Management and Reporting Standards as a basis for recording private support data in your database. The need for reports is one of the best reasons for adhering to the CASE standards. They provide universal definitions of what constitutes an alumnus and what can be considered unrestricted giving, to name just two topics. When you use the standards and analyze data from peer institutions that do likewise, you can feel confident you are comparing apples to apples and getting reliable results.

Before you begin to create a set of comparative reports, identify both their purpose and the audience . . .

Let's examine the subject of reports in two parts. First we will look at the basic steps in gathering and organizing your data. Then we will discuss the best ways to handle the three most important types of reports.

Reporting Basics

Before you begin to create a set of comparative reports, identify both their purpose and the audience you are targeting. These will determine the types of reports you create and the results they bring to your development office.

The data collection process at Case Western Reserve University dates to 1985. We first used it to measure our performance against that of other private research institutions as a means to educate our administration about the realities of fundraising. Those early findings helped convince our president and the trustees that although we were spending only 3 cents to raise a dollar, we were

Forecasting Capital Campaign Results A Formulaic Approach to the Question, 'Will We Reach the Goal?'

About halfway through the public phase of a capital campaign, fundraisers often bring up questions about the ultimate total of the campaign. Usually they ask, "Will the goal be met?" Whether the institution is doing well and wants to explore increasing the goal, or whether some believe reaching the goal is in jeopardy, the campaign cabinet, board of trustees, comptroller, treasurer, and your campaign staff may want to know the answer to that question at some point.

The following models can be used to forecast the end result of a campaign. Gathering data on closed campaign prospects (whether they have made a gift or pledge to the campaign or were removed from the pyramid) by rating level, and using those data to model how prospects at the same rating level will act during the balance of the campaign, will result in a pair of projections for the final total.

These models will yield distinct results—one based on the yield to capacity of donors to date, the second based on the median campaign giving of donors to date. The yield-to-capacity model will generally forecast a higher result than the median model, but running both models will give a range of potential results.

Because the models are based on past performance, at least two years' public-phase data are needed for them to be as accurate as possible. Otherwise, there is a chance that enough data will not be accumulated to make a good estimate.

The data needed for these models are the following:

1. **Number of closed prospects per prospect financial-rating level.** Find out how many prospects have been moved off the campaign pyramid, whether by signing a pledge card, saying no to a proposal, or having a major gift officer report that a person is not a viable prospect in the campaign. Include prospects who have died during the campaign in this total.

2. **Total campaign giving for the above closed prospects per rating level.** For these data, adjustments may be necessary, as no doubt outliers will appear. Someone rated as a $10,000 donor may have given a planned gift that is countable at more than $250,000. That will be rare but will skew the data set. A good rule of thumb is to remove from the data all gifts that are 10 times more than the rating level ($100,000 for a $10,000 donor, and so on). After removing the outliers from that data set, calculate the total giving and the median giving for each of the prospect groups. (Using the median instead of the mean is a more conservative approach in this analysis.)
3. **Number of remaining prospects on the pyramid per prospect rating level,** no matter where they are in the cultivation cycle.

Yield-to-Capacity Model

Step One: Figure the yield percentage of your current closed prospects.

Min. Rating	Closed Perspective	Capacity of Closed Perspective	Total Campaign Gifts for Closed Prospects	Actual Yield
$10,000	228	$2,280,000	$4,300,466	188.62%
$25,000	132	$3,300,000	$1,819,196	55.13%
$50,000	132	$6,600,000	$4,031,487	61.08%
$100,000	98	$9,800,000	$7,001,342	71.44%
$250,000	23	$5,750,000	$3,753,895	65.28%
$500,000	17	$8,500,000	$10,040,622	118.12%
$1,000,000	13	$13,000,000	$10,474,161	80.57%

Adjusted Gifts For Closed Prospects	Adjusted Actual Yield
$2,213,457	97.08%
$1,819,196	55.13%
$2,337,228	35.41%
$7,001,342	71.44%
$3,753,8956	5.28%
$4,738,322	55.74%
$10,474,161	80.57%

The yield of a group of prospects is calculated by taking the total campaign gifts for all closed prospects and dividing it by the total capacity of the closed prospects. The capacity is the minimum rating of the prospect groups multiplied by the number of prospects in that group. To be conservative, use the minimum rating, so even though a prospect might be rated at $75,000, she would fall in the $50,000 range in this model (assuming the prospect range is $50,000 to $99,000).

Remember, closed prospects include all prospects closed, not only prospects you have closed a gift on and moved to stewardship.

The adjusted gifts for closed prospects exclude any considered outliers, which would skew the results greatly. If the results seem high, reexamine the individual data sets in each rating group to see if other outliers should be removed.

Step Two: Project the remaining campaign prospects.

Min. Rating	Prospects	Total Capacity	Adjusted Actual Yield	Projected Yield Percentage
$10,000	389	$3,890,000	97.08%	$3,776,469
$25,000	349	$8,725,000	55.13%	$4,809,845
$50,000	218	$10,900,000	35.41%	$3,859,967
$100,000	105	$10,500,000	71.44%	$7,501,438
$250,000	21	$5,250,000	65.28%	$3,427,200
$500,000	11	$5,500,000	55.74%	$3,065,973
$1,000,000	9	$9,000,000	80.57%	$7,251,342
Total	**1102**	**$53,765,000**		**$33,692,234**

In this step, multiply the percentage yield and total capacity to come up with a projected yield.

Step Three: Add the projected yield to the current campaign total.

Projected Yield:	$33,692,234
Campaign Total to Date:	$70,754,176
Final Campaign Total:	$104,446,410

(Note: The Campaign Total to Date will not equal above total campaign gifts of closed prospects because of gifts from donors not rated, gifts from corporations and foundations, matching gift expectancies, unexpected bequests, and other gifts and pledges).

Median Campaign Giving Model

Step One: Calculate the median campaign giving for each group of prospects.

Min. Rating	Closed Prospects	Median Campaign Gift per Closed Prospect
$10,000	228	$5,223
$25,000	132	$4,288
$50,000	132	$5,640
$100,000	98	$45,125
$250,000	23	$112,514
$500,000	17	$241,343
$1,000,000	13	$1,264,451

The median campaign giving should be calculated after the outliers (the same as in the other model) have been removed, to provide the most accurate projection.

Step Two: Project the remaining prospects using the median giving as calculated above, multiplying the median for the prospect rating range by the number of prospects left in that range.

Min. Rating	Prospects	Median Campaign Gift per Closed Propsect	Expected Median Campaign Gift
$10,000	389	$5,223	$2,031,553
$25,000	349	$4,288	$1,496,338
$50,000	218	$5,640	$1,229,618
$100,000	199	$45,125	$8,979,875
$250,000	21	$112,514	$2,362,804
$500,000	11	$241,343	$2,654,774
$1,000,000	9	$1,264,451	$11,380,057
Totals	**1196**		**$30,135,019**

Step Three: Add the projected yield to your campaign total.

Projected Yield:	$30,135,019
Campaign Total to Date:	$70,754,176
Final Campaign Total:	$100,889,195

The closer you get to the end of the campaign, the more accurate the model will be in forecasting the campaign total.

You may need to consider other factors while calculating the models. If the economy suddenly shifted downward during the campaign, then it might be prudent to use data only from the most recent 18 months or two years of campaign activity to calculate the yield and the medians. Also, if the quiet or silent phase of the campaign raised an exceptional amount but the public phase of the campaign has not been so stellar, then it might be prudent to calculate the models based just on the results of the public phase to date. The key is to be as conservative as possible when constructing the data set and the models.

These models may also be used for calculating the fundraising totals for a specific project. If there is a campaign to restore the library, for example, and prospects interested in giving some restricted dollars to the library have been identified, then the same models can be run using the past prospects for the library as the data set for the yield and median. When calculating the yield and median giving for the models, be careful to use only the restricted dollars the past prospects have given toward the specific project, not their overall giving to the campaign.

I tested these models at Wabash College during a capital campaign that ended June 30, 2004. After running these models for two years (starting in late 2001), we decided that because the economy had dramatically shifted downward over the past few years, we needed to concentrate on our yield and median gifts for the previous 24 months when calculating the projections. The median gift projection gave us a total of $134.1 million dollars, the yield-to-capacity projection gave us a total of $141.0 million, and we achieved a total of $136.1 million dollars. Even though the yield projection was $4.9 million dollars high, it was within 3.6 percent of our actual campaign total.

The key to projecting the final campaign total is making sure accurate data are in your database, not only for current prospects but for prospects who have moved off the pyramid. Without this information, the data will lack credibility, and the projections may be skewed.

Above all, remember this is a projection; events out of the institution's control can affect the results of the campaign down the road. However, these calculations do serve as useful tools to determine where the capital campaign is heading, and they can help the institution develop the courses of action needed to achieve its ultimate goal.

—Scott Fendley, Director of Advancement Services, Wabash College

raising much less than our peer institutions, and we needed to invest more in our fundraising programs.

We also used our data collection to identify for both internal and external decision makers our fundraising "competition" and set our sights on national peers, not the smaller nonprofits in Cleveland. We did this exercise not to compete for dollars with other private research institutions, but rather to say that Case Western Reserve University should be doing in Cleveland what Duke does in Raleigh-Durham and Washington University does in St. Louis.

Gathering Data

One of the most important decisions you must make before you begin your research is how to define your data source or sources.

One of the most important decisions you must make before you begin your research is how to define your data source or sources.

For internal data comparisons, you must decide whether to extract your data from historical, hard-copy reports or pull the data from your computer system. If you use reports produced historically, you'll be reporting data as recorded in the year the report was produced. Obviously, this is the optimum choice.

However, the downside to using historical report documents is that you may not have the data in the form you need if the information was not classified then as it is today. In this case, you have no choice but to use the data in your computer system, provided your institution has stored historical data in its database.

There is also a disadvantage in doing extracts of historical data from your computer system. Over time, changes in entity types, source codes, pledge status codes, and others may have affected the data in your database. These data changes may mean that the totaled information does not match the final reported totals of any given year. If this happens, you need to footnote any data discrepancies on the comparative reports.

You can choose to use a mix of historical reports and computer extracts to acquire the data needed, but again, remember to note any data deviations that appear. And always indicate your data source or sources on the bottom of the comparative reports, so you know the origin of the information.

For national and peer group comparisons, the Council for Aid to Education (CAE) *Voluntary Support of Education* (VSE) survey is the best source of data for both your institution and other institutions. The VSE survey provides extensive information for comparative analysis, such as total private-support data, data by source, capital and current operations totals, information on planned gifts, corporate matching-gifts data, and statistics on education and general expenditures, endowment market value, and enrollment.

VSE Data Miner, accessed via the Web, is an outstanding tool to use when gathering data about other institutions. It gives access to 10 years of VSE survey data for educational institutions participating in the survey (approximately 1,000), among other things. Many of Data Miner's features make data gathering fast and efficient. It is also easy to create charts and graphs. Data Miner is available by annual subscription from CAE. It is well worth the annual subscription fee if you plan to do regular comparison reporting.

Choosing the Best Format

Comparison reports can be as simple as a list sorted high to low, or as complex as a multilevel graph. For example, if you want to display alumni giving trends, a list of 10 to 15 years of total alumni giving may suffice; or you might want to create a graph using software such as Harvard Graphics.

You also can compile more complex reports that compare averages over a certain number of years or display pre-campaign, campaign, and post-campaign giving. Again, keep in mind the point of your analysis and the audience for the report. These two factors will determine how simple or how complex your report format should be.

Specific Report Types

Internal Comparative Reporting

Internal comparative reports give a historical perspective on your institution, identify its strengths and weaknesses, and track institutional philanthropic trends. Internal comparative statistics are helpful if your institution is doing strategic planning or contemplating a capital campaign. The following are examples of internal comparative report formats.

1. Historical analysis of private support totals. These data show whether your institution is continuing to increase private support annually. A simple graph produced in Harvard Graphics, with time on the X-axis and dollars on the Y-axis, is an excellent format to use to display these data. You also can add a trend line to plot private support trends *(see Figure 1)*. A fiscal-year giving comparison that compares last year's to this year's attainment is also useful. Reports can compare giving on a specific date to the previous year at the same time *(see Figure 2)*.

Figure 1: Historical Analysis of Private Support

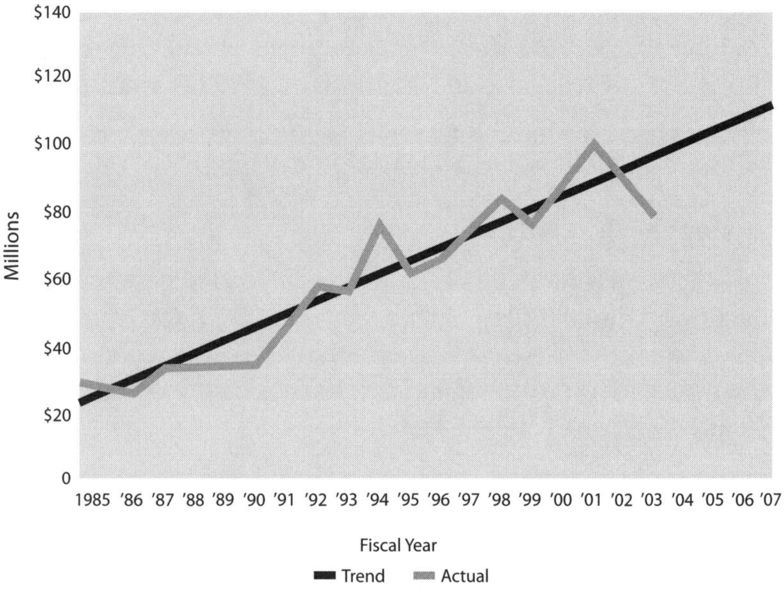

Figure 2: Fiscal Year Giving Comparison

Fiscal Year	Private Support Total for FY	Private as of Report Date	Commitment Total for FY	Commitment as of Report Date
2006	$65,444,724	$65,444,724	$72,060,948	$72,060,948
2005	$67,897,673	$52,163,151	$81,309,202	$44,007,194
2004	$75,646,485	$62,128,777	$71,954,706	$56,765,640
2003	$97,705,233	$69,433,803	$87,674,852	$56,589,573

2. Historical analysis of private support by school within your institution. Just like the historical analysis of private support, this is best done in a Harvard Graphics chart with time on the X-axis and dollars on the Y-axis. Another way to display the data is with a simple chart called the box *(see Figure 3)*. This format shows how much money each of your schools has raised over time. You can present the chart with or without a box drawn around a particular school on which you want to focus attention.

Figure 3: Private Support by School or College

Fiscal Year	1	2	3	4	5
2006	Medicine $29,179,979	Management $15,502,202	Arts & Sciences $9,988,477	Engineering $8,717,507	Law $2,379,588
2005	Medicine $29,423,921	Engineering $28,734,079	Arts & Sciences $13,679,496	Management $12,616,286	Law $2,367,582
2004	Arts & Sciences $95,156,576	Medicine $36,070,808	Management $19,135,748	Engineering $11,316,968	Law $3,125,069
2003	Engineering $36,242,201	Medicine $29,446,628	Arts & Sciences $15,277,936	Management $6,853,022	Law $3,746,127

3. Historical analysis of private support by source. This report gives perspective on VSE survey sources such as alumni, corporations and corporate foundations, foundations and family foundations, associations, friends, parents, and trustees. You can easily graph these data or put them in a box chart. You also can use this format for a historical analysis of private support by source for each school in your institution.

4. Historical report of private support by fund account. This report gives historical perspective on endowment, current support, and capital dollars. These data are easy to graph to show trends over time.

In addition to these four, two other types of historical comparative report are useful. One graphs cost per dollars raised. By comparing your development budget to private support dollars raised, you will be able to track fundraising effectiveness *(see Figure 4a and 4b)*.

Another is an analysis and comparison during pre-campaign, campaign, and post-campaign years. One way to format these data is to graph your private support attainment during these three periods, calculate your averages, and display them on the graph *(see Figure 5)*.

Figure 4a: Development Budget vs Cash Raised
Cash Attainment

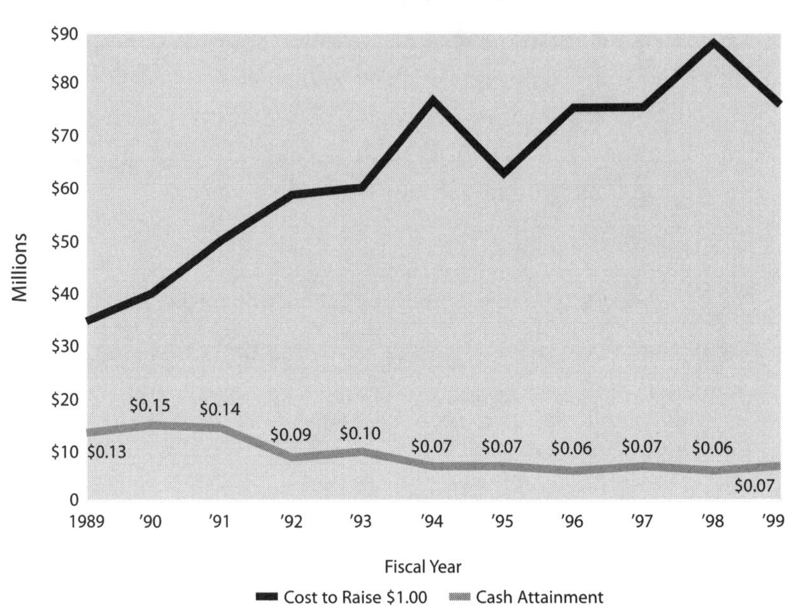

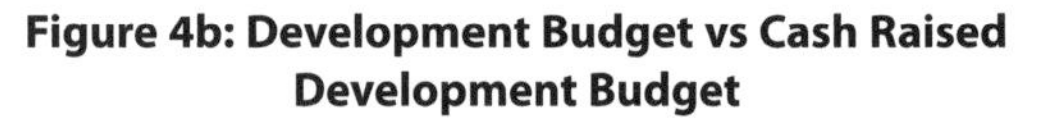

Figure 4b: Development Budget vs Cash Raised
Development Budget

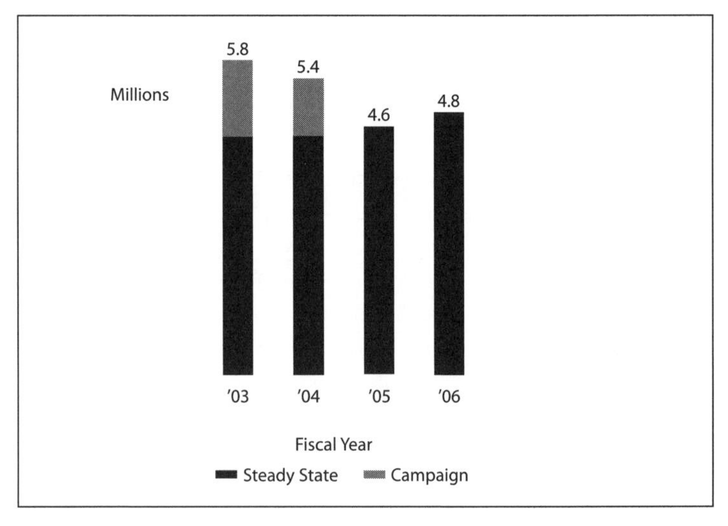

Figure 5: Fiscal Year Private Support: 1985-2002
Cash and Cash Equivalents

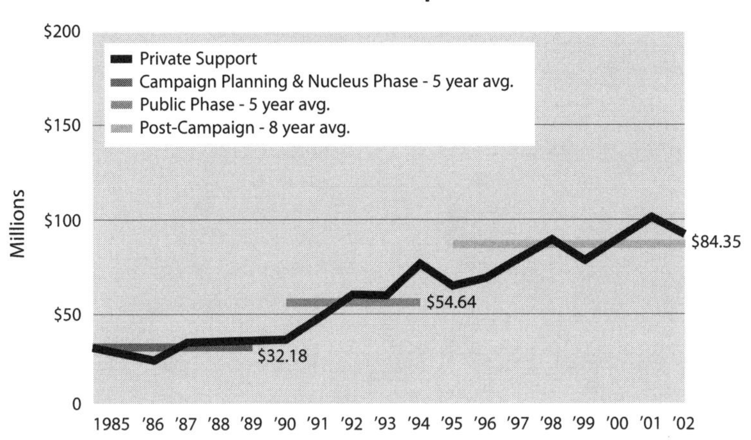

Again, this type of report is invaluable for strategic or campaign planning because it tracks fundraising performance over a significant period.

National Ranking Reports

These reports are important for measuring your institution's fundraising performance against that of other national institutions. One of the most basic formats is a comparative list of the top 25 or 50 institutions in the country, ranked high to low in terms of total private support. To measure trends, your report also should include the same ranking for the previous fiscal year. This format makes it easy to see the movement in rank among the institutions *(Figure 6)*. It also may be helpful to display more than one comparative fiscal year so that trends over a more significant period can be identified.

Figure 6: Comparative List
Private Research Universities
Total Private Support (In Millions)

Institution	RANK	Private Support 2006	Institution	RANK	Private Support 2005
Stanford University	1	580.4	Harvard	1	451.6
Harvard	2	485.2	Cornell	2	341.3
Duke University	3	407.9	Duke University	3	330.9
Yale	4	358.1	Stanford University	4	319.5
Cornell	5	308.6	Columbia	5	284.4
Johns Hopkins	6	304.0	University of Pennsylvania	6	270.0

Figure 7: Analysis of Private Research Universities
Source: Operating

School	Average Change 95-00 v. 01-06	School	Average Change 95-00 v. 01-06
University A	105.76%	University L	50.20%
University B	97.19%	University M	43.88%
University C	87.96%	University N	40.52%
University D	79.16%	University O	38.63%
University E	71.08%	University P	37.74%
University F	57.02%	University Q	36.65%
University G	56.43%	University R	36.62%
University H	56.04%	University S	32.92%
University I	55.27%	University T	30.66%
University J	53.85%	Mean Average Change:	56.05%
University K	53.38%		

A set of reports comparing your institution with others at the national level also should include comparisons for your Carnegie classification group. This subset is often more relevant and interesting because the institutions are similar. For example, if you are at a major private research university, you are naturally most interested in comparing your institution with similar ones. You should prepare comparative reports for total private-support rank for your Carnegie classification group, as well as by source and fund account.

It is also useful to analyze comparative data over time for your Carnegie classification group. Doing a two-year comparison by laying out the data side-by-side on a report is simple. It also is interesting to analyze data over five- or 10-year periods; you can display this comparison in a graph prepared in Harvard Graphics or in spreadsheet format. Doing a giving analysis over a significant period will give a true sense of philanthropic trends for your particular group.

Another way to look at comparative giving is to calculate the percent change in giving between two distinct periods. First, gather 10 years of total private-support data for your Carnegie classification group. Then compare the average total private support for the first five years of giving with the average total private support of the second five years and calculate the percent change between the two averages. Once you have your percent change data, you can rank the institutions based on these numbers *(see Figure 7)*. This type of comparative analysis works for data by source and fund account as well. When calculating your averages, you might want to eliminate the high and low figures for each school to guard against averaging in high one-time gifts or windfalls.

Using average-percent-change data for institutional comparisons is an excellent way to display your institution's strengths. Let's say your institution ranks 30th in the country in total private support, but you know that you have been particularly strong in raising dollars for buildings over the past decade. When you calculate your average percent change over the past 10 years and compare it with that of others in the buildings category, you could rank No. 1 nationally.

Another useful way to analyze fundraising performance in your Carnegie classification group is to do comparisons based on total private support by student. This analysis is helpful when you compare large institutions with smaller ones because it puts the dollars raised into perspective based on institutional size.

Peer Group Reporting

Whittling your Carnegie classification group down to peer groups allows you to make more extensive and relevant comparisons. For one thing, your comparison group is smaller and easier to manage; for another, the data for the institutions to which you are comparing yourself are significantly more pertinent because you are comparing similar institutions. Peer group comparisons are particularly helpful when you are measuring fundraising performance and trends. These reports can show strengths and weaknesses within your institution, as well as educating internal constituencies about your advancement team's goals and priorities.

When compiling your peer group, consider, among other things, size of endowment, size of enrollment, number of alumni, and the structure of the institution. Ten or 12 institutions are usually enough to provide relevant comparisons.

Once you have identified your peers, any and all of the reports discussed previously will work well. It is easy to show total private support by peer group, again, either in box charts or by graphing total private support using Harvard Graphics *(see Figure 8)*. Ten to 12 years of comparative data for each institution will give a sense of the trends. Be sure to include private support by source and by fund account in your reports as well.

Figure 8: Peer Group Giving
Private Support Comparison: Based on 2003-2006

Fiscal Year	1	2	3	4	5	6
2003	University A $139,179,979	University B $118,502,202	University C $91,955,477	University D $81,717,507	University E $41,861,564	University F $33,789,092
2004	University A $149,423,921	University D $138,734,079	University C $123,679,496	University B $92,616,286	University E $84,054,170	University F $29,102,154
2005	University C $195,156,576	University A $136,070,80	University B $100,135,74	University D $91,316,968	University F $79,640,335	University E $74,423,457
2006	University D $156,242,201	University A $139,446,628	University C $125,277,936	University $111,685,302	University E $96,793,970	University B $94,742,109

So there you have it: the many reasons that gathering, analyzing, and presenting data in comparative reports are important tasks for your advancement services office. If you have not done such reports before, starting now will be a great benefit for years to come. After all, reports that make your institution look good can make you look good as well.

Advancement
SERVICES

Section II: Prospect Research and Management

CHAPTER 5

An Overview of Research in Advancement

By Jonathan A. Lindsey, Ph.D. CFRE | Assistant Vice President, Donor and Information Services | Baylor University

Art? Science? Combination? Playing hunches? Taking educated guesses? All or none of the above?

Research in advancement has come a long way in more than three decades. Nevertheless, much about it is still hard to define. Even describing a typical workday for a typical researcher is nearly impossible because of the different ways we conduct our work and the different issues that arise from the research enterprise. No two research units are organized or integrated into the advancement process in the same manner.

To understand the full scope of prospect research, we need to give broad consideration to the significant changes of the past 35 years. In this chapter, I will start with research's conceptual issues, profile, and changing procedures. Then I will address the electronic data deluge. This overview of research will end with a look at the issues the new century raises, including analysis vs. research, data and data source reliability, trustworthy dipsticks, and the essential quality of our questions.

A Look Back

Until the early 1980s, only a few major educational institutions had formal research units in their advancement offices. At about that time, progressive development officers were beginning to recognize the value of market research to direct mail and telemarketing. Particularly in higher education, fundraisers grounded their efforts in class loyalty, reunion-class giving programs that grew out of the annual fund, capital campaigns, and other standard activities. Only through careful personal cultivation did development officers explore issues related to giving ability, such as net worth, expendable income, and potential inheritance. The standard literature of the time is replete with warnings not to make assumptions about information the prospect did not provide.

In the mid-1980s, however, a not-so-subtle change took place. Thanks to fast-moving cultural transformations on Wall Street, money became a subject about which even polite people could converse. Information about money became more public. Concurrently, but probably unrelated to this cultural phenomenon, advancement offices in large educational institutions began to appreciate what research could reveal about well-known individuals. Development officers who had carefully clipped newspaper articles for their files began to combine that information with knowledge about networking, board memberships, philanthropic activities, and other facts that provided a critical mass of information for evaluation.

Thanks to fast-moving cultural transformations on Wall Street, money became a subject about which even polite people could converse.

By combining an entrepreneurial approach with a little academic savvy, enterprising development officers saw an opportunity to focus on an area that had a new feel to it. Research! Find out what you can about an individual or family. Then look for ways their interests coincide with campus interests and needs.

Thus the development/advancement profile was born. One of the first standard profiles appears in *Prospect Research: A How-to Guide* (CASE, 1986) edited by Bobbie J. Strand and Susan Hunt, which benchmarks the early practices of the field. With the exception of changes wrought by online data sources, remarkably little has changed since. Most institutions' standard prospect profiles still include name, residential and business addresses and phones, personal history, educational history, special interests, gift history, significant relationships, family history, indications of affinity, philanthropic interests, and other idiosyncratic items deemed necessary at each institution. For example, one campus had a place in its profile for "emotional valence," which a development officer translated as "hot buttons."

Fundraising staff completed this new instrument after conducting painstaking bibliographic and documentary research in development offices and libraries. A standard checkoff list ensured that those in training looked for information in all potential resources, duly copied it, and then transcribed it into the profile. Of course, each time the profile was reworked, the whole document had to be retyped. Also by the mid-1980s, relief came to most advancement offices in the form of word processing. This provided a cut-and-paste environment for creating profiles on demand.

Yet another notable development in advancement research was related to progress in information delivery. Dialog, originally developed for science, began to branch into other areas, such as biographical information. Other databases began to emerge, as did newspaper indexes, so we no longer depended on the *New York Times* Index alone. These indexes at first were in print, then on microfilm. Their early digital format was magnetic tape, then compact disks. After 1995 and the growth of the internet, this information became generally available online.

A Look Standing Still

The microchip, invented in the third quarter of the 20th century, spurred the technological advances that in turn prompted significant leaps forward in managing information. What was once possible only via massive mainframe computers became easy to do on desktop units that could stand alone or be connected to networks. Furthermore, enterprising computer scientists began to manage business data the way advancement services needed; thus, a whole new area of software was born. Here are just a few examples of how technological changes in other realms stimulated further breakthroughs for researchers:

- As American industry developed digital modes of inventory control, librarians adopted this type of technology and developed library systems that eventually furthered advancement research.
- When business came up with digital methods for maintaining sales records and tracking customer contacts, advancement officers benefited from parallel developments.
- At one time complex data, particularly about securities holdings, were available only in government depositories, and their recovery required laborious manual research. Once this information was collected in digital format, it became easily and quickly accessible via mediated online services and then on CD-ROM.

Advancement Services: How Many Hats?

In addition to the plethora of new rules and regulations advancement services professionals must understand and help fundraisers and donors comprehend, they must master another level of knowledge. The umbrella of "advancement services" covers more than data processing; many advancement services operations are now responsible for such support areas as prospect research, stewardship, and event planning, with publications, communications, and Web design thrown in for good measure. In some cases, they recruit and support human resources for institutional advancement, as well as carry out more traditional tasks of demographic data entry, gift processing, and reporting.

One of the reasons the range of advancement services continues to grow is that technological resources—hardware or software—are taking exponential leaps forward. Advancement services professionals continually have to juggle the needs of the institution, adhering to external reporting requirements and catering to individual needs and requests for recognition or privacy. Even if we don't make the outright ask for money, everything that supports the methods and means for realizing fundraising is related in some way to what advancement services professionals do.

Advancement services now has a substantially broader definition than it did 20 years ago. No longer are advancement services professionals escapees from a central information systems department. Institutional advancement has raised its demands on fundraisers to manage information in a more technically savvy manner, and that cannot happen without varied methods of operation to support fundraising. One role advancement services professionals still fill is that of technical manager of advancement hardware and software. But the work also includes developing concepts, such as coding, that support statistical analysis in the form of data mining, as Brian Dowling discusses in Chapter 16. These did not exist in any notable form before the turn of the 21st century.

The ever-changing technology that can be used to support institutional advancement is a comparatively new and rapidly expanding domain of knowledge. Those in the back offices of institutional advancement need to acquire a great deal of expertise. Every large nonprofit organization now has at least a home page, and those in the academic area have made tremendous strides in maintaining contact with alumni through use of online communities and e-mail blasts. That said, those who have become adept at using the internet as a tool are well aware that it can be a bane and a blessing for any nonprofit organization. The Web readily provides not only overwhelming information resources about constituents but also the means through which those constituents can be kept engaged with and supportive of the institution.

No longer do we live in an age when paper reports in floppy folders or clumsy binders are the best means of keeping information at the fundraiser's fingertips. Advancement support professionals are called on to assess and implement the most current and sophisticated methods for pulling, organizing, and storing countless bits of information about constituents. They are responsible not only for importing data from external resources, but also for doing the initial RFP outline for vendor selection and software implementation. They study the data structures, formulate the design of technological bridges through which information is both pushed and pulled, and use all the software tools for institutional advancement. Cell phones, PDAs, and laptop computers are the cutting-edge tools of prospect management and cultivation. The electronic pipelines between each piece of hardware and the person who conveys them to the institution are only as strong as the staff members who design and maintain those fragile connections.

The key to providing the greatest amount of data and the most current constituent information is to build a safety structure behind which constituents can retreat if they choose. Advancement services staff are the definers of coding structures and information sharing policies and procedures that take into account both governmental restrictions and constituents' instructions. It is for those who build and operate the database structure to forge the invisible bridge each institution tries to build to its constituents.

—Amy J. Phillips, Gift Registrar, Smithsonian Institution

The combination of easily available financial data, census data (in digital format since 1990), and other information collected by entrepreneurs opened another industry mentioned in Chapter 7 by David Lamb: electronic screening. By screening your database electronically, vendors promise to identify wealth indicators that signal near-millionaires, millionaires, and multimillionaires. Business journals cooperate in this trend by seeking information about significantly rich persons and Fortune 500 companies, and publishing lists of them. Complex formulas calculate the presumed net worth of individuals and families.

In the mid-1990s, access to information exploded when the internet became popular. While revolutionizing attitudes about how readily available information should be, the internet created a clear dichotomy between the haves and the have-nots: those with computer access and those without.

At the vortex of this revolution is the advancement researcher.

All these information breakthroughs created instant access to large quantities of information. Combine that access with inquisitive minds and well-trained, computer-literate college graduates, and you have a research revolution. Add the sophisticated computer information systems many campuses use to store and manage information, and you have an advancement revolution.

At the vortex of this revolution is the advancement researcher. This person is normally a college graduate, computer literate, likes the chase as much as the answer, has an analytical mind, and—oh yes—realizes that the human side of creating the advancement services infrastructure is still immensely important.

A significant outcome of using the internet for advancement research is a shift from information provision to information analysis, a shift that involves knowledge management. Achieving this change requires intellectual retooling for many researchers. We need to develop skills in interpreting financial data, some of which are extremely complex. We become close followers of business activities, not just those of principal donors or potential donors but of international markets where ownership is multinational. We might even need to use several languages in filtering and assessing information.

In contrast to the "old days," today we no longer have so much trouble finding timely data. Often, fresh information is available almost instantly from a variety of electronic sources: home pages, business profiles, industry directories, real estate records, political contribution filings, auto and luxury item registrations, professional membership directories, and census records. All provide so much data that sifting and analyzing are now vitally important skills. But given the fact that some electronic sources are more reliable than others, another essential skill is the ability to spot the spurious.

Because of the immense amount of information available about any individual, some say conducting research is like looking for a needle in a haystack. I prefer the metaphor of the automobile dipstick. We must develop the means to reach directly into the core of information relevant to our particular institution. Markers on your dipstick will be similar to the categories developed for the advancement research profile during the 1980s—with one significant difference. Synthesizing information, spotting relationships, thinking in a matrix, reviewing constituent data, and making suggestions to major gifts officers requires strong knowledge of advancement protocols, in addition to the ability to find information.

Because of the immense amount of information available about any individual, some say conducting research is like looking for a needle in a haystack.

Tools of the Trade

Moving from developing communication based on demographic segments to creating analytic programs based on data that profile and predict philanthropic behavior is a recent wave among major universities, many colleges, and other nonprofit organizations. Major consulting firms that support fundraising provide profiling and predictive models. But the creative use of SAS, available on most campuses, can lead to parallel results.

Peter B. Wylie's approach to data mining employs a less complex, desktop model that researcher/analysts with a modicum of statistical background can use with ease. Wylie, author of *Data Mining for Fund Raisers* (CASE, 2004) has an approach that establishes clear definitions of terms, particularly variables, and a comfort level for communication.

Whether you use a simple or complex statistical approach to analyze your data, being perceived as the predictor of philanthropic behavior may cause others to ascribe godlike attributes to you.

It's All About the Data

In the olden days of information management, say five or 10 years ago, the leadership in development, or institutional advancement, usually referred to advancement services as the "back office" (if they referred to it at all). Those of us toiling away in advancement services jobs then comprised a hidden or almost invisible organization. We were, and often still are, housed in windowless, airless basements or attics in very old buildings. People stumbled on our offices by chance, usually looking for a restroom or an exit door.

In the past three to five years, however, to quote Bob Dylan, "The times they are a-changin'." And they are a-changin' very rapidly as a result of new information technologies and sophisticated software that allow us to analyze, package, and deliver data and information on an anytime/anywhere basis. They also require new, sophisticated skills from our staffs and the people we hire.

In addition, we are being held more accountable for the information we provide. External agencies' mandates and additional internal business reports are required from us because of state and federal laws and ever-changing internal or external audit requirements. Also, we now have a generation of donors who pay close attention to and hold us strictly accountable for how our institutions use their gifts. This is a busy time for all of us in those basements and attics, and this is not going to change anytime soon because of the ever-increasing importance of the information and data we collect and store.

Who Knew?

As those on the support-services side (more than on the relationship-building side) of development know, this information-management business is not easy. The amount of information we now need to collect and store has expanded considerably since the early to mid-1990s. Moreover, sophisticated relational databases and information systems and technologies enable us to collect and store much more information about our constituencies than ever before.

Let's think about the data for a moment. Something as simple and straightforward as an out-of-date address, phone number, or e-mail address means that time and money are wasted in unfulfilled solicitations. We spend both of those precious resources on finding and updating the information, on returned mail costs, and on not connecting with someone who might have given a gift if we could have contacted the person.

Bad prospect data can jeopardize relationships with major donors if we do not have some of the most basic information about them correct. If we do not know the donor has changed jobs or retired, and we still attempt to contact him at a former business address or pester him to get his former employer to match his gift, he is likely to become annoyed and wonder why we cannot even get the obvious information correct. It could be worse. Upon review of insufficient or incorrect data, we could formulate a wrong approach to a donor or cultivate him or her in an inadequate way when planning to ask for a major gift. We could ask for a gift that is too low or for a project in which the donor has not the slightest interest. We could embarrass our institutions and ourselves. It all comes down to the basic building block of our work—good data.

It takes savvy advancement officers and leaders to capitalize on and fully appreciate the value that good information adds to their fundraising efforts. Good information is timely, accurate, easy to access, and, most of all, useful. Information stored in a database or file cabinet is really not valuable until someone acts upon it—to make a decision, solve a problem, advance a strategy, inform, or communicate. If the information is out-of-date, inaccurate, or inaccessible, then bad decisions could be made, problems worsened, inaccurate reports generated, and other valuable assets, such as time and money, wasted. Information is an easy resource to take for granted since it is ubiquitous. It also is an organizational asset whose value can be difficult to measure. Understanding how to apply and use data and information effectively is crucial.

Information Infrastructures

The components necessary to create a solid information infrastructure for today's development or advancement organization include not only accurate, complete, and up-to-date data, but also skilled people who understand and can maintain, retrieve, analyze, and package them. They also include the information technologies needed to refresh the data, acquire and store new information, and mine the database. The fundamental role of advancement services always has been to support our organizations' friend-raising and fundraising efforts by managing the information infrastructure and the large amounts of data and information collected. Consider the following primary functions in advancement services, the information intensiveness of each, and the place each occupies in our fundraising efforts from start to finish of the development cycle:

- **Prospect identification and research.** Information includes biographical, academic, student activity, demographic, institutional affiliations, employment, and gift-giving data. We use these data to determine our prospects' financial capacities and philanthropic inclinations, their interests in our institution's goals, and the appropriate projects they might want to fund. The data also are used in developing the most appropriate cultivation strategy for donors. The Web offers an information warehouse that saves researchers a great deal of time searching for information; thus, more time can be spent analyzing and suggesting actions based on their findings. Internal information combined with external information provides the most comprehensive profiles of our prospects.
- **Information technology and database management.** These high-tech tools enable the storage, retrieval, and manipulation of vast amounts of alumni and development information, the ability to format information into meaningful reports and analyses, and to deliver the results electronically to anyone with an e-mail address or access to the internet or an intranet who has been cleared as having a need to know.
- **Alumni, friends, and donor records and file management.** Entering and maintaining gift, biographical, and prospect data comprise the foundation on which successful fundraising and alumni relations activities grow. Without what is often referred to as directory information—accurate addresses, phone numbers, and e-mail addresses—we have no way to contact our alumni, donors, or prospects for soliciting via phonathons and direct mail, mailing publications, building relationships, inviting to events, or accepting online donations. The value of a good address and phone number or e-mail is that we have at least a

50 percent chance of securing a donation because we are able to contact a potential donor.

- **Donor relations and stewardship.** Assuming the best donors are our previous donors, then thanking and recognizing current donors is one of the most important things we can do. We need accurate gift and pledge data to ensure we have correct contact information when acknowledging and recognizing gifts or volunteer work. First, the gift and data entry staff need to receive correct donor and gift information, and second, they must receive it in a timely manner so the database can be quickly updated.
- **Reporting.** Using gift, biographical, and prospect data, we generate a variety of reports on fundraising progress, alumni participation rates, sources and types of funds, endowments, status of various projects, prospect tracking and moves management, and audit reports, as well as the reports we do for CASE, CAE, FASB/GASB, IRS, or *U.S. News & World Report*, among others.
- **Data mining and predictive modeling.** By looking for associations, patterns, or sequences in our data, we can begin to forecast future actions. When we learn who gives consistently, whose gifts are increasing, and what the indicators are for a potential major donor, we can increase the likelihood of more successful solicitations. We also have a better chance of success in asking for the right gift amount for the right project. Predictive modeling allows us to analyze our database and prioritize potential donors from the top down. Finding the needle in the haystack is faster and easier with some of the statistical analysis tools we have at our disposal today. Data mining, combined with the information gleaned from external prospect or database screenings, offers us the potential to determine very quickly who in our databases are the most affluent and philanthropic and what areas of our institutions are of greatest interest to them.

Good, accurate information helps fundraisers make better decisions about where to travel, who to meet, what to ask for, how much, and when. Used effectively, good information can help ensure that we all can:

- Maximize or manage our time more efficiently
- Avoid duplication of effort

- Stop unproductive activity
- Inform and communicate
- Benchmark and measure progress
- Meet goals and objectives
- Reduce costs
- Avoid the consequences of being uninformed
- Focus on priorities

Out of the Attic

Despite the importance of the alumni and development-related data and information we collect and store and the technology and skilled personnel needed to manage them, advancement services is still generally the back-office for many in the advancement profession. Although probably not meaning to, they seem to regard advancement-services professionals' work as less important than fundraising—the front office. This is an outdated view. Today, those who lead and manage advancement services offices would do well to have a law degree, an accounting degree, a computer science degree, a library and information science degree, or an MBA. A law, business, or accounting degree would be very useful given FASB/GASB requirements, planned giving vehicles, IRS regulations, Sarbanes-Oxley, new privacy laws, and many other emerging rules and requirements.

The proliferation of information technologies, information products, and information services requires at least an elementary knowledge of computers, networks, and relational databases. Wireless technologies, phishing, SPAM, identify theft, cyber-hacking, and computer viruses provide enough security issues to ensure sleepless nights, not to mention the continual software upgrades, bug fixes, and patches that far too often we must apply to our information systems. Don't forget the hardware upgrades and plethora of handheld computing devices that can be easily lost, stolen, or dropped on the floor. A computer science or information technology degree just might ease the angst of this "behind-the-scenes-until-it-is-broken" aspect of our business. The amount of information we collect from a variety of sources, pay large amounts of money for, store in a variety of devices, and deliver to end-users in a variety of formats must be organized, retrieved, analyzed, formatted, and refreshed; hence the need for the library or information science degree.

It is time to raise collective awareness that our advancement services staffs are the generalists who have, or should have, a very big picture of our entire advancement operations and organizations. Our knowledge of the business of development encompasses fundraising progress to date, donor-giving levels and recognition societies, numbers of prospects, fundraising priorities, campaign progress, and bequest expectancies, to mention a few. We seek to understand and interpret IRS rules, FASB/GASB requirements, CASE standards, and National Committee on Planned Giving guidelines. We must know about the donors and their pledges and gifts, alumni and their addresses and mailing preferences. We have to send accurate, timely tax receipts, pledge reminders, and thank-you letters while remembering, "The customer is always right"—even if she isn't. We need to have experience and expertise in using spreadsheet software, merging documents, authenticating users, providing secure access to data on our end-users' laptops, PDAs, databases, and cell phones, our intranets and the internet, especially when wireless technologies are employed. We engage in fierce arguments with our auditors over conditional versus unconditional pledges, calm annoyed donors who want yet another copy of a tax receipt, and train development officers to understand and use the data we store.

Mission-Critical

When or how did the prospect researchers, techno-geeks, gift and bio clerks, and other information services folks become so mission-critical to successful fundraising? Information technologies, donors who demand more accountability and reports on the use of their gifts, and federal and state legislative mandates are among the primary drivers in changing the roles of the back-office.

It is no longer wise to view this area as overhead, because without the data, information technology, and knowledge to be gained from tapping our invaluable information resources fewer funds would be raised and the time frame for doing so would be longer. Institutional advancement offices that recognize the changing role of the back office should invest strategically in their advancement services organizations, information infrastructure, and the people who run them. The ultimate result will be more and happier donors and more charitable contributions to our organizations. In addition, the fundraisers for our institutions do not have enough time to raise money and create all those reports and files for our auditors, campaign managers, CASE, NACUBO, *U.S. News & World Report*, various trade publications, research projects, grant applications, donors, deans, athletic directors, vice presidents, presidents, boards of trustees, volunteers, vendors...

—Linda Bennett, Vice President of Development, Mercyhurst College

A second place for advancement researchers/analysts is at the management table—or at least the table where solicitation strategy is developed. The advent of moves management as a process for solicitation generated the need for meaningful interpretation of the data. Many research personnel have moved into the prospect management vacuum and are supporting solicitation through contact data entry, analytic reports, and strategy development.

Prospect management is a nice euphemism for solicitation accountability. The results of prospect management systems are being used to hold gift officers accountable for their constituent relationships and their productivity.

A third tool of the trade is a clear understanding of the roles and implications of research and analysis in the larger scheme of organizational dynamics. In spring 2005, FundSvcs—one of the fundamental discussion listservs in advancement—entertained a question about the integrated activities of advancement, from research to cultivation to ask to stewardship.

Your local organization may not totally resemble this diagram—in fact, mine does not—but the common elements of it outweigh the differences.

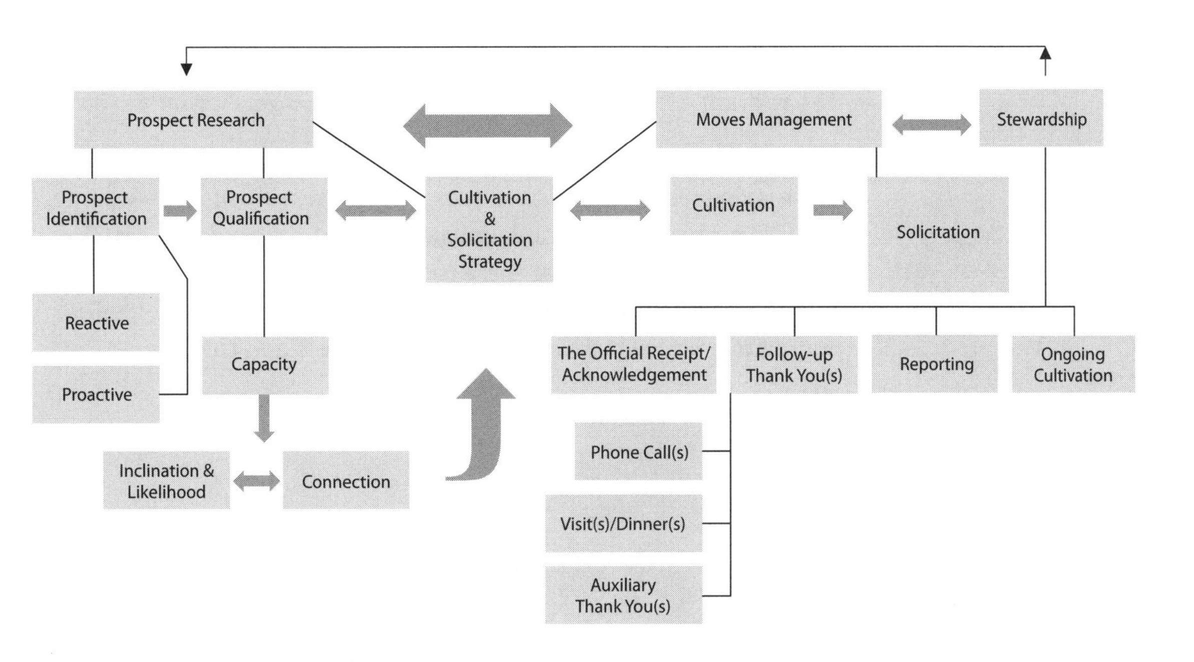

The fourth tool of the trade is best described as cultivating the blink factors. Good researchers/analysts develop a skill that allows them to sense potential in a prospect. Malcolm Gladwell, author of *Blink* (Little, Brown & Co., 2005) says this rapid-fire response is based on accumulated knowledge and experience and demonstrates itself in settings from art evaluation to police behavior.

The fourth tool of the trade is best described as cultivating the blink factors.

Researchers/analysts, particularly those involved in prospect management, subliminally develop a body of information with which they subconsciously compare each new research subject. In a blink they can predict with considerable accuracy—or accuracy parallel to some statistical studies—a prospect's probable philanthropic behavior. Combined with data mining, profiling, and predictive modeling, this intuitive response should be honed and valued.

Finally, the most valued tool of the researcher/analyst is the basic one: critical questions. By the end of the 20th century, prospect research had moved from being a predominantly reactive form of behavior that provided answers—sometimes to unasked questions—to a proactive and analytical questioning mode. The quality of the questions is critical to the success of facilitating philanthropy. Each research activity or set of results leads to a new set of questions. Knowing wealth indicators is only one piece of the puzzle. Interpreting wealth indicators as part of the constituent gestalt involves knowing the relationship with the constituent via gift officers' contact reports.

Critical question skills will be applied to new and more powerful microchip power, to statistical analyses that result from data mining, profiling, or predictive modeling, access to more powerful search engines, and the results of these tools. But no new tool or technology can replace the unique ability of the human mind and its essential inquisitiveness, which lead to a new synthesis and the "a-ha" of discovery.

CHAPTER 6

Setting Up a Research Office

By Brenda Eckles | Director of Advancement Services | Rhodes College

When you undertake any new endeavor, it is good to remember why you are doing it. So it is with establishing a research office. Your actions and moves should always be guided by the two underlying purposes of prospect research: to match a prospective donor's interests and giving capability with the institution's goals and needs, and to preserve the institution's memory of a prospect.

Five elements of prospect research contribute to the goal of matching a prospect to an institutional need:

1. Prospect identification. The best place to start is with people or organizations that already have a connection with your institution. For educational institutions, trustees, alumni, and parents are the most logical groups. Others include local corporations or foundations. Medical nonprofits usually include grateful patients in their prospect identification work. Museums certainly look at their membership rosters. You get the idea. Be creative.

2. Prospect screening. Once the initial pool is defined, individual screening allows you to focus your research on the best prospects. Prospect screening is any one of several methods that identify individuals most likely to make a gift to your institution and most capable of making a major gift. Methods include staff, peer, or volunteer review, donor group selection, or electronic screening by outside vendors who cross-reference your prospects with information in their databases. Using any or all of these methods should allow you to put your time and resources to best use.

3. Information development. This is the element most of us consider first when we think of prospect research. It is systematically gathering useful information and presenting it in a usable format. Note I said useful information, not all information. Part of information development is filtering the gathered pieces to report only those that further the two purposes mentioned above: matching the prospect to an institutional need and preserving institutional memory.

. . . your organization must be willing to commit staff and budget resources to this effort.

4. Prospect classification. The resulting profile should provide the background to develop an informed strategy to cultivate and solicit your best prospects. Cultivation methods will vary, depending on how involved prospects already are in your institution and what their charitable interests are. The amount and purpose of the gift will depend on the prospect's interests as well as institutional needs. Whether your office should solicit in the near future or many months from now depends on the cultivation process and the amount requested. The prospect profile should provide you with the information necessary to classify prospects properly in all these respects.

5. Prospect tracking. The prospect pool must be tracked and managed through the cultivation, solicitation, and stewardship stages. Relevant questions include the following: What cultivation steps are planned for a prospect, and what steps have been completed? Is the time right to ask for a gift? Should a staff member, a volunteer, or both make the ask?

After the gift is made, stewardship must be managed so the donor feels good about the gift. Effective stewardship prepares the donor for the solicitation. A good tracking system maintains and manages all this information.

Getting Started

Two things are certain about setting up a research operation. First, your organization must be willing to commit staff and budget resources to this effort. Second, your chief development officer must be convinced of the value of prospect research and willing and able to make it happen. If your development leadership is not committed, you might try contacting colleagues at similar institutions and asking them to share success stories, so you can strengthen your case for setting up a research office. You need to make the case that sound research pays off in more and larger gifts.

Once you have that commitment, what is next? Most research positions include more than just research. My own position always has included information management as well as research; stewardship was added a few years ago. Do not let the task overwhelm you. Break it down into manageable pieces. As the ancient Chinese philosopher Lao-tzu said, "A journey of a thousand miles begins with a single step."

One of the first steps relates to the purpose of research. To match a prospect with organizational needs, you must be knowledgeable not only about your prospects, but also about your institution. You must become as familiar with your institution's missions, goals, and needs as you are with your research tools.

In learning about your institution, you should become familiar with the people who shape it. For me, this meant learning about the governing board. When I set up shop, the first group I researched was the board of trustees. I gathered information and developed a prospect profile for each board member. This initial project helped me learn prospect research skills and become familiar with a group that plays a crucial role in forming institutional goals and needs.

The next group to focus on is major gift donors not on the governing board. The way major donors express their personal interests, by making specified gifts, will certainly shape the direction of the organization.

Do a couple of things as you gather your institutional knowledge. First, start to review two or three local periodicals, whether in print or online. Look especially for names of the members of your governing board and major gift donors. This will help you access those names faster and bring you up-to-date on your local community.

Second, set up a research profile form, using either a word-processing application or database software. Some development software packages feature a research module that includes a profile form. The profile should include several categories of information. Even though you almost never will gather all this information for any one prospect, having the categories listed constantly will remind you of what information might be helpful to include:

Personal Information

- Name, address, phone numbers, e-mail address
- Vacation home address and phone and periods spent there
- Marital status, children, parents, other relatives (note any institutional connections)
- Date and place of birth
- Hobbies, sports, leisure activities

Business Information

- Company, employee title, address, phone numbers, assistants, type of business
- Employment history
- Corporate board memberships
- Professional affiliations and awards

Educational Background

- Class year, degree, area of undergraduate, graduate, and postgraduate study
- Honorary degrees

Civic Information

- Civic board memberships
- Awards
- Social club affiliations

Financial Indicators/Estimates of Wealth

- Salary, stock/option holdings, property ownership
- Inheritances, lifestyle indicators

Philanthropic Information

- Nonprofit board memberships
- Gifts to charities
- Volunteer work for charities

Engagement With Your Institution

- Events attended
- Volunteer work, including dates
- Giving history (detailed)
- Liaisons (relatives, friends, business colleagues, etc.) and their relationship to your institution
- Contacts by staff members
- Strategy

Rhodes College recently enhanced the prospect profile form by including not only the categories of information listed above, but also our standard list of research references. We always want to use certain references when developing a profile; having a list ensures we do not leave any out. We place a check mark next to references that yield useful information and include the checklist as part of the completed profile. Our development officers find it helpful to know where we obtained the information included in the profile.

Once you have completed the prospect profile form during the initial research phase, do not treat it as a closed file. Update it as your office uncovers new information and makes new contacts with the prospective donor.

Once you have completed the prospect profile form during the initial research phase, do not treat it as a closed file.

Target Your Research

Focus your efforts by doing prospect screening and choosing appropriate levels of research for different prospects. After all, you do not have time to research everyone on your constituency list, and you do not need to research everyone in depth.

The simplest screening method in a new research office is to target members of specific groups mentioned above: the governing board, major donors, and your most effective volunteers. Another good screening tool is to concentrate on staff requests and in-house leads. A new research office is usually awash in staff requests!

As you develop your research operation over time, you may want to consider peer screening reviews. Peer screening consists of carefully chosen volunteers who review prospective donor names, either in a group setting or individually. For people the volunteers know personally, they can advise regarding gift capability as well as interest in your institution.

Another approach to consider as you become established is screening by outside vendors. They study and analyze your prospect pool and cross-reference it with many kinds of information in the vendor database. The firm then presents the results with the goal of identifying the most promising prospects in terms of gift capability and inclination to give to your institution. Most vendors package their output in software that aids the prospect research effort in various ways. As you might imagine, this can be expensive. Institutions usually do it only in the planning stages of a major campaign.

My office defines two levels of research:

Level I (Basic) is all the information that can be pulled directly from our computer database. For us, this includes considerable data, since our database storage capability and data gathering efforts have improved over the past decade. Information in a basic profile includes the following:

- Name
- Relationship to our organization
- Personal information, such as birth date and maiden name
- All contact information, including home, vacation home, and business
- Family information, including family connections to our organization
- Business affiliation and title
- Educational background
- Giving history
- Specific areas of volunteer or charitable interest within our organization
- Involvement with our organization, such as volunteer work, events attended and specific interest areas
- Prospect management details, such as staff member assigned to the prospect and next solicitation

Level II (Complete Profile) is useful information compiled from all available sources. The first page of a Level II complete profile is the Level I basic profile. Succeeding pages include the other categories of information listed above for a prospect profile form.

Where to Look for Information

Office Files

It is hard to know where to look for information when you first set up a research operation. Start by determining the sources already available to you. Some of your best information may be waiting in your in-house constituent files. With electronic archives becoming more accessible (many free of charge), paper files of clippings seem to be growing redundant. But do not overlook them. Like me, you may be fortunate to have in-house files of clippings going back 40 or 50 years or more. Years ago, a staff member was extremely thorough in reviewing and clipping local periodicals; I have reaped the benefits of his work time and time again.

In addition to old clippings, staff contact reports can be a rich source of facts. Constantly encourage development officers to write contact reports and to do so carefully. As in the research profiles, respect the individual's privacy rights. Also remember that your prospects may very well have the legal right to examine any information you may have gathered on them. Contact reports should be thoughtfully worded. Include only facts useful for securing a gift or preserving institutional memory. Remind your colleagues often how valuable contact reports are for the continuity that must be maintained through staff turnover and changes.

In-house files often contain other bits of information drawn from surveys or correspondence from the constituent. Surveys sometimes reveal clues to areas of interest for possible gifts, as well as attitudes toward your institution. Correspondence can yield several kinds of information, depending on the subject.

. . . select only those volunteers who are convinced of the worth of prospect research and ask only questions that are above reproach.

Volunteers

In a one-to-one setting, a volunteer who knows and trusts you may feel comfortable talking about the prospective donor and answering some questions. For this reason, you should be included whenever possible in development group meetings with volunteers. By getting to know the best volunteers personally and developing a rapport with them, you will instill a sense of trust in your professionalism and the value of your work.

If you do take this approach, pick your volunteers carefully. Be certain you select only those volunteers who are convinced of the worth of prospect research and ask only questions that are above reproach. You never want any volunteer to question your motives for gathering information on a prospective donor.

Libraries

A new research office usually has to get established with the barest of budget resources. Sometimes it is necessary to stretch your funds by making use of references available in nearby municipal or campus libraries. Useful general references include the *Who's Who* directories, which present biographical sketches of prominent individuals in a region or industry, and specialized biographical directories, such as *Contemporary Authors*. Most municipal libraries also have a local history section that may include periodical clippings or other information on prominent citizens.

Public Records

In public records you can find business information, corporate filings with government agencies, property records, unclaimed property, professional licenses, and court filings. By law, public records are available to anyone who asks to view them. In the past, this meant you had to visit the office that maintained the record to which you sought access. Now many public record databases are available online. One good search engine for public records is Search Systems *(www.searchsystems.net)*. You can browse public records by geographic link, or you can search by keyword for a public record database.

Government records may disclose property ownership and value. These records usually are housed in county tax assessor offices. Many counties now make their real estate records available on the internet. Christina Pulawski, formerly director of development and donor services at Loyola University Chicago, has developed a Web site with links to many county tax assessor offices *(www.pulawski.com).* If records are not available online, anyone who visits the office in person may request information. Often county clerks will answer questions by phone, but they are not required to do so.

Other public documents that prospect researchers sometimes access include probate records. As a will is executed, information outlining the value of the estate and distribution of bequests to beneficiaries is provided to the court to prove the executor is carrying out the decedent's instructions. This information becomes public record, but few probate records are available online. Again, some court clerks will answer questions by phone.

Publicly traded companies are required to make their Securities and Exchange Commission (SEC) filings, including annual reports and proxy statements, available to the public. The proxy statement is a rich source of information regarding compensation and stock ownership of directors and top officers. Most companies are now filing electronic reports with the SEC, making their retrieval easier than ever if you have internet access. The SEC maintains an online database that can be searched through their Edgar (Electronic Data Gathering, Analysis, and Retrieval) system *(www.sec.gov/edgar/searchedgar/webusers.htm).*

Internet

Easily the biggest revolution in prospect research is the advent and growth of the internet. I already have noted many resources available online. Even researchers with modest budgets can access an array of tools that hardly could be imagined a few years ago. If you work on a campus that already has internet access, obviously you can connect for free. If not, internet access fees may be the best research money you spend.

You have numerous no-cost sources from which to choose. For instance, SEC corporate filings mentioned above are available at no charge via the internet on the SEC Web site *(www.sec.gov)*. Stock ownership information on directors and top officers, gleaned from proxy statements, can be enhanced with quotes of current or historical stock values from several internet sites, such as Microsoft Investor *(www.investor.msn.com)* or MarketWatch *(bigcharts.marketwatch.com/historical/)*. The Martindale-Hubbell site *(www.martindale-hubbell.com)* and West Legal Directory site *(lawyers.findlaw.com)* include free access to directories of legal professionals, complete with search capabilities. Every researcher has favorite sites; one of mine is the Business Journals page *(www.bizjournals.com)*. This site has links to regional business journals across the country, as well as a search engine that allows you to search the entire site or the business journal of a specified city.

APRA offers members and nonmembers alike a collection of Web resources for advancement research *(www.aprahome.org)*. This incredibly rich site contains links to Web collections compiled by prospect researchers representing several different types of institutions. It is one of the best resources available on free internet sites for prospect research. Another invaluable collection is offered by SupportingAdvancement.com, a volunteer-run site that offers resources for those working in the development and advancement fields. Its Research home page *(www.supportingadvancement.com/research/research.htm)* has links to many resources of interest to prospect researchers.

Many vendors charge for their information tools. Since new research offices usually must husband their resources, you should thoroughly examine these tools before signing any contracts. With that caveat in mind, here are some sources you might want to investigate.

- **Dialog.** Among the general information vendors, Dialog has one of the largest collections of databases. It contains many of the reference directories cited above, as well as a wealth of other information. The databases can be searched through Dialog's Web site *(www.dialog.com)*. Each database has variously defined searchable fields and an index listing databases in which a search phrase yields results. Free training is available to new users in most urban locations, and Dialog has developed user-friendly search capabilities on its Web site.

- **Lexis/Nexis.** While Lexis/Nexis *(www.lexisnexis.com)* originally began by providing information to legal research offices, it has expanded to users in other disciplines. Like Dialog, it contains reference databases beyond periodicals archives. Lexis/Nexis has developed a product tailored specifically to the needs of prospect researchers: Lexis/Nexis for Development Professionals *(www.lexisnexis.com/academic/universe/devpro)*. It brings together the types of resources prospect researchers use most often. The free customer support and one-on-one training available will help you make the most of this product.
- **ProQuest.** Another general information vendor popular among prospect researchers, ProQuest *(www.proquest.com)*, formerly called DataTimes, provides a deep database of current periodicals and newspapers, from international publications to regional journals. In some instances, it has digital images of the full back runs of the most popular newspapers.
- **Business and financial.** Some vendors specialize primarily in business or financial data. For example, Dow Jones News Retrieval *(www.dj.com)* concentrates on this area. Thomson Financial News *(www.thomson.com/solutions/financial)*, focuses on real-time market, business, and industry news. Dun & Bradstreet is one of the best sources of information on privately held companies. With an internet presence *(www.dnb.com)* and a desire to expand its customer base, it has begun offering flexible pricing options that make it more attractive to low-volume users. Its most popular publication is the "Business Information Report," containing a factual summary of information from public records and company officer interviews. Dun & Bradstreet databases are searchable by company name, phone number, or executive name.
- **Consultants.** Vendors have begun developing databases primarily for prospect screening and research. Most compile information from wide-ranging sources and screen your prospect database against their information. They usually deliver a product that identifies the best prospects in a constituent population and provide software to help manage prospect research. Those mentioned with some frequency by prospect researchers include

Bentz Whaley Flessner *(www.bwf.com)*, Grenzebach Glier & Associates *(www.grenzebachglier.com)*, Major Gift Identification/ Consulting or MaGIC *(www.majorgifts.net)*, Prospect Information Network or P!N *(www.prospectinfo.com)*, and Target America *(www.tgtam.com)*. A more comprehensive list of vendor links may be found on the Research page at SupportingAdvancement.com *(www.supportingadvancement.com/research/research.htm)*.

Training and Professional Development

As limited as your time and money may be, you still will find it worthwhile to invest what you can in conferences, networking opportunities, and periodicals on prospect research.

Conferences

CASE *(www.case.org)* serves fundraisers, alumni administrators, and communications professionals who work in higher education or at independent schools. One of its best offerings for prospect researchers is its Annual Conference for Development Researchers, a two- to three-day gathering. You can meet with colleagues to discuss new challenges in the field, find solutions to current problems, share experiences and proven strategies, and make valuable connections. Another popular conference, the CASE Summer Institute in Advancement Services, offers workshop sessions on prospect research, as well as other advancement services functions, such as gift processing and stewardship. You also can attend individual sessions on research and find broader networking opportunities at CASE's eight district conferences, which take place regionally from December to April, and its annual conference in July.

The Association of Professional Researchers for Advancement *(www.aprahome.org)* hosts an international conference each summer devoted to prospect research topics. Its organization of workshops includes nine tracks from which you can choose, based on your experience and interests. In addition, vendor exhibits, a computer lab (you can browse fee-based vendors free!), and a model library give participants the opportunity to gain hands-on experience with a variety of research resources. APRA symposia are focused learning opportunities offered two or three times a year. One, usually offered for beginning researchers, features experienced faculty, low student/instructor ratios, and moderate registration fees. APRA Virtual Seminars offer a Web-based meeting with faculty presenting selected topics and moderating live, question-and-answer sessions. APRA also offers regional conferences sponsored by some 25 APRA chapters nationwide that feature inexpensive programs in one- and two-day sessions. APRA's mentor program links veteran researchers with those who have limited experience or are new to a geographic region or type of nonprofit. These partnerships are designed to provide one-to-one support as researchers set up and manage their operations.

Some lists generate many messages, usually more than you can read and still get your job done.

The Association of Fundraising Professionals *(www.afpnet.org)* serves development officers at a broad range of nonprofits. Prospect research sessions are among the national conference workshop offerings and are usually offered in local workshops sometime during the year.

Development consulting firms often sponsor workshops or one-on-one training sessions. If your institution has a contractual relationship with a firm, you may be able to participate.

Listservs

These days, some of the best networking takes place on free e-mail discussion lists. Prospect researchers have their own group, PRSPCT-L, founded in 1992 and currently host to nearly 3,500 members. A quick way to subscribe is to send a blank e-mail to *PRSPCT-L-SUBSCRIBE-REQUEST@CharityChannel.com*, or you can visit *http://charitychannel.com/archives/prspct-l.html.* To post a message to the subscriber group after you join, e-mail *PRSPCT-L@CharityChannel.com.*

As you might expect, subscribers to the various discussion lists range from novices to seasoned professionals. Some lists generate many messages, usually more than you can read and still get your job done. Protect your limited time by using the subject line to cull messages; read only those you are interested in or need. (To see a list of other e-mail discussion groups in which you might be interested, visit *www.case.org* and click on "Listservs."

Small, Not Smaller: A Small Shop Does Not Mean a Smaller Job

After I made a career move from a large research institution to a small liberal arts college, a former colleague asked if I were enjoying the "smallness" of my new position. Sure, my new school has less than 5 percent of the addressable alumni and a fundraising goal less than 10 percent of my previous employer's. We are definitely a small (by comparison) shop. But does that translate to a smaller job? Not even close.

We perform the same functions. We record and acknowledge gifts. We maintain databases and files. We plan events. We manage information systems. We produce reports. We identify and research prospects. We oversee budgets tasks. Although the scale is different, the variety and significance of the responsibilities are not.

We also have many of the same issues. At both schools, for example, the same tensions exist between advancement services and annual giving departments as the compressed fundraising cycle challenges internal systems. The annual giving staff's need for up-to-the-minute results and increasing demands for data can seem excessive to those of us in advancement services, but we must strive to balance internal and external demands and expectations, always remembering that we exist to support the entire advancement operation.

Another commonality between both shops is the challenge of keeping constituent records up-to-date, although we have different approaches to data collection. At Franklin & Marshall College, we track much more detail about all our alumni. For example, we collect information about favorite professors and courses, hobbies, and personal interests. Although potentially useful, it would be impractical to manage this level of detail for the masses at my former institution.

The most significant difference between my current and past employers, however, is the lack of resources. As well as fewer staff, we also have fewer technical and financial resources and often compete institutionwide for both. On the other hand, it is a great environment in which to be innovative, since fewer obstacles prevent growth and development. In addition, although at times we may continue to work in our own silos, they certainly seem shorter.

Given the differences, do similar strategies work in both large and small shops? Absolutely.

Invest in staff. A properly trained staff is more efficient and effective, and a cross-trained staff is crucial for covering planned and unplanned staff absences and surviving crunch times. To minimize training costs, staff can attend or host regional training, or take training via the Web. Another option is to seek formal training for an enthusiastic staffer and have her train the rest of the staff ("train the trainer"). Require staff to share training, conference materials, and notes with those unable to attend.

Document, document, document. Documented policies and procedures can be a lifesaver for staff when they work outside daily routines. It is a best practice to know what you do and why you do it.

Work as a team. Teams work toward common goals. Teamwork can be more visible in a small shop, since we often operate with "all hands on deck," particularly on large projects like our Annual Report of Gifts or an event weekend on campus. But it should translate to the little things as well—sharing news of a promotion with a major gift officer and the alumni magazine staff; pitching in on gift processing at calendar-year's end; helping get a mailing out the door, and so on.

Collaborate. I have found that my department has much in common with the operations function of our admissions office. As a result, we have been able to collaborate on diverse issues such as defining geographic regions in our databases, software purchases, and other technology initiatives.

Invest in tools and technology. Buy the best equipment you can afford, and implement a replacement cycle. The increased productivity is worth it.

Don't reinvent the wheel. Numerous resources on best practices are readily available. I have found listservs and their archives to be excellent sources of information. I also am a huge fan of the Web sites *www.supportingadvancement.com*, *www.fundsvcs.org*, and *www.case.org*.

Right is right. When it comes to ethics, the same high standards apply no matter how pressing our institutional needs or how limited our resources. IRS regulations govern our acceptance and acknowledgment of charitable contributions. Industry standards dictate how we report our progress.

Finally, be flexible. In a small or large shop, advancement services professionals wear many hats. If nothing else, such variety keeps our minds challenged and our days interesting.

References

Evans, Gary A. "Ethical Issues in Fund Raising," *Handbook of Institutional Advancement*, 3rd ed., CASE, 2000.

Fitzgerald, Nancy. "Small Office: Creative Hiring," CURRENTS, July/August 1999.

Palm, Patricia. "Manager's Portfolio: On the Ball: Managing Big Demands in a Small Shop," CURRENTS, May/June 2005.

—Becky Wile, Director of Advancement Services, Franklin & Marshall College

Periodicals

Some of the professional associations mentioned above offer publications as a benefit of membership. CURRENTS, a nine-times-a-year magazine published by CASE, covers topics in prospect research several times each year. APRA publishes *Connections*, a quarterly professional journal devoted exclusively to prospect research. You do not need to join an association to subscribe to *The Chronicle of Philanthropy*, a trade newspaper that often publishes articles on research trends. The *Internet Prospector (www.internet-prospector.org)*, published by a national network of volunteer prospect researchers, offers free subscriptions to its e-mail monthly newsletter, which is devoted to prospect research on the internet.

After you get your research office established and running, you need to develop the other components of a good, proactive research operation—prospect identification, prospect screening, prospect classification, and prospect tracking. Methods for many of these components are discussed in other chapters.

A Word About Integrity

The old Aretha Franklin song says it all: R-E-S-P-E-C-T. Respect for the prospect should always be foremost in your mind. Confidentiality is a must in all development work, and certainly in prospect research.

Respect for the prospect should always be foremost in your mind.

To help you set standards, write a research policy for your office, and do it sooner rather than later. Researchers at peer institutions are usually willing to share such documents. Your chief development officer and office colleagues probably will want to provide input. The APRA Advancement Research Standards collection *(www.aprahome.org)* may be useful as you write your policy. Once you have completed your policy, review and revise it each year. *(See Chapter 7, Privacy.)*

But no matter what, make certain your files are secure, both on computer and paper. Share research profiles only on a need-to-know basis and only with development staff. If a volunteer needs some of the information, write a meeting brief containing only the facts the volunteer must have to do the task requested. Even then, guard confidentiality closely.

Finally, when writing a research profile, include no unnecessary information. Here we end with the principles with which we began. You must be familiar with all aspects of development to make good judgments about what is valuable information and what you should not include in a research profile. In all your work, remember the purpose of prospect research—to match a prospect's interests and giving capability with the institution's goals and needs and to preserve the institutional memory of a prospect.

References

APRA Skill Sets: Prospect Research Fundamentals, Advanced Prospect Research, Research Management, Relationship Management.

APRA Position Paper, "The Strategic Role of Research in the Development Process," August 1998.

APRA Position Paper, "Privacy and Prospect Research," December 2000.

Dickey, Marilyn. "Fund-Raising Veterans Offer Advice on Setting Up a Donor-Research Unit," *Chronicle of Philanthropy,* October 16, 2003.

Eynon, Matthew K. "All Hands on Deck: Use a team approach to build donor relationships and maintain institutional memory," CURRENTS, January 2005.

Hogan, Cecilia. Prospect Research: *A Primer for Growing Nonprofits.* Jones and Bartlett Publishers, 2004.

CHAPTER 7

Privacy

By David F. Lamb | Prospect Research Consultant | Blackbaud Analytics

I was late checking into the hotel after a long day of business travel. I trudged up to the second floor and slipped my keycard into the door reader. The green light flashed and I opened the door.

Slam! The door stopped abruptly against the security bar, which was set from the inside of the room. Surprised as I was by this, I was even more surprised to see a cheek and an eye, peering out at me suspiciously, appear in the crack.

"Who is it, Don?" called a tremulous female voice from inside the room. "What do you want?"

"I'm so sorry," said I in embarrassment. "This was the key I was given at the front desk. Please excuse me."

The door slammed shut without further comment, and I returned to the desk to get a less crowded room.

Finally getting into a blessedly vacant room, the first thing I did was to set the security bar on the door! As I unpacked what I needed for the next morning, I thought about what had happened. It was discomfiting for me, but it had to be vastly more disturbing to the couple whose privacy I had violated.

The next morning, as I was eating my breakfast just off the hotel lobby, I thought I saw the same eye and cheek from the night before, along with the rest of the unhappy guest, in earnest conversation with the person at the front desk. I'm sure the occupants of that room received some kind of accommodation from the hotel. For a moment I thought maybe I should have sought some compensation from the hotel. As I mulled it over, though, I realized that I was not the injured party. I was the innocent bystander, but the slight embarrassment I felt was not troubling enough to make me seek redress. On the other hand, if I had been one of the occupants of that room, I would have been truly shaken.

Most of us present a version of ourselves to the public that we hope is attractive or at least inoffensive. In our own rooms with the door closed, all our defenses are down. All our imperfections are unprotected—and who cares? We are safe from exposure there. The closed, locked room is the place where we least want to be viewed by someone not invited into our private domain. To find that this sanctuary can be violated without our consent interferes with deeply rooted cultural assumptions about privacy.

Most of us present a version of ourselves to the public that we hope is attractive or at least inoffensive.

Those we allow into this private space are there because (we hope) they understand the context of our lives. They are less likely to judge us unfairly, since they know us as complex people with both attractive and unattractive qualities. If you know the whole context of a person's life, an isolated example of an unseemly quality will probably seem less offensive. That is the theory, anyway.

If someone who does not know us observes us in our private space, it feels like a terrible invasion of privacy. It is not just a physical intrusion that triggers this sense of violation. Being subject to observation, either directly or by access to private information about us, is enough to cause the injury. We fear that facts about us may be taken out of context and used to harm us.

Here we come to the crux of the problem of privacy and the prospect researcher. The prospect researcher's job is to gather information about potential donors. Prospect researchers are quick to point out that they limit themselves to public information sources and do their work with respect for prospective donors. Nevertheless, if you tell people that your job is to collect facts about donor prospects, the chances are good that they will look at you as if you had confessed to voyeurism.

Trouble at the ACLU

The American Civil Liberties Union has been the subject of much negative publicity lately because of its plans to engage a vendor to do prospect research on donors and other constituents. The *New York Times* on December 18, 2004, broke the story, "ACLU's Search for Data on Donors Stirs Privacy Fears." The ACLU's executive director had hired a firm to screen its database for donor prospects capable of contributing to the upcoming fundraising campaign. An

A Brief History of APRA

To understand how prospect research has emerged as a profession, you need to know something about the evolution of the Association of Professional Researchers for Advancement (formerly the American Prospect Research Association). APRA provides a distinct professional identity for both hands-on researchers and those who manage that activity as part of advancement services.

The association got its start in the early 1980s, when researchers in Minneapolis-St. Paul met to address specific research issues. The first gathering took place June 12, 1981, at Augsburg College. Members of the group called themselves fundraising researchers (and briefly considered becoming a sub-unit of the National Society of Fund Raising Executives). In 1983 they took the name Minnesota Prospect Research Association; by 1986 they had developed a guiding document about the rights and responsibilities of researchers.

At its July 1987 board meeting, the group adopted the name American Prospect Research Association, and APRA was incorporated in Minnesota on January 11, 1988. The first national meeting took place September 15-16, 1988, in Spring Hill, Minnesota. The annual conference topics since then show the changes that have taken place in technology, research methodology, and the role of research as the basis of fundraising, particularly in higher education and at medical centers.

Since incorporation, APRA's membership has grown to more than 1,600, with approximately half attending meetings in recent years. Leading the organization is a board of directors; it contracts out membership services and conference management. In 1992, the association adopted a statement of professional ethics that was revised in 1998. In the mid-1990s, the board also considered whether to certify researchers. A task force considered but decided not to pursue certification at that time, and instead APRA has produced basic and advanced skills sets for researchers.

Recognizing that research has gone international (as evidenced by members from Canada and Europe), in 1995 the organization became the Association of Professional Researchers for Advancement.

At the end of its first formal decade, APRA has gained respect for the services these professionals provide and grappled with the impact of a membership sizable enough to need multitrack conferences. The association publishes a professional journal, *Connections*, as well as a newsletter. All these services have earned APRA a distinctive place among the organizations that support the fundraising profession.

—Jonathan A. Lindsey Ph.D. CFRE, Assistant Vice President, Donor and Information Services, Baylor University

ACLU officer accidentally learned about the project and took word of it to the board of directors. Their privacy policy explicitly stated that the ACLU would gather personal information only with the permission of members and donors. It also said it would not sell or transfer information to a third party or use it for marketing. Making things worse, after the staff member blew the whistle, this wording was changed to more ambiguous language. Several directors objected to this use of the database and felt it was hypocritical because the ACLU criticizes large corporations for their use of consumer information in a way that endangers privacy.

. . . if your policy states you do not do research, or certain kinds of research, you jolly well better not do it.

The *Times* article noted that it is common for nonprofits to "collect information about their donors to help their fundraising, using technology to figure out giving patterns, net worth, and other details that assist with more targeted pitches." There were three problems with the way ACLU administrators went about this, however. First, the ACLU historically has taken a hard line on privacy issues. Second, the executive director took pains to obscure the fact that he had engaged a screening company to identify prospects. Third, the ACLU's published privacy policy was changed specifically to allow this kind of data mining without the board's agreement.

Let me be clear about the issues raised by the ACLU debacle. This episode does not bring into question the ethics of doing prospect research. It does point out that if your policy states you do not do research, or certain kinds of research, you jolly well better not do it. If you decide to change your policy on what you do with donor data, you should change it publicly, so that the donors are duly warned.

I will return to the importance of a clear privacy policy—and sticking to that policy.

Prospect Researchers Love Privacy Too

Ironically, prospect researchers as a group tend to be strong privacy advocates. Knowing that sometimes privacy lines can be crossed with relative ease, prospect researchers are vigilant not to cross them.

The Association of Professional Researchers for Advancement is the international organization that promotes and supports the activities of prospect researchers. A history appears on page 93. APRA has taken a strong stand on privacy. Its positions are laid out in several documents that can be found on its Web site *(www.aprahome.org)*. These include APRA's "Statement of Ethics" and a position paper, "Privacy and Prospect Research." Here are some of the main points of that position paper (reprinted by permission of APRA):

- The availability of information in the public domain does not drive the collection of data nor supersede ethical principles and practices concerning its use.
- As outlined in APRA's Statement of Ethics, the fundamental principles that drive our work include:
  - The protection of confidential information
  - The accurate recording of all data
  - Relevance of the information sought
  - Honesty in revealing our identities and the purpose of our work
  - Taking responsibility and being accountable for our actions as professional researchers
- APRA members follow all applicable federal, state, and local laws governing the collection, use, maintenance, and dissemination of information.
- Policies and procedures are amended to address changes in laws and available technologies while preserving the underlying ethical standards.
- It is our professional responsibility to require information vendors to disclose the sources of their data and their use of any data our organizations might provide to them.

- We utilize only those resources and work with only those vendors that meet our ethical guidelines.
- We abide by the principles of confidentiality and appropriateness when sharing internal information between departments and between organizations.
- We seek only information needed for effective fundraising for our organizations and avoid the collection of unnecessary peripheral data that might compromise an individual's privacy.

Several themes emerge here that are important to the conduct of prospect research that respects the privacy of donor prospects. First, researchers have something akin to a fiduciary relationship with the subjects of their research in the sense that they keep the information collected in trust, protect it from misuse, and have the best interests of the prospect in mind at all times. Second, the actions of researchers are limited by legal and ethical boundaries. And third, the researchers hold vendors who supply data to researchers to the same standard of conduct that they (the researchers) impose on themselves. Let's unpack these themes.

Fiduciary Relationship

The *Merriam Webster Dictionary of Law* defines a fiduciary as "one...who obligates himself or herself to act on behalf of another (as in managing money or property) and assumes a duty to act in good faith and with care, candor, and loyalty in fulfilling the obligation." If a prospect researcher acts like a fiduciary, it is not money that he or she manages; it is *information*. The researcher has an obligation to use and communicate that information to appropriate development staff members in good faith with the prospect, considering the prospect's best interests and sensibilities.

Legal and Ethical Boundaries

The Fourth Amendment notwithstanding[1], there is no Constitutional right to privacy. Over the past 100 years, however, the courts have

[1] *The Fourth Amendment says, "The right of the people to be secure in their persons, houses, papers, and effects, against unreasonable searches and seizures, shall not be violated, and no warrants shall issue, but upon probable cause, supported by oath or affirmation, and particularly describing the place to be searched, and the persons or things to be seized."*

upheld "the right to be left alone." With this as a starting point, according to *21st Century Money, Banking and Commerce Alert* (Fried, Frank, Harris, Shriver & Jacobson, 1998) legally recognized invasions of privacy can be boiled down into four distinct categories:

1. The unreasonable intrusion upon the seclusion of another
2. The appropriation of another's name or likeness
3. The unreasonable publicity given to another's private life
4. Publicity that unreasonably places another in a false light before the public

Advancement researchers shall be truthful with regard to their identities and purpose . . .

While all of these should be avoided while doing donor research, the first invasion is most likely to tempt prospect researchers. A healthy ethical orientation is the best safeguard against "intrusion on the seclusion" of our prospects. APRA provides good guidance in its Statement of Ethics. I quote several salient lines:

- Advancement researchers shall seek and record only information that is relevant to the cultivation, solicitation, and/or stewardship strategy with the prospect.
- Advancement researchers shall be truthful with regard to their identities and purpose and the identity of their institutions during the course of their work.
- Advancement researchers should not evade or avoid questions about their affiliations or purpose when requesting information in person, over the phone, electronically, or in writing. It is recommended that requests for public information be made on institutional stationery and that these requests clearly identify the requester.
- Advancement researchers should use the usual and customary methods of payment or reimbursement for products or services purchased on behalf of their institutions.
- Advancement researchers should be experts on the reliability of sources (print, electronic, and otherwise), as well as the sources utilized by third parties to gather information on their behalf.
- Advancement researchers shall present information in an objective and factual manner; note attribution, and clearly identify information that is conjecture or analysis. Where there is conflicting information, advancement researchers should objectively present

the multiple versions and state any reason for preferring one version over another.

I cannot emphasize the last two points enough. It is not sufficient to limit oneself to public information. The quality of the information in the public domain ranges from rock-solid truth to outright lies. Researchers must do their best to discern the quality of the information they find and report only what is truthful. Whenever possible, the researcher should find two or more reliable sources that agree with each other.

Some might say even these guidelines are not restrictive enough. Information that is relevant and truthful still may be too personal to be recorded. They argue that collection of any information, even if it is publicly available, requires too great an intrusion on the prospect's "seclusion" to be tolerated. Those who criticize the ACLU's screening project might take this position. While I understand and respect it, I find the position unnecessarily restrictive. I will explain why later.

Prospect researchers at certain types of nonprofits must pay attention to industry-specific laws. I speak here primarily of hospitals, governed by HIPAA regulations, and educational institutions, governed by FERPA. It behooves researchers employed by healthcare and educational institutions to read the law and know the parts that are relevant to their work. *(See Chapter 9, Operating in the Context of Federal Privacy Requirements.)*

Working with Vendors

In the world of prospect research, a "vendor" is a business that aggregates and sells data useful to prospect researchers. These companies include Dun & Bradstreet, Hoovers, 10K Wizard, DIALOG, and Lexis-Nexis. They collect, organize, and index news, business, and asset information. The researcher usually accesses all this information through a Web page with simple search commands, retrieving large amounts of data in a short time. Collectively, these vendors are known as commercial data brokers.

The power of the search capability provided by data brokers is impressive, but it is limited. Much of the data they collect must be disclosed by certain individuals and companies. Everyone has a right to see it. The data brokers just make it easier to access.

A public company insider (defined as a top officer, director or 10 percent shareholder of a public company) has enormous potential to make decisions that affect the company's profits. The government recognizes that the company's shareholders and the public at large (for the most part not insiders) have a legitimate interest in knowing if the insiders bought or sold shares in the company, and how much of the company each insider owns. This openness is designed to reduce the ability of a company's leaders surreptitiously to take actions that harm the stockholders and the economy. However, a person could own stock worth billions of dollars and not meet the criteria for an insider. A noninsider's stock is invisible to the prospect researcher. Since most people are not insiders, their stock is safe from examination by strangers. On the other hand, insiders know and expect strangers to be interested in their stock holdings.

Every time you use your credit card or hand your grocery discount card to the clerk at the checkout counter, data about your tastes, interests, and buying habits are being collected.

Insider stock data are just one example of a huge and growing number of data streams funneled to commercial data brokers. Every time you use your credit card or hand your grocery discount card to the clerk at the checkout counter, data about your tastes, interests, and buying habits are being collected. We willingly cooperate in this collection of information about us in exchange for discount prices or the convenience of credit cards.

Here is where privacy advocates start to ring the warning bells. Once data are collected, you have virtually no control over how they are used. This is why certain laws have been passed to help prevent improper use of your personal information. Over the past 35 years, successive laws have been designed to protect consumer privacy. Two that are relevant to the data sources used in prospect research are the Fair Credit Reporting Act (FCRA) of 1970 (Privacy Initiatives, *www.ftc.gov*) and GLBA, also known as the Financial Modernization Act of 1999.

The FCRA sets rules for how consumer-reporting agencies (such as Experian, Equifax, and TransUnion) store, allow access to, and permit corrections to data they collect on consumer credit. GLBA includes provisions to protect consumers' personal and financial information held at financial institutions. Neither of these laws, nor many others related to privacy that have cropped up, is perfect. Privacy watchdogs such as the Electronic Privacy Information Center *(www.epic.org)* keep a close eye on consumer reporting agencies and government agencies that aggregate personal information.

Some have suggested that the problem is not as great as it seems. In June 2004, *Reason Magazine* published an issue devoted to the "Database Nation" *(www.reason.com)*. In the cover story, Declan McCullagh argues that those who would fight the "databasification" of American society fail to consider the many benefits it brings. He says:

> *Markets function more efficiently when it costs little to identify and deliver the right product to the right consumer at the right time. Data collection and information sharing emerged not through chance but because they bring lower prices and more choices for consumers. The ability to identify customers who are not likely to pay their bills lets stores offer better deals to those people who will. In films like* The Net *and* Changing Lanes, *Hollywood tells us that databases can be very dangerous. The truth is more complex. Being a citizen of a database nation, it turns out, can be very good for you.*

Whether you endorse McCullagh's sunny attitude toward consumer databases or the more suspicious stance of EPIC, it is important for researchers to be aware of the provenance of the information their vendors provide to them. Only information that is legally and ethically collected may be used for the purposes of prospect research. The question remains, "How do you know when there's a problem?"

Consider the kind of information that might be purchased from a commercial data broker:

- **Insider stock holdings.** The government collects and publishes this information for the good and protection of the public. It is easily accessed from the government's own Web site, although data brokers improve the ease of search and retrieval.
- **Real estate values and descriptions.** The government records property values for tax purposes. The information is made available to the public to ensure that taxes are evenly and fairly administered. Data brokers obtain the information from county assessor offices and index it for ease of searching.

- **Private company directories.** Much like a phone directory, these sources allow customers and suppliers to find and evaluate companies with which they might do business. Some vendors—Dun & Bradstreet, for example—also serve a credit reporting function to analyze a company further. For most researchers the credit report is too expensive and too detailed to bother with. However, basic descriptive information like sales, top officers, and number of employees is less expensive to buy from a data broker. All of this information is self-reported by the companies.
- **Biographical directories.** Most of the information in biographical directories like *Who's Who* is self-reported. *Who's Who* researches a small number of celebrities because of the general public interest in them.
- **Foundation affiliations.** The only tax returns open to public scrutiny are called 990PFs, filed by foundations. You do not need to go through a commercial data broker to read these, but the data brokers index them for more efficient searching. Other vendors do additional research about the foundations and publish profiles of them in directory form.
- **Direct marketing databases.** Direct marketers collect data from many different sources and perform statistical analyses to answer the question: Who is likely to buy which product? If you are statistically similar to someone who buys golf clubs, you probably will get advertisements for golf clubs. This helps the companies that sell golf clubs because they do not waste money advertising to people who do not know a fairway from a runway. It helps the golf aficionado learn about the latest golf gadgets.

The obvious application to fundraising is that you could use the same technique to answer a different question: Who is likely to make which kind of gift to my organization? The data come from many sources, including the census, surveys, polls, behavioral research, consumer-supplied data (as when you register new software), magazine subscriptions, and credit transactions.

The bomb in that sentence is "credit." One could imagine prospect researchers checking the credit rating of prospects to see if they "qualify" to make major gifts. Nothing could be further from the truth. It is, in fact, inappropriate for a researcher to have direct access to any credit information. Researchers do have a way, however, to use credit information appropriately without violating privacy.

In the past two decades, a number of vendors have created screening tools that apply the lessons of direct marketing to fundraising. ACLU contracted one of these, which stirred up all the trouble. But remember, screening is not unethical. It was the ACLU's failure to follow its own policy that caused the problem. By including aggregated credit information, along with all the other typical data sources used in direct marketing, these vendors create a statistical profile of someone likely to make a gift to a particular organization. All the people on the nonprofit's database then can be scored according to this model. The credit data for any one person are not revealed. The prospect becomes part of a composite "likelihood" score.

Companies that provide this modeling service are known collectively as screening vendors. Keep two points in mind with respect to credit data when using a screening vendor. First, even the screening vendor should not see the details of a person's credit record. The vendor sees only aggregated data from groups with similar credit profiles. Second, request assurance that any credit reporting agency used by a screening vendor complies with the FCRA.

Why Worry?

Considering social fears about lost privacy and bad publicity for nonprofits like the ACLU, why would a respectable nonprofit want to do prospect research at all? Do you not risk offending major donors by doing research on them? My answer is no.

Do you not risk offending major donors by doing research on them? My answer is no.

At a recent fundraising conference, a panel of wealthy donors responded to questions about what it was like on the other side of the tin cup. The moderator asked, "What is something that you find annoying as a donor?" Without hesitation, one panelist responded, "It's the volume of requests for money from organizations I care nothing about." The other panelists generally agreed with this complaint. Wealthy people are often besieged by solicitations from organizations that need their support. Usually, the only ones they fund are those in whose mission they are personally involved. The others are like a swarm of annoying flies. If you do not want your organization to be perceived as an annoying fly, you'd best do some research to find out what plucks the heartstrings of your most capable prospects. That way you can present your project to the prospect in the most appealing light.

Another panelist noted that he could tell when a fundraiser had not done his or her homework. "They'll ask for too much or too little." It is almost a cliché in development that if you ask for too little, the prospect will get out her checkbook and write you a check for the amount you requested. Usually it is less of a problem to ask for too much, but this still usually results in a smaller gift. The prospect may be flattered but will probably counter with an amount that is less than her capability. The ideal request will be an amount the prospect must stretch to make but is well within his capacity. This will make the prospect think long and hard about his depth of commitment to your cause, and when the gift is made, the prospect's joy in giving will be all the greater.

This is the noble role of the fundraiser: to help generous people do the good things they want to do with their money. It is the noble role of the prospect researcher to ascertain the right project and the right amount for the right donor. When that happens, everybody wins.

Let's be clear. Doing your homework does not extend to gathering every scrap of data and gossip available about a prospect. When collecting prospect information, a researcher should be able to answer "yes" to all these questions:

- Is it truthful?
- Is it relevant to the mission of the organization and the fundraising process?
- Is it respectful of the prospect?

Make a Statement

Thanks to laws like FCRA, FERPA, and HIIPA, privacy statements abound on documents related to healthcare, education and finance. Most commercial Web sites have links to the corporation's privacy statement. Legislation about what nonprofit organizations must guarantee in terms of privacy is less well formed.

Charity Navigator *(www.charitynavigator.org)* evaluates nonprofits to help donors make informed decisions about which organizations should receive their charitable dollars. One of the things Charity Navigator looks for is whether the nonprofit provides a privacy statement to donors. This statement must "have a donor privacy policy in writing, guaranteeing that they will not sell or trade their donors' personal or contact information to anyone else. Furthermore, the policy must be prominently displayed on the charity's Web site or in its marketing and solicitation materials."

In December 2004, Charity Navigator reported on a study of how 3,282 of the nation's largest charities and nonprofits were implementing their privacy policies—or if they had one at all. The results of the survey became part of Charity Navigator's ratings of these organizations. Here is what they found, as reported on their Web site:

- 18 percent have donor privacy policies that Charity Navigator's analysts were able to verify (depicted on Charity Navigator's ratings page with a latched padlock);
- 7 percent said they either had no policy or had not taken the time to put their policy in writing (depicted on the ratings page with an unlatched padlock); and
- 75 percent chose not to respond to the inquiry (identified on the ratings page with the term "no response").

As concerns about identity theft and erosion of privacy continue to rise, nonprofits can ill afford to be among those whose privacy policy is ambiguous or nonexistent. While prospect researchers can lead the initiative to publish clear privacy policies, they cannot do it alone. Donor privacy must be safeguarded at every level of the nonprofit organization.

The purpose of a privacy policy is to let donors know that you understand your fiduciary responsibility for their information, you abide by strong ethical standards, and you insist that the vendors you hire do the same. It should answer the following questions:

- What information is collected?
- How will the personal information be used?
- How will the personal information be saved? How is it protected? Who will see it?

- Will the personal information ever be disclosed? Shared? Sold?
- Should users expect to be contacted only when permission is granted? Without permission? By third parties?
- When a person submits personal information, is implied consent granted? If so, what is implied?
- What other information (for example, demographic information) may be kept, used, and shared?

The above list was supplied by the University of Washington. Several Web sites listed in the Resources section at the end of this chapter can assist an organization that wishes to create a privacy policy.

Any nonprofit's privacy policy should have a section on prospect research.

Any nonprofit's privacy policy should have a section on prospect research. The following sample language is excerpted from a handout Lona Farr, a partner in Farr Healey Consulting, provided at the 2004 AFP International Conference in a session on donor privacy:

- Prospect research enables ABC Charity to obtain highly confidential background and wealth information on prospects and donors. This policy is intended to protect these individuals' privacy, to control the gathering of that information, and to control the costs of purchased internet prospect research.
- Prospect research will be used only to gather information about potential ABC Charity prospects and donors and will not be utilized by any other person for any other purpose.
- Requests for prospect research on individuals must be cleared by the chief development officer. It is suggested that the gift potential triggering these requests is in excess of $25,000.
- Prospect research will be conducted only by a designated advancement officer or the chief development officer. All requests for prospect research will be logged in by this person.
- Only a designated advancement officer or the chief development officer will have the password for any search services purchased for the purpose of prospect research.
- A designated advancement officer or the chief development officer will compile the research information in a composite form, to be viewed only by personnel involved in preparing briefings for meetings and solicitations. This information will be maintained in a highly confidential manner.

- This information will not be included in the computerized data available about the donor or prospect. It will be filed alphabetically in hard copy in a filing cabinet accessible only to individuals approved by the chief development officer.
- A code or note in the donor's or prospect's computer file will indicate that additional information is available in hard copy.

Not every organization will adopt a research policy exactly like this, but these points bear discussion. A point on which some may disagree is the method of profile storage. Some would argue that if the proper security measures are taken on a nonprofit enterprise's database, keeping the donor information in electronic format is every bit as secure as putting hard-copy documents under lock and key.

A privacy statement is only as good as the follow-through.

A privacy statement is only as good as the follow-through. Just ask the ACLU. The same is true with a hotel's guarantee. I happen to know that the hotel I mentioned at the start of this article has a money-back guarantee if the guest is not satisfied. One couple was dissatisfied, and they had a right to complain. They might not stay there again. But other customers put greater confidence in that hotel chain because of their public statement that they strive to give 100 percent satisfaction. If on a rare occasion they miss the goal, it is because human beings operate the company. Mistakes happen, but they cannot be tolerated. If mistakes go uncorrected, that hotel chain will soon be out of business. If you violate the privacy of your donors, so will you.

Resources

Association of Professional Researchers for Advancement
www.aprahome.org

Online Privacy for Nonprofits: How to Protect Members' Privacy and Personal Information, Fact Sheet 28, *www.privacyrights.org*

The Nature Conservancy, *www.nature.org*

TRUSTe Model Privacy Policy, *Privacy Resources, www.truste.org*

TRUSTe Guide to writing an online privacy policy, Privacy Resources, Your Online Privacy Policy, *www.truste.org*

CHAPTER 8

Tracking Prospects: The Right Gift From the Right Person at the Right Time

By Robert Weiner | President | Robert L. Weiner Consulting

Karen Rhodes | Director of Campaign Planning | College of Engineering
University of California, Berkeley

Your newest colleague, a major gifts officer, wants your help. She needs to get acquainted with her prospect pool and decide where to focus first. To get started, she wants to know:

- Have any of her prospects been rated as having a high-gift capacity?
- Which of them have the strongest connections to your institution?
- How is her pool divided among prospects in cultivation, solicitation, and stewardship?
- Which prospects are ready to make a gift in the immediate future?
- How much have her prospects given in the past and what did they support?
- What actions took place recently and what follow-up is needed?

For some answers, she will seek out colleagues, volunteers, board members, and perhaps her predecessor. At the same time, the advancement services office and advancement database should help her fill in the blanks, track the new information she gathers, and stay focused on the best prospects.

(Note: Although corporate and foundation fundraisers need to answer the same questions, the focus of this chapter is on major gifts from individuals.)

Every organization has its own way of tracking prospects. The fields and codes listed below are provided as examples, not as the "right" answers or "best practices." A best practice is what works best for your organization.

Who?

. . . it does not matter how wealthy someone is if she does not care about your institution and will not answer calls from your fundraisers.

Top prospects are those with an optimal combination of capacity (they are likely to make a large gift), inclination (they are strongly committed to your institution), and readiness (they might be able to make a gift in the near future). Capacity is the most seductive of the three. However, it does not matter how wealthy someone is if she does not care about your institution and will not answer calls from your fundraisers.

How Much?

Gift potential, or capacity, is a good starting point for prioritizing prospects. Ratings are derived from staff and volunteer interactions with the prospect, prospect research, peer ratings, and electronic wealth screenings. Gift potential is not the same as net worth or disposable assets; it should reflect the likelihood of a gift to your institution. Below are sample gift potential ratings for an institution that classifies a major gift as $10,000 or more:

$5 million+
$1– $4.9 million
$500,000 – $999,999
$250,000 – $499,999
$100,000 – $249,999
$50,000 – $99,999
$25,000 – $49,999
$10,000 – $24,999
Less than $10,000 (not a major gift prospect)

How Committed Are Your Prospects?

Ideal prospects have inclination or affinity, as well as capacity. Inclination is a subjective rating of the prospect's interest in giving a significant gift to your institution. It is based on the prospect's previous support of your institution (or organizations with similar missions), the degree to which your project aligns with the prospect's interests, and the strength of the prospect's relationship with your institution.

One institution uses the following codes:

1 Strongest inclination to give at rated potential: We are their top priority.

2 Strongly inclined, but we may not be their top priority.

3 Moderate inclination; worthy of pursuit. Could be inclined to give at potential if engaged properly.

4 Low inclination; worthy of pursuit. With proper attention, they could become more inclined to give at potential.

5 Not interested in us. No amount of cultivation will bring them around.

6 Interested, but health or personal situation prevents giving at this time.

7 Unknown inclination.

Another institution uses:

1 HIGH: Trustee, major donor, active on boards and committees, solicitor of others.

2 MEDIUM: Active, regular volunteer, significant donations made, committee person.

3 LOW: Moderately active or formerly active, periodic donor at lower levels.

4 QUESTIONABLE: Minimal interest, sporadic donor, participant, meeting attendee, etc.

5 NONE: Not involved, no record of interest.

Others categorize their prospects as hot, warm, or cold.

Inclination and readiness to give are often demonstrated by a history of interactions with your institution, including past giving. If you are not able to combine giving history with your prospect tracking data, it may be time to look for a new donor database. This topic is discussed in Section V of this book and in the *Handbook of Institutional Advancement,* 3rd ed. (CASE, 2000).

Tracking Contacts

Your database and contact reports should tell you who did what with whom and when. You should be able to tell whether any prospects are expecting calls, meetings, or proposals. The contact reports should provide more qualitative information about interests, inclination, and readiness (but nothing you would not want the prospect to read).

Your tracking system should tell you at least whether a prospect is in initial investigation, being actively solicited, or has declined a previous ask. There are many ways to track prospect status. For example, one organization uses the codes:

A Identify

B Involve

C Align

D Ask

E Close

Often, a prospect status hierarchy looks like the following:

A Identification

B Research

C Qualification

D Cultivation (some institutions use a separate Renewal status)

E Solicitation

F Stewardship

G Not a prospect

A fully detailed hierarchy may look something like the following. But even if you choose a simpler or shorter format, many of these stages are worth adopting:

A **Pending or Internal Tracking:** The prospect is awaiting research or qualification.

B **Research**

C **Not a Prospect:** The prospect is not viable.

D **Potential or Introductory:** The prospect is awaiting classification by a fundraiser.

E **Initial Cultivation:** Used during the early stages of getting to know the prospect.

F **Cultivation:** The prospect has displayed interest or is a previous major donor who has been moved back into cultivation. A prospect might remain in cultivation for months or years.

G **Active:** A solicitation strategy is being developed. Used just before scheduling and making the ask.

H **Inactive:** The prospect is not able to make a major gift/ commitment at this time but has potential for the future.

I **Ask Scheduled:** The anticipated ask date and amount have been set.

J **Ask Made:** The solicitation took place and a decision is due.

K **In Negotiation:** The prospect may have made a commitment but the specifics of the gift are still being worked out.

L **Closed Solicitation/Yes:** The prospect agreed to the ask.

M **Closed Solicitation/No:** The prospect declined the ask.

N **Closed Solicitation/Not Now:** The prospect declined the ask but will consider an ask in the future.

O **Stewardship:** Stewardship would follow Closed Solicitation/Yes.

P **Renewal:** Renewal follows a period of stewardship.

Readiness

You have looked at capacity, inclination, past giving, and past actions. Many institutions also track the likelihood of a gift within a specific period. This coding may be called *readiness, timeline,* or *stage*, among other things. For example, one institution uses the codes:

C1 0 – 6 months until solicitation

C2 7 – 12 months until solicitation

C3 13 months or more until solicitation

The C indicates that they are in cultivation (so you can pull a list of all the Cs), and the number tells you when an ask might come.

Putting it All Together

In reviewing all the prospects assigned to your new fundraiser, you identify 50 prospects coded as actively cultivated (let's say they are coded "C") and a dozen coded for stewardship ("S"); they made a gift in the past and may be ready for another approach.

Five of the Cs and two S prospects are rated with gift potentials above $5 million (substitute your own amounts based on your organization's historical performance). However, their inclination ratings are all low or unknown. They might be wealthy, but they are not ready to be approached (and never may be).

On the other hand, 30 of the Cs and 10 of the S prospects with the highest inclination have gift potential ratings above $500,000, and a few are rated at $1 million. The inclination codes were entered within the past six months, so the information is relatively current. This group goes at the top of your fundraiser's list. Unfortunately, the previous fundraiser did not track readiness, so you do not know if any gifts are imminent. The new fundraiser promises to do better at tracking readiness.

The fundraiser decides to focus her immediate attention on the Cs with the highest inclination ratings, capacity ratings of at least $500,000, and recent significant contacts with the institution. She also will work on re-engaging the S prospects.

Meet the Prospects

As the fundraiser gets to know her prospects, she will want to record her results. If she is raising funds for more than one purpose, she needs to track which prospects are interested in what. Many institutions do this with interest, project, or campaign codes. These might be general (Music, Engineering, Building, Scholarship, or Endowment), or specific (Building Addition Campaign). If you are recording projects only as free text in a spreadsheet, contact report, or comments field, it will be difficult to produce a list of prospects by project. Instead, you need a defined set of codes, so that "emergency relief funds" are always "ERF," rather than a random set of acronyms and abbreviations.

As the fundraiser builds relationships with her prospects, she should track prospect status (cultivation, solicitation, etc.), along with dates showing when the status code was assigned. Many fundraisers also track the following:

- What action needs to be taken next (such as arranging lunch with the department chair)? This is usually entered as a free-text comment.
- Who needs to take the action? In large offices, the action may be delegated to another fundraiser or an assistant. Some databases allow tasks to be assigned to someone else. The person who made the assignment then can monitor the status of the task.
- When should the action take place? Many databases include a "tickler" system to remind fundraisers of upcoming actions. The ticklers might be displayed when the fundraiser logs into the database or might arrive via e-mail.

However you track them, it is important to retain a record of past actions.

However you track them, it is important to retain a record of past actions.

If your institution has more than one fundraiser, you will want to assign a solicitor to active prospects. Some institutions assign multiple solicitors. They might include a manager who helps develop strategy and oversees all approaches, a volunteer who helps with cultivation, and a fundraiser (or perhaps a dean or director) who will make the ask.

A related topic is prospect clearance: Who is authorized to make contact with a prospect?

Large organizations often assign a prospect manager who is not necessarily the solicitor. The manager needs to be informed of all cultivation and solicitation plans. Clearance might be granted only for specific types of activities (such as ongoing cultivation but not solicitation). Clearance also might be granted for a set period. At the end of this time, the clearance may be extended if tangible steps have been taken and progress is being made. Otherwise, it may be withdrawn.

What Else do You Need to Track?

Fundraisers must avoid the trap of spending all their time tracking data at the expense of raising funds.

The list seems endless. It includes wealth ratings from electronic and peer screenings, the value of stocks, options and properties, board memberships, gifts to other organizations, *Who's Who* entries, news reports, and much more.

No system has defined fields for everything. Much prospect data will be entered as free-text comments. If possible, however, you should categorize comments so they can be retrieved or mined easily.

Fundraisers must avoid the trap of spending all their time tracking data at the expense of raising funds. Leave the tracking to the advancement services specialist—the fundraiser needs to meet and engage people. In addition, some information changes daily and is not worth transferring to a database. If you have a small shop or no researcher, stick to the basics: status, inclination, interests, capacity or ask amount, last action, and next action.

The Right Gift, the Right Person, the Right Time

Some databases allow you to enter a proposal record for a prospect. A single prospect could have multiple proposals. A proposal record lets you track the solicitor, project or purpose, planned ask amount, planned ask date, and any notes. You then can record a series of activities and dates related to the ask. Some institutions also record a confidence level for a planned ask. For instance, it might be targeted at $1 million, with a 75 percent confidence level.

Some development offices use a pipeline report to track major gifts activities and forecast revenue. Such a report might summarize how many prospects are in each stage of activity for each fundraiser, department, region, or campaign. It might list the predicted value of pending and planned solicitations, and, if tracked, the level of confidence the asks will be successful.

Your challenge is to help fundraisers identify the best prospects, prioritize their work, and stay in touch with previous donors without getting bogged down in record keeping. A good prospect tracking system also turns information about prospects into an asset that is available long after any particular fundraiser has left the institution.

CHAPTER 9

Operating in the Context of Federal Privacy Requirements:
FERPA, HIPAA, and GLBA

By Alan S. Hejnal | Director of Advancement Services | University of Richmond

Privacy concerns arise from respect for our donors and for professional and organizational standards. In addition, federal and state laws apply to fundraisers in general and prospect researchers in particular. Federal privacy laws include the Family Educational Rights and Privacy Act (FERPA), the Health Insurance Portability and Accountability Act of 1996 (HIPAA), and the Financial Modernization Act of 1999, also known as the Gramm-Leach-Bliley Act (GLB Act or GLBA).

Each was passed to address privacy rights in the respective area of concern: educational records, health information, and records of financial institutions. These laws were *not* created as a result of concerns related to the fundraising profession. Nevertheless, the privacy rights they established apply to and restrict fundraisers' use of information in those areas.

These acts are subject to interpretation. They are relatively recent, and the regulations implementing them are newer still. A limited number of court rulings test the application of the laws in specific contexts.

Because these laws are general and not directed toward fundraising in particular, their terms and restrictions need to be interpreted in this context. In addition, definitions and policies are left to each institution to define. FERPA, in particular, requires each institution to establish and publish policies further specifying key terms defined by the act.

For all these reasons, it is very important that each institution's legal counsel be closely involved in establishing policies under these laws. The information that follows is intended as a general overview, not as legal advice.

Education Records and FERPA

FERPA states that with explicit exceptions, education-related information is private and should be treated as confidential.

Passed in 1974, FERPA is the earliest of the federal privacy laws, and its elements are echoed to some extent in the later legislation. It defines the institutions to which it applies and the type of records that fall within its scope. It provides specific rights to individuals, restricts the use that institutions may make of the specified information, and requires them to make disclosures to various individuals.

FERPA applies to any educational institution or agency that receives federal funds. It applies to "education records" directly related to a student and maintained by an educational agency, institution, or party acting for the agency or institution.

FERPA states that with explicit exceptions, education-related information is private and should be treated as confidential. It grants precise rights to parents or guardians of students under age 18, including the right to control the release of information and to review and correct education records. It transfers rights to "eligible students" when they turn 18 or attend a postsecondary education institution.

FERPA and Fundraising

Much of FERPA and the regulations implementing it have little to do with advancement. For example, specific provisions apply to releasing information to law enforcement agencies or in connection with a health or safety emergency.

The area in which fundraisers most commonly encounter FERPA has to do with restrictions it places on development officials' use of information from education records. Even in this specific context, it is apparent that FERPA treats different types of information differently. Several provisions of FERPA govern whether fundraisers are allowed to use various types of information:

Former Students' Educational Records

In advancement, we typically make a distinction between a currently enrolled student and an alumnus or alumna, a graduate or other former student. FERPA makes a similar distinction, up to a point. FERPA's definition of education records does not include records that only contain information about an individual after he or she is no longer a student at that agency or institution. For example, FERPA does not apply to records of attendance at reunions, employment information, address changes, or other information specific to the time when the individual was no longer a student. On the other hand, information that applies to the student while in attendance is considered part of the education record, and FERPA continues to apply even after an individual is no longer a student.

Directory Information

For information that is part of the education record, FERPA makes a distinction between "directory information" and other information. Broadly speaking, disclosure of directory information generally would not be considered harmful or an invasion of privacy.

FERPA requires each institution to define what it considers directory information and to give parents and eligible students notice of these definitions. It might include a student's name, address, telephone number, date and place of birth, major, participation in recognized activities and sports, weight and height for members of athletic teams, dates of attendance, and degrees and awards received.

In general, provided an institution has given notice of its directory information policy and offered parents and students the opportunity to opt out, institution officials may make public and otherwise use any data they have defined as directory information without prior written consent from the parent or eligible student. However, a parent or eligible student may restrict the disclosure of any or all directory information. Here again, former students are treated slightly differently from current students. Institution officials may use or disclose directory information about former students without making provisions for them to restrict the information further.

Legitimate Educational Interest

Much of the institutional information of interest to a development official is available under one of the provisions considered so far. However, fundraisers might want to make use of additional information that is part of the educational record but is not directory information, or is directory information further restricted by a parent or eligible student. For example, a researcher might want to use a Social Security number to locate a current address for a lost alumna. Or the Parents' Fund might want to use the name and address of a current student's parents to send them a parents' newsletter. FERPA protects this information, and advancement officers may use it only if such use qualifies as an exception to the privacy protections.

For most institutions, maintaining contact with alumni is a strong, legitimate educational objective.

Fortunately, FERPA includes a provision that permits institutional officials who have a "legitimate educational interest" to use information from education records. Here again, each institution must disclose its criteria for determining who campus officials are and what constitutes a legitimate educational interest.

The U.S. Department of Education model disclosure states, "A school official has a legitimate educational interest if the official needs to review an education record in order to fulfill his or her professional responsibility."

For most institutions, maintaining contact with alumni is a strong, legitimate educational objective. Advancement officers cannot build or maintain relationships with alumni without being able to locate them. Similarly, one can understand the legitimate educational interest in communicating with the parents of current students.

Still, institutions vary in their interpretation of FERPA and their assessment of what qualifies as a legitimate educational interest. Some institutions have decided that finding lost alumni, or even fundraising in general, is not a legitimate educational interest under the law. These institutions do not give their advancement staff access to nondirectory information or restricted directory information under FERPA.

Written Consent

Regardless of any other considerations, an institution is free to disclose information from the educational record if the parent or eligible student has given written consent to the disclosure. Certain requirements apply to this written consent. It must specify the information to be disclosed, the context in which the information may be disclosed, the person or persons to whom the information may be disclosed, and so on.

For example, participants in intercollegiate athletics might be asked to give written permission for information such as name, age, class year, major, home town, position or event, height, and weight, to be disclosed in sports programs and news releases.

Putting It All Together

An illustration shows how these considerations apply to a particular case. Suppose a current student is awarded an endowed scholarship, and the advancement office wishes to tell the donor the name of the recipient, the recipient's class year and course of study, and the student's grade point average. This information is all clearly maintained by the institution and directly related to the student, so it would fall under the privacy protections of FERPA.

Institutions typically define a student's name, class year, major, and scholarships and awards received as directory information. If the institution's disclosure of directory information includes these items, and if the student has not further restricted release of this information, it may be provided to the donor.

However, if the information cannot be disclosed as directory information, the donor probably would not be considered an education official with a legitimate educational interest in the information.

It still would be possible to disclose the information to the donor if the student gave written permission for this specific information to be provided to the scholarship funder. The GPA probably could not be disclosed to the funder without the student's written permission.

To simplify the business process, the institution might implement a policy that as a condition of receiving a named scholarship, students give written permission for the institution to tell the donor the student's name, class year, and course of study, and optionally for the donor to learn the student's GPA.

Health Records and HIPAA

HIPAA addresses a range of topics related to healthcare and health insurance. One of these is the privacy of individually identifiable health information. HIPAA's Standards for Privacy of Individually Identifiable Health Information ("Privacy Rule"), which implement its privacy-related provisions, apply to health plans, healthcare clearinghouses, and health providers that electronically transmit health information. The rule applies to "health information," defined as information "created or received by a healthcare provider, health plan, public health authority, employer, life insurer, school or university, or healthcare clearinghouse" that "relates to the past, present, or future physical or mental health or condition of an individual, the provision of healthcare to an individual, or the past, present, or future payment for the provision of healthcare to an individual." It prohibits wrongfully disclosing or obtaining "individually identifiable health information."

The Privacy Rule defines and limits the circumstances in which covered entities may use or disclose an individual's protected heath information. Except in specific permitted instances, protected health information may be used or disclosed only with the written authorization of the individual who is the subject of the record (or the individual's personal representative).

The Privacy Rule also includes the principle of "minimum necessary" use and disclosure. Only the minimum amount of protected health information may be disclosed. The HIPAA Privacy Rule also grants other rights to patients, including the right to review their own health records and request corrections.

HIPAA and Advancement

A great deal about HIPAA, and the regulations implementing it, has nothing to do with fundraising. Fundraisers most commonly encounter HIPAA in reference to the strict restrictions it places on use of information from health records.

Fundraising for the benefit of the covered entity is one of the activities HIPAA considers to be "healthcare operations." However, unlike most of the identified healthcare operations, fundraising is subject to additional limitations on the use of protected health information. Specifically, the only protected health information available for fundraising purposes without the patient's specific authorization is basic demographic information and dates of healthcare provided to an individual.

In this context, basic demographic information refers to name, address, other contact information, age, gender, and insurance status. It specifically excludes any information about an illness, treatment, diagnosis, or services.

Other protected health information may be used for fundraising only if the individual provides specific authorization. Specific requirements for such authorization include the provision that it must be in plain, readily understandable language. It also must describe the information to be used or disclosed, identify the purpose of the use or disclosure, identify the person or class of persons authorized to make use of the information, specify the period during which the information may be used or disclosed, and include a signature and date.

Covered entities that engage in fundraising of any kind, . . . must include that use of information in their Notice of Privacy Practices.

Covered entities that engage in fundraising of any kind, even if they intend to use only basic demographic information and dates of service, must include that use of information in their Notice of Privacy Practices. In addition, fundraising communications are required to include information about opting out of receiving further communications. Fundraising also must be distinguished from marketing.

Before HIPAA, it was common for healthcare fundraising to reflect information about the individual's health or healthcare. Former patients might be solicited, based on the type of healthcare they had received. Patients treated for diabetes might be solicited to support programs related to diabetes. Patients with unfavorable outcomes might be excluded from solicitation.

Under the Privacy Rule, such information cannot be used for fundraising. Since basic demographic data are available, it is possible to send solicitations and other mailings to former patients. Because information is available about the dates the healthcare was provided, it is possible to solicit former patients only for a set period, such as a year, after they receive care.

Other Types of Information

The HIPAA Privacy Rule applies specifically to protected health information. Other information not about the past, present, or future health of the individual, or about healthcare provided to the individual, is beyond the scope of the Privacy Rule.

For example, without specific authorization, a former patient may be solicited only on the basis of basic demographic information. That solicitation might be general, or the former patient might be sent several solicitations related to different medical areas. However, if the patient responds indicating an interest in supporting the treatment of lymphoma, that is not protected health information, and it can be used in further fundraising activities.

Financial Records and GLBA

GLBA covers a wide range of topics related to financial services, including mergers of banks, brokerage companies, and insurance companies. With respect to consumers' personal financial information held by financial institutions, it includes three main provisions: the Financial Privacy Rule, the Safeguards Rule, and pretexting provisions (essentially prohibiting the use of information under false pretenses).

The Financial Privacy Rule applies to "financial institutions," which include not only banks, brokerage companies, and insurance companies, but also companies providing a wide variety of financial services to consumers. The rule applies to customers' personal financial information. In particular, it distinguishes between customers and consumers and applies to the collection and disclosure of customers' "nonpublic personal information."

The Financial Privacy Rule requires companies to give consumers privacy notices that explain their information sharing practices. In turn, consumers have the right to limit some—but not all—sharing of their information. The Financial Safeguards Rule requires financial institutions to have a written information-security plan to protect the confidentiality and integrity of personal consumer information.

GLBA and Fundraising

A great deal about GLBA and the regulations implementing it has nothing to do with fundraising.

It may not be immediately clear that GLBA and the Financial Privacy Rule have anything at all to do with nonprofit organizations that engage in fundraising. However, among the broad range of financial activities covered by GLBA are "making, acquiring, brokering, or servicing loans," and institutions of higher education participate in activities such as making federal Perkins loans. As a result, FTC regulations consider such educational institutions to be financial institutions for GLBA purposes.

At the same time, colleges and universities are not typical financial institutions and are already subject to an existing set of privacy requirements, namely the privacy provisions of FERPA. Therefore, the regulations implementing the GLBA specify that if a college or university complies with FERPA, it will be considered in compliance with the privacy requirements of GLBA. Colleges and universities are, however, still required to comply with GLBA's Safeguards Rule.

Advancement
SERVICES

Section III: Gift and Data Considerations

Operating in our Standards-Based Environment: Understanding the Requirements of IRS, CASE, and FASB/GASB

By Alan S. Hejnal | Director of Advancement Services | University of Richmond

At least three sets of standards apply to the day-to-day work of gift recording in the United States. The Internal Revenue Code and Internal Revenue Service (IRS) regulations govern the deductibility of charitable contributions for federal income-tax purposes. CASE Management and Reporting Standards are the benchmark for standardized and comparative gift reporting. And the Financial Accounting Standards Board (FASB) and Government Accounting Standards Board (GASB) promulgate financial accounting standards.

Anyone who has worked in gift processing probably has encountered cases in which a gift is treated differently under different standards. This really is not surprising, because each set has a different goal and addresses different concerns. It may be more surprising that the various standards agree as often as they do. To understand why differences arise, it is useful to consider why each set of standards exists, what each is trying to accomplish, and how each applies in different circumstances.

The Internal Revenue Code and IRS Regulations

As discussed in detail in Chapter 11, IRS Rules and Regulations, nonprofit institutions have special status under the Internal Revenue Code: A broad range of organizations—from religious, educational, and charitable institutions to fraternal organizations—is considered exempt from federal income tax. Because of their religious, educational, or charitable purposes, some nonprofits are authorized to receive contributions that donors may deduct from their taxable income. These organizations are sometimes called "qualified organizations" but are more commonly called "501(c)(3) organizations," after the section of the tax code that authorizes them. Most organizations apply to the IRS to establish their qualified status and receive from the IRS what is sometimes called a "501(c)(3) letter," granting that status.

. . . the federal tax code provides that when a gift is tax-deductible, the federal government has agreed to forgo any income tax otherwise due on a corresponding amount of income.

Once a qualified organization establishes its tax-exempt status, one of the main ways it engages the IRS is through the receipt, and receipting, of charitable contributions. The Internal Revenue Code and IRS regulations determine what is and is not considered a tax-deductible, charitable contribution. Requirements govern receipts for charitable contributions, and others are placed upon organizations that receive charitable contributions. These additional requirements include reporting to the IRS, nondiscrimination, and record keeping.

At a very basic level, the federal tax code provides that when a gift is tax-deductible, the federal government has agreed to forgo any income tax otherwise due on a corresponding amount of income. Determining what sorts of gifts are eligible to receive that special treatment under the Internal Revenue Code is entirely up to the federal government. Regardless of other circumstances of a gift, the Internal Revenue Code limits such deductibility to three broad categories of contributions:

- Contributions of cash
- Contributions of property other than cash
- Out-of-pocket expenses incurred while providing voluntary service to a qualified organization

Property other than cash spans a broad range, from securities such as stocks and bonds to real property such as land and buildings, tangible personal property such as artwork and jewelry, and intangible property such as patents and intellectual property. These three categories exclude certain sorts of contributions. For example, contributions of services are not deductible as charitable contributions for federal income-tax purposes, regardless of any other criteria they might meet.

Contributions of property other than cash are subject to the further requirement that (except in a handful of specific and unusual cases), the donor must give the entire interest in the contributed property. In particular, if a donor only allows a qualified organization free use of property—a so-called "partial use" arrangement—this is not a charitable contribution for federal income-tax purposes. So a donor who transfers an office building to a qualified organization may have made a gift, but a donor who lets a qualified organization use office space in an office building has not.

Further conditions must be met for a gift to be considered deductible. The contribution must be voluntary and made with charitable intent. As a result, payments made under contractual relationships or under a court settlement are not deductible as chartable contributions.

The recipient organization must be able to use the gift for the religious, educational, or charitable purpose for which it received its tax-exempt status. This is clearly not an issue with a cash gift. In most cases of gifts of property other than cash, if an organization cannot use the property, it may sell the property and apply the proceeds to its charitable mission. However, the donation of property which an organization can neither use nor sell does not qualify as a deductible contribution.

In addition, the donor must not receive or expect to receive anything of equal value in return for the cash or property. Such a transaction, where the donor receives something of equal value in return, is called an *exchange transaction*. A purchase in a college bookstore or a museum shop may support the mission of the college or museum, but it is not considered a gift because the person who made the purchase received something of equal value in return.

The deductibility of specific transactions is evaluated according to these broad provisions, as well as additional provisions and regulations that may apply in particular cases. In some transactions, the donor receives something of lesser value in return for the contribution. This is sometimes called a quid pro quo transaction. *(See Chapter 11 for details.)*

The IRS provides specific guidance in situations that arise frequently. One helpful list of these cases is in IRS Publication 526. For example, any transaction where the donor enters a raffle, drawing, or other game of chance is not considered a deductible contribution. The rationale here is that the donor already has received something valuable, namely the chance to win a prize, as part of the transaction. The value of that chance is considered to be the full amount of the contribution that was the basis of the donor's eligibility for the prize, so there is no gift.

Another specific case addressed by the IRS is that a donor cannot specify an individual beneficiary of a contribution. For example, a donor may establish a scholarship and even specify general criteria for the selection of recipients, but the donor may not select the specific recipient. A gift to a specified individual is considered to benefit the individual rather than the organization. If, on the other hand, the organization controls selection of the recipient and does so in a manner consistent with its charitable mission, the gift is understood to benefit the organization rather than the individual.

It is the taxpayer's responsibility to determine whether to claim a charitable deduction, the period in which to claim, and the amount to claim.

Charitable deductions for out-of-pocket expenses incurred when providing voluntary service to a qualified organization are also subject to certain limitations. For example, deductions for travel expenses are allowed only if the trip is made just to provide the voluntary service. If the trip is combined with vacation, travel expenses are not deductible. Also, deductions may be limited to expenses considered reasonable. Travel to provide service does not commonly require the donor to purchase an airplane to make the flight, for instance, when tickets on commercial air carriers are readily available.

Several other observations are worth making at this point. The deductibility of a specific gift, and the extent of any such deduction, always depends on the individual or corporate taxpayer's unique circumstances. These are matters beyond the knowledge and concern of the recipient organization. If the contribution meets the criteria outlined here, the recipient organization may appropriately issue a tax receipt that meets the detailed requirements addressed in Chapter 11. But that does not, of itself, mean the donor will or should claim a deduction.

IRS regulations make some things the responsibility of the taxpayer and others the responsibility of the recipient organization. It is the taxpayer's responsibility to determine whether to claim a charitable deduction, the period in which to claim, and the amount to claim. Deductibility is further affected by circumstances such as overall limits on the amount that may be deducted. The tax status of the contributed property also affects the deductibility. The amount of the deduction for the contribution of securities may depend on the length of time the donor has held them. Such matters are beyond the scope of the recipient organization, and so it never should attempt to offer tax advice. It can be helpful to be aware of such matters, however, to understand why the donor may have certain concerns.

The charitable organization, in turn, may be asked to certify it is a qualified organization, if it has received the property in question, and if it provided any substantial goods or services in return. In the case of a donor's out-of-pocket expenses incurred in providing voluntary service, the organization may certify it is qualified and that the donor provided specific services on specific dates, and specify if the organization provided any substantial goods or services in return for the donor's service.

The federal government appears to be increasingly concerned about the valuation of contributed property.

While a deductible gift must contribute to the mission of the recipient organization, the deductibility of a gift is not linked to the details of that benefit. For example, the purchase of a ticket to a fundraising dinner may be deductible to the extent that the contribution exceeds the fair market value of the dinner the donor receives in return. If the host organization paid a caterer the fair market value of the dinner, the benefit to the organization is roughly the same as the donor's tax deduction. On the other hand, if the organization paid nothing for the dinner, the full ticket price may be available for the organization's charitable mission. However, that does not affect the deductibility of the donor's gift, which still is limited to the excess of the contribution over the fair market value of the dinner received.

Similarly, the services of a building contractor may be of great value to the organization, which otherwise would have to buy those services on the open market, but they still are not deductible as a charitable contribution for federal income-tax purposes.

The federal government appears to be increasingly concerned about the valuation of contributed property. Recent changes have related to types of property that frequently have been overvalued, such as motor vehicles, boats, and airplanes. In general, any contribution whose value is not readily apparent and requires a qualified appraisal is difficult for the IRS to assess. This category includes most gifts other than cash or publicly traded securities. The IRS is making efforts to limit contributions in such cases to a more objective standard, such as what the donor actually paid for the property. In the case of appreciated property, this would have the effect of reducing the donor's tax deduction, significantly in some cases.

CASE Standards

The purpose of CASE's Management and Reporting Standards has nothing, directly, to do with the deductibility of gifts. Rather, the standards are intended to provide a useful way to measure contributions to charitable, particularly educational, institutions. These standards are for the use of those who manage such institutions. In addition, they set out to provide a consistent measure of contributions generally and a way to make meaningful comparisons between different institutions. Organizations use them internally and externally for reporting on the Voluntary Support of Education (VSE) Survey of the Council for Aid to Education (CAE) and CASE's Campaign Report.

To a considerable extent, CASE standards start with IRS regulations. For the most part, if a type of gift is not deductible as a charitable contribution for federal income-tax purposes, it is not countable under CASE standards.

At the same time, CASE reporting is not based on the particular donor's circumstances. A gift that meets the general principles is countable under CASE standards, regardless of whether the donor's deduction was further limited to the amount that the donor paid for the contributed property, for example, or whether the donor elected not to take a deduction at all. Similarly, even though private foundations do not pay income taxes, and therefore do not make deductible contributions, their contributions are counted under CASE standards.

Governmental entities also do not pay income tax. However, because CASE standards are intended to measure *private* support, they exclude all support from governmental sources.

CASE standards extend to information not of concern to the IRS. For example, although deductible contributions must advance the mission of the recipient, the IRS generally is not interested in the particular program a gift supports. CASE standards, as they apply to the VSE survey, distinguish among current gifts, capital gifts, and gifts to endowment. They further distinguish among certain programmatic areas, such as unrestricted gifts, gifts restricted to student financial aid, gifts restricted to community service, gifts restricted to athletics, and so on.

In addition, CASE standards seek information about the donor's relationship to the recipient institution. They classify individual donors as alumni, parents, grandparents (in the case of private secondary schools), or other individuals and also identify members of the institution's governing board. For institutions of higher education, alumni are further identified as those who received an undergraduate degree, those who received a graduate but not an undergraduate degree, and those who did not receive a degree. Organizations are classified as corporations, foundations, fundraising consortia, religious organizations, and other organizations.

The VSE also extends to the overall population of constituents, as well as donors, collecting the number of alumni of record and alumni solicited, plus similar statistics for other donor categories. These figures are combined with the number of donors in a category to determine participation levels, an important measure for assessment of fundraising programs.

The IRS is interested almost exclusively in completed gifts, cash, or property transferred from the donor to the recipient. The CASE Survey of Cumulative Campaign Activity extends further to pledges —irrevocable commitments to make specific contributions at a specified future time. This is important because campaign management takes place during an active campaign period, while pledge payments may extend for several years. Understanding the progress of the campaign requires understanding those commitments, even though there is no deductible gift until pledge payments are made. CASE standards also provide definitions of capital campaigns with respect to length of the campaign, length of pledge payment schedules, relationship to previous campaigns, and so on.

Financial Accounting Standards

These standards exist, first and foremost, to provide an assessment of the financial position of an institution. The organization's leaders, such as its governing board and executives, as well as external entities such as creditors and donors, use this assessment. Financial accounting standards apply to the institution's expenses as well as its revenues and to its liabilities as well as its assets. Contribution revenue, or gifts, is one part of that larger picture.

These standards exist, first and foremost, to provide an assessment of the financial position of an institution.

Accounting for nonprofit organizations is somewhat different than in for-profit organizations. Until the 1990s, the respective accounting rules significantly differed. However, in that decade significant changes were made in the accounting standards for nonprofit organizations. This was done partly to make financial reports more useful to nonprofit governing boards, which tend to be much more familiar with for-profit accounting. Thus, Financial Accounting Standard (FAS) 116, *Accounting for Contributions Received and Contributions Made*, and FAS 117, *Financial Statements of Not-for-Profit Organizations*, came into being. Both these standards had a direct effect on gift recording.

One distinctive characteristic of gifts, as opposed to other sorts of revenue, in financial accounting is that donors are allowed to place restrictions on them. For example, a donor may place a permanent restriction on a gift, specifying that it be invested and that only the investment earnings be spent. The donor may restrict the purpose for which the income may be spent, such as to financial aid for students majoring in mathematics. A donor also may place a restriction that allows the gift itself to be spent, but only for a specified purpose, such as construction of a new science building. These donor-stipulated restrictions are binding on the recipient organization. In fact, they can be very difficult to set aside, even if the specified purpose is no longer practical or even possible.

This characteristic of gifts is really quite distinctive among sources of income. Most income is unrestricted, available to be spent in any manner that the institution's board and executive leadership determine (consistent, of course, with applicable laws and the institution's religious, educational, or charitable mission). For example, someone making a tuition payment or purchasing a textbook at the bookstore cannot say he wants his payment used only to fund scholarships in the humanities.

Donor-imposed restrictions can be extremely significant in assessing the financial position of the institution. An organization may have considerable assets, but if they are subject to restrictions, it may not be free to use them to meet general expenses. For example, if an organization's assets are restricted to provide financial aid to students, those assets are not available to meet general expenses such as paying salaries, utility bills, and so on. As a result, situations may arise in which an organization with considerable assets cannot meet its obligations, whereas another organization with fewer but unrestricted assets may be in a much better position.

Donor-imposed restrictions can be extremely significant in assessing the financial position of the institution.

To address such issues, financial accounting standards classify all revenue in one of three fund classes: unrestricted income, temporarily restricted income, and permanently restricted income. Financial accounting standards also require organizations to track restricted funds and ensure that they are used in a manner consistent with those restrictions. It is important for gift recording staff to work closely with their finance counterparts to classify gifts in these classes, as well as providing specific information about, and documentation of, any restrictions.

The financial position of an organization also involves its assets and liabilities. One type of asset is what is commonly considered "accounts receivable," funds an organization is owed by some other individual or organization, such as outstanding payment for goods and services an individual or organization has agreed to purchase. Outstanding tuition payments are an example of such a receivable.

One of the changes FAS 116 made is that pledges of charitable contributions are now classified as revenue, just as tuition is considered revenue even while its payment is outstanding. FAS 116 considers a pledge as an *unconditional promise to give*, further defined as a *written or oral agreement to contribute cash or other assets to another entity*. The Government Accounting Standards Board (GASB) followed with similar rules in 1998 when issuing its Statement No. 33.

According to financial accounting standards, revenue is recognized when a pledge is made. Pledge payments, then, are not considered revenue, but only the payment of outstanding debts due to the organization. A pledge payment might be considered a new, deductible gift for federal income-tax purposes, and as a new, completed gift for reporting on the VSE survey, but not as new revenue for either financial accounting purposes or inclusion in campaign totals. This illustrates the importance of precise gift recording, accurately classifying gift transactions, and reporting them appropriately in each context.

Additionally, because the purpose of financial accounting standards is to reflect the financial position of the organization and not to determine whether a donor should receive a tax deduction, financial accounting standards treat certain sorts of transactions differently than the tax code and CASE standards do. One important example of this difference is that certain gifts of services can be recognized under financial accounting standards. Specifically, FAS 116 provides that *contributions of services shall be recognized if the services received (a) create or enhance nonfinancial assets or (b) require specialized skills, are provided by individuals possessing those skills, and would typically need to be purchased if not provided by donation.*

Suppose a contractor contributed professional services to construct a building for the organization. Since the contribution consisted of services, the contractor could not claim a deductible contribution for federal income-tax purposes. However, as a result of those services, the organization has a significant additional nonfinancial asset, the new building, and its financial statements should account for that asset. This is true regardless of the fact that the IRS, which is concerned with the collection of taxes and not the reporting of the organization's financial position, did not grant the contractor a tax deduction for providing those services.

Similarly, an organization may require specific professional services, such as those provided by an auditor, investment manager, or attorney. Purchasing those services is an ordinary business expense, possibly a significant expense. If, instead, those services are contributed, that expenditure is not required, and the organization is in a different financial position as a result. Therefore, the value of those contributed services can be recognized for financial accounting purposes.

CHAPTER 11

IRS Rules and Regulations:
What You Need to Know to Stay Out of Trouble

By Alison L. Paul | Deputy Director | Montana Legal Services Association

Nearly every nonprofit in the United States conducts fundraising activities of one kind or another. These range from seeking small gifts via direct mail to sponsoring fundraising banquets to soliciting large donations through a complex planned giving program. To conduct these activities successfully, the development professional must understand the IRS regulations that apply to a 501(c)(3) organization, both to protect the tax-deductible nature of the donations and to shield itself and donors from IRS penalties.

Although it may be hard to believe, the IRS rules and regulations discussed in this chapter were not developed solely to torture development professionals. These rules are intended to guard against income-tax fraud by donors. Unfortunately, the complexity of these rules can also trap the unwary. If you take the time to master the tax rules regarding the three key parts of a charitable contribution, you should be able to comply with IRS requirements. This chapter will help you make sense of basic IRS rules that determine exactly what makes an individual or corporate gift a tax-deductible, charitable contribution. For income-tax purposes, the three key aspects of a charitable contribution are:

- The contribution itself, since only certain types of donations qualify as tax-deductible, charitable contributions
- The organization, because a tax-deductible, charitable contribution must be made to a qualified recipient organization
- The receipt, since the donor must be able to substantiate the charitable contribution, as the IRS requires

The Contribution

To be considered a contribution for income-tax purposes, the gift must involve the transfer of money or property to a qualified charitable organization. Gifts of cash or stock are obvious examples of the types of gifts that qualify as tax-deductible, charitable contributions.

If you work for an organization that receives only cash gifts, you can stop reading here and skip to the next section. If you are not that lucky, however, it is important to identify what types of transfers to nonprofits fail to qualify as tax-deductible charitable contributions. A fundraiser who inadvertently gives a donor incorrect information about tax deductibility risks bringing the wrath of the IRS upon both the organization and the donor who claimed the deduction.

Here are common types of contributions that do not qualify as tax-deductible, charitable contributions:

- Payment for a raffle ticket
- Payment earmarked for lobbying activities
- Payment that is earmarked for an individual, regardless of the charitable nature of the payment

Time

Volunteer time is not considered a gift for tax purposes. For example, an attorney who gives your organization pro bono legal advice may not take a charitable deduction for the billable value of that time. However, a volunteer may deduct out-of-pocket expenses, such as mileage, parking, or supplies.

Conditional Gifts

A gift that is conditional on a future event also does not qualify as a tax-exempt contribution. For instance, if a couple gives a painting to a university but keeps it for three months before moving it to campus, the gift is not official until the painting is transferred to the university. Or a donor transfers stock to a charitable organization but retains voting rights over the stock until the end of the year. The gift is not complete until the charitable organization has control and ownership of the stock. *(See Gifts of Securities, page 139.)*

Gifts of Securities: Steps to Ensure Timely and Responsible Receipt

In many institutions of higher education, the receipt and processing of gifts of securities and mutual funds are left to the accounting or treasurer's office. The thought is that they are the only ones authorized to determine when to sell the asset; therefore, they should handle its receipt. This may be fine from a purely administrative perspective, but this policy often gives rise to serious donor relations issues.

Occasionally, when a business office handles the receipt and processing of gifts of securities, it does so in the context of a business transaction. The office tends to be more concerned about the asset—and selling or investing it—than about donors. This can lead to the opening of numerous brokerage accounts across the country, sometimes with the institution's authorization, sometimes without, to facilitate the transfer of a gift within the brokerage firm. Frequently the business office first realizes that a gift has been made when it receives a statement or check from that firm. Therefore a minimum of 30 days might pass before an acknowledgment can be sent to the donor. And if the business office did not have prior knowledge that a gift was going to be made, it might never determine from whom the gift came. The development office finds out when the donor calls to complain that the donor never was thanked!

To eliminate this donor relations problem without removing the responsibility for the actual sale or investment of assets from the business office (and actually enhance its control), I suggest the following:

1. Close unnecessary brokerage accounts. Ideally there should be a single account at a brokerage firm or bank for the receipt of gifts of securities. You should have online access to your gift account. This could be either a true online, real-time ability to look at gift activity or the ability to download, on a daily basis, a report reflecting gift activity from the previous day. As mentioned above, donors and brokers open many accounts without proper authorization from the nonprofit organization. But even if the nonprofit has authorized the opening of such accounts, they are unnecessary.

In today's world the transfer of stock can take place electronically the same day to any account in the country. The consolidation of all activity in a single account gives you both greater control and a stronger hand to negotiate a reduced brokerage fee. Certainly, situations arise when it is prudent to keep an account or two open (the major donor's brother-in-law is the broker; the broker is a highly regarded alumnus), but these should be few and far between.

2. Inform donors of the change in procedure. Your database should be structured so that all gifts of securities can be readily identified. In most advancement systems, a unique payment type to identify stock gifts does this. Using this identifier, obtain the name and address of any individual who has donated stock within the past three years. A short letter should be sent to these individuals, indicating that you are changing your procedures for accepting gifts of stock and that if they wish to contribute securities in the future, they or the broker should contact your office for the most current electronic delivery (DTC) instructions. You should not publish these instructions anywhere—not in the letter, not in a brochure, not on your Web site. Nor should you disseminate them to your development officers. The entire organization simply should be told that if donors ask how to make a gift of stock, they should be referred to your office. You might consider publishing a flier that outlines your preference for DTC and asks donors to contact your office in such a case, but also explains how to physically deliver certificates.

3. Develop a tracking system. When stock is sent by DTC, it rarely carries the name of the donor. All you "see" is the name of the security, the number of shares, and the firm initiating the DTC. Your task, then, is to match a gift with a donor. Therefore, you must know ahead of time which donor is sending what. Hence the prescribed procedure of having the donor or broker contact you first. When contacted, and before releasing the DTC instructions, you should obtain the donor's name; brokerage firm; name, phone, and fax number of broker or agent; name of stock and number of shares (or approximate target dollar amount); and purpose of gift. The information should be recorded in a searchable database. This is important for two reasons. First, even though you will tell the donor or broker always to contact your office in the event of future stock gifts to confirm the transfer instruction, you will run into the occasional donor or broker who will send a gift without informing you first. By retaining information concerning prior gifts in a searchable format, you can query the database when a "rogue" gift comes in. Often, a donor will send the same stock a second time. Second, you can and should query the database on a regular basis to identify notifications of gifts that are more than a week old and have not been received. A follow-up call might be appropriate.

4. Communicate with your broker. It is important that your broker know what gifts are expected. This way, should she receive an unexpected gift, she can raise a flag more quickly. The easiest way to alert her as to what is coming would be to fax a copy of your tracking sheet to the firm. Ideally, when gifts are received, your broker will match the stock with a tracking sheet and append the donor's name to the report of gifts she prepares for you. If a match cannot be made, your broker should communicate this information to you immediately by phone, fax, or e-mail. The brokerage should provide you with the name of the transfer agent (firm), the name of the stock and number of shares, and the approximate gift amount. With this information, you can query your database and check other internal sources to identify the donor.

5. Return unknown gifts. It is important that gifts whose donor you cannot identify be returned immediately. Do not "hold" these transfers for more than 48 hours. The gift may not belong to you! For tax purposes, have your broker add a comment to the DK (Don't Know), requesting the initiating firm to contact your office immediately upon receipt of the returned shares. As long as they contact you before crediting the shares back to the donor's account—and you can ascertain who the donor is and have the shares re-sent—the donor still should be able to claim the original date of transfer as the gift date. The donor never regained control of the asset. The donor will need to confirm this with a tax adviser.

6. The donor and department should receive equal credit. Certainly, your donor should receive gift credit equal to the legal value of the gift. So, too, should the department benefiting from the contribution. This should occur regardless of brokerage fees or whether the stock is ultimately sold for a gain or at a loss. That is simply the price of doing business. Therefore, all proceeds from sales of stock (excluding restricted or closely held stock) should be credited to a single "clearing" account. You then debit this account for the legal amount of the gift and credit the benefiting department. Ideally, your general ledger interface will automate this process. The clearing account will absorb all fees, gains, and losses. It can be proven that over a period of years, the net is always a positive one. The institution can determine how often, if at all, to flush this account and transfer the net to a spending account.

7. Closely held and restricted stock requires different accounting. In these cases the timing of sale is beyond the institution's control. Although the donor should certainly receive gift credit equal to the legal value of the stock, it would not be appropriate for the institution to absorb the potential loss resulting from sale in its clearing account. The exposure is too great. Therefore, the benefiting department should be contacted first to determine if it wishes to accept the closely held or restricted stock, understanding that it might not realize the "legal" amount of the gift. Usually it will—something is better than nothing! When the stock is ultimately sold, all proceeds should be credited directly to the department.

8. Outline procedures for physical delivery of stock. Many donors own physical shares of stock not held in a brokerage account. These shares cannot be delivered electronically. Be prepared to advise the donors of safe and efficient methods available to deliver these shares. The first would be to hand-deliver the certificate to the institution and "endorse" the shares over to it in the presence of an official of the institution. A second way would be to mail the unendorsed certificate and a "signature guaranteed" stock power to the institution in separate envelopes. The donor should be advised that the legal date of gift in these cases is the later postmark date on the two envelopes. If a third party such as Federal Express delivers the stock, the correct date is the date of receipt by the nonprofit. Some donors prefer to skip the stock-power step and would rather sign the certificate over and then mail it. If they do, suggest that they complete the line indicating the name of the institution receiving the gift. You also may recommend that the donor use certified or registered mail in this case. A final method available for delivery of physical shares is for the donor to send the certificate back to the issuing corporation and have a certificate issued in the recipient's name. This is not advisable because it significantly delays turnaround time. Furthermore, the legal date of gift in such cases is the date the certificate is registered in the name of the receiving institution. That date could be weeks or months before the donee has physical possession of the certificate.

9. Mutual fund donations require alternate procedures. More often than not, mutual funds cannot be transferred by DTC, but only to a like account and then sold. Therefore educate your donors that to make a gift of a mutual fund, they should begin well before the end of the year. It could take a month to complete the paperwork to open an institutional account with that firm. And your business office or other department authorized to establish banking and financial institution relationships will have to be involved. Once the account is opened, provide the donor with your account number and the donor can initiate the transfer. Although your business office probably will instruct the firm to sell the shares upon receipt, do not close the account. Rather, develop a list (in alphabetical order) of mutual fund accounts that have been opened, including account number, client number (if applicable), and contact phone number. You never know when another, or the same, donor will wish to transfer shares in the same fund.

10. Don't forget the receipt! The IRS regards gifts of appreciated assets, such as stocks and bonds, as property. (see IRS Publication 561). In theory, then, only a description of the asset given is required on the receipt, per IRS Publication 1771. However, many donors transfer these assets to satisfy an existing pledge—they want to know how much might be outstanding. It might be appropriate to state a value indicated as "for internal purposes only" in addition to the description. You might also enclose a disclaimer with the receipt and direct the donor to seek professional tax guidance. Remind donors that they might need to file IRS form 8283 to claim this gift as a deduction. In most cases, the receiving organization does not need to sign the 8283 for gifts of securities.

—John H. Taylor, Principal, Advancement Solutions

Use of Property

The use of a donor's property by a charitable organization does not qualify as a tax-exempt contribution. For example, if a donor allows a charity to use his beach house without paying rent, the donor is not allowed to deduct the fair market value of the rent as a contribution to the charity.

Quid Pro Quo

A quid pro quo contribution is not a tax-deductible contribution. If donors receive something in exchange for their contributions, then only part of the amount paid is tax-deductible. The most common example is a fundraising dinner; in return for contributions, donors receive the right to attend a fancy (or not so fancy) social event. The only part of this "contribution" that the IRS considers tax-deductible is the amount paid over the fair market value of attending the event. Another example of a quid pro quo contribution is payment for an item at a charitable auction. (The disclosure requirements imposed on charities with respect to quid pro quo contributions are discussed below.)

Token Gifts

Under certain circumstances, when donors receive a small item or a benefit of token value, the entire amount of the contribution is fully deductible. A benefit is considered a token if:

- The payment occurs in the context of a fundraising campaign in which the charity informs contributors what amount constitutes a deductible contribution; *and*
- The fair market value of the benefits received is not more than 2 percent of the payment, or $89, whichever is less; *or* the payment is $44.50 or more and the only benefits received are token items bearing the organization's name (such as a mug or T-shirt). The cost (not fair market value) of all of the items received must be less than $8.90.[1]

[1] *Rev. Proc. 2006-53 (11/9/2006). These amounts are indexed each year for inflation and are current for 2007 contributions. The IRS releases updated amounts for the next tax year in November or December of each year.*

Tickets

Certain parts of a payment by a donor for the right to purchase tickets to athletic events are not considered gifts. Under IRS regulations, 80 percent of such payment is treated as a charitable contribution and 20 percent as a payment for the right to purchase the tickets. For example, if a donor pays a university $400 for the right to purchase basketball tickets, the substantiation receipt the university furnishes must show that the taxpayer received a benefit of $80 for the right to purchase the tickets. The taxpayer may then treat $320 as a tax-deductible, charitable contribution.

Promotions

Payment to a charity for publishing or otherwise publicizing a gift acknowledgment that includes an endorsement or other comparative language concerning a donor's products or service are not considered charitable gifts. In a case like this, the amount is considered a payment for advertising rather than a charitable contribution. This is true unless the payment is considered a "qualified corporate sponsorship payment" under IRC 513(i) and its interpreting regulations. If a corporation's payment qualifies as a "qualified corporate sponsorship payment," the IRS will consider it a charitable contribution. To qualify for a deduction, the corporate contributor may receive an acknowledgment of the contribution from the charity, but any further language will be considered advertising. To comply with this regulation, a charity may divide a single payment by a corporate sponsor between a qualified sponsorship payment and a payment for advertising services.

Clearly, IRS regulations about deductibility are many and varied. But other issues come into play as well.

One important issue is the question of when the charitable gift occurs. Although this seems easy, determining it can become quite complicated because of the many different forms the gift may take. The basic rule is that a charitable gift is complete when the charity receives the cash or property. However, the IRS has stated that a charitable gift made by check is complete at the time the check is delivered or mailed, provided the bank eventually honors the check.

One important issue is the question of when the charitable gift occurs.

For example, a check mailed December 30, 2006, would be considered a 2006 charitable contribution, even though the nonprofit did not receive the check and the funds did not clear the bank until January 2007.

As a development professional soliciting gifts from individuals or corporations, you need to understand which organizations the IRS considers qualified organizations.

A gift made by credit card payment is complete when the charge is made, regardless of when the credit card bill is paid. The charge is considered made when processed by the recipient. So if a donor filled out a charge slip December 27, 2006, but the charity did not process the charge until January 3, 2007, the donor would be treated as making the gift in 2007 rather than 2006, as she intended.

A gift of securities or stock is made when the certificate is delivered or mailed to the charity with a transferring document, such as a signed stock power. If a stockbroker completes the transaction, the gift is considered made when the stocks are re-registered in the charity's name. Accordingly, if a charity receives a letter stating that the donor has transferred 50 shares of stock to a charity December 29 of one year, but the securities are not re-registered until February of the next year, the transfer did not actually occur until the second year.

The Recipient Organization

As a development professional soliciting gifts from individuals or corporations, you need to understand which organizations the IRS considers qualified organizations. If you work for an independent school, college, university, or other established nonprofit, you do not need to be concerned about proving your organization is qualified. However, if you have to address the deductibility of contributions to other, related organizations, such as independent auxiliaries, some of your charitable organization's programs, or payments under a matching gift program your organization operates. In such cases, it is important to understand which organizations the IRS considers qualified.

An individual or corporation may deduct contributions to organizations described in Internal Revenue Code Section 170(c). For practical purposes, most organizations described in Internal Revenue Code Section 501(c)(3) also qualify under Code Section 170(c). In addition, institutions such as hospitals, universities, and churches generally qualify to receive tax-deductible, charitable contributions, even though they may not be 501(c)(3) organizations.[2]

However, other types of tax-exempt organizations are not recognized recipients of tax-deductible, charitable contributions. For example, the IRS does not allow deductions under Section 170(c) for contributions to social welfare organizations exempt under Section 501(c)(4), for contributions to business leagues exempt under Section 501(c)(6), or for contributions to social clubs exempt under Section 501(c)(7).

To be described in Section 501(c)(3) of the Internal Revenue Code, an organization must be organized and operated exclusively for religious, charitable, scientific, literary, or educational purposes. No part of its net earnings may inure to the benefit of any private individual. No substantial part of its activities may carry on propaganda or otherwise attempt to influence legislation. The organization may not intervene or participate in any campaign on behalf of or in opposition to any candidate for public office. Every charitable organization described in Section 501(c)(3) is presumed to be a private foundation unless it establishes otherwise to the satisfaction of the IRS. Whether a 501(c)(3) organization is considered a public charity or a private foundation is important only if a private foundation is making the contribution. Individual and corporate donors may make tax-deductible, charitable contributions to either type of organization.

Donor-advised Funds

Generally established by a charity or investment firm, donor-advised funds are considered 501(c)(3) organizations. These funds are designed so that a donor may make a sizable gift to the fund in one year and then "advise" the fund on the future distribution of the money in smaller amounts. For the donor-advised fund to qualify as a 501(c)(3) organization, the donor must give up all control over the money contributed to the fund. The donor may not require that distributions be made to certain organizations in the future; the donor only may make suggestions. Practically

[2] *Hospitals, educational institutions, and churches may receive tax-deductible, charitable contributions under IRC § 170 without obtaining 501(c)(3) status if they meet the specific requirements of §170.*

speaking, however, the donor-advised fund almost always will honor the donor's suggestions.

The tax distinction between the fund and the individual is important to the donor.

Because the donor-advised fund is itself a charity, gift checks from a donor-advised fund will be signed by the fund, not by the individual who established the account. Accordingly, the gift receipt should go to the fund, not the individual (although you may wish to thank the individual for making the "suggestion"). The tax distinction between the fund and the individual is important to the donor.

Verification of Tax-Exempt Status

A donor may want verification that your organization is a qualified recipient. The most reliable way to verify tax status is to give the donor a copy of your organization's IRS determination letter. This letter states the type of 501(c) organization and whether it is a private foundation or a public charity. If this letter is more than five years old (as it often is), a donor also may request a signed statement that no material changes in your organization's tax status have occurred since the letter was issued.

If an organization cannot find its IRS determination letter, the organization may write to the IRS for confirmation or verification that it is a 501(c)(3) organization and get a copy of the IRS letter.

Be aware that hospitals and educational institutions may not have a determination letter from the IRS, since they are not required to apply for 501(c)(3) status. Accordingly, many donors do not require verification of the tax status of these types of organizations. If they do, a corporate officer may verify by signed statement that the organization is qualified to receive tax-deductible contributions under Internal Revenue Code Section 170(c).

The second most reliable way to demonstrate your organization's tax status is to confirm that it is listed in IRS Publication 78 (the renowned "Cumulative List"). The IRS updates this publication regularly and lists organizations to which gifts are tax-deductible. Between updates of the list, revocation of tax-exempt status is published weekly in the Internal Revenue Bulletin and listed at *www.irs.gov.* You may download IRS Publication 78 from the Web site or access the online, searchable database.

Filing and Recordkeeping Requirements

Questions regarding best practices, industry standards, or even government regulations pertaining to retention of constituent-related documents routinely surface at most nonprofit organizations. People struggle with the boundaries limited space imposes on information storage. At times the battle takes a personal turn, as people consider conservation of natural resources. Bottom line: Do we really need all that "stuff"? Which tidbits of data are truly critical to prospect cultivation and management aspects of our institutional advancement mission? How long should we keep those odds and ends of information we determine are important? Are there government regulations that mandate records retention policies? What do other institutions define as the most important pieces of constituent information to store?

Initial responses to a survey conducted at *SupportingAdvancement.com* in 2005 might lead one to believe that there are no definitive answers to questions about records management. Seventy-two percent of respondents indicated the existence of a records management policy at their institutions, with 21 percent saying their institution has no defined policy; 7 percent were uncertain. Even so, few patterns indicate trends that could be defined as industry standards or best practices to which any institution could be enticed to adhere.

Although some institutions have managed to take advantage of the options today's technology offers for maintaining electronic records, most rely heavily—if not completely—on hard copies of constituent information stored in paper files.

When developing a records management policy, advancement services professionals must consider what pieces of information to retain, in what order to organize the information, and how long to keep information that might still be relevant to current operations.

Roughly 70 percent of survey respondents said they regularly retained copies of matching gift forms, media clippings, and acknowledgment letters or receipts; 86 percent retained copies of other general correspondence. Almost 98 percent stated that they kept copies of pledge and gift agreements in the donor files.

Among the most controversial types of information retained are copies of donor checks. Almost 91 percent of respondents said they retained check copies. Many matching gift companies ask for copies of donor checks for match requests of $250 or more. There is a common misconception, however, that the IRS demands that charitable organizations retain copies of donor checks.

IRS publication 4221 contains the following statement related to types of information nonprofit organizations must retain:

Transactions such as contributions, purchases, sales, and payroll will generate supporting documents. These documents—grant applications and awards, sales slips, paid bills, invoices, receipts, deposit slips, and canceled checks—contain information to be recorded in accounting records. Keep these documents because they support the entries in books and the entries on tax and information returns. Keep them in an orderly fashion and in a safe place. For instance, organize them by year and type of receipt or expense.

The prevailing interpretation of the reference to canceled checks in this statement seems to be those issued by the nonprofit organization.

More than 70 percent of respondents refer to an historic institutional precedent having an impact on the amount of time records are retained. Some institutional staff responded to the effect that their organizations never get rid of constituent information. Most did narrow the time frame to a more specific period. More than half indicated information was stored on site for more than 10 years; roughly one-third stated that their organizations kept records on site for three to 10 years. The majority of institutions indicated no access to off-site record storage, but for those with such storage space the inclination was to keep information for more than 10 years.

Keeping records in a locked or restricted-access location is a best practice because of the institution's sense of accountability and also because of donor relations offices' concern to minimize the chance that unauthorized individuals might gain access to sensitive information. Slightly more than 72 percent of respondents kept constituent records in a locked or restricted area; roughly 25 percent indicated no restricted access. The rest were uncertain.

IRS publication 4221 discusses the amount of time charitable institutions must retain records:

Exempt organizations must keep records as long as they may be needed to administer provisions of the Internal Revenue Code. Generally, this means you must keep records that support an item of income or deduction on a return until the period of limitations for that return runs out. The period of limitations is the period of time in which an organization can amend its return to claim a credit or refund, or the IRS can assess additional tax. The most common limitations period is three years after the date the return is due or filed, whichever is later.

Often with limited resources to support conversion from paper files to electronic records management, many institutions are still relying on hard-copy records of constituent information. Twenty-one percent of respondents stated that the conversion from paper to electronic records management was already in progress. Of those planning a conversion, 16.3 percent were making such plans for the near future, and 55.8 percent said they would move to electronic records "somewhere down the road." Only 7 percent hold onto the idea of keeping only paper records both now and in the future.

The final question—how to dispose of records—sis an area of agreement: Shredding constituent information is the known practice of 83.7 percent of respondents, and 9.3 percent incinerate documents no longer needed; the remaining 7 percent are unsure.

Although no common standards have yet evolved for records management, the onus is on those supporting institutional advancement in the back offices to find the methods and means to organize constituent information. Because of increasing competition for donor dollars and the need for information to be available at the fundraiser's fingertips while on the road, there is an inexorable drive toward using technology to store constituent data in a manner easy to access and review. The best plan is to develop a policy for how your office manages every aspect of information about your constituents.

—Amy J. Phillips, Gift Registrar, Smithsonian Institution

The Receipt

> **It is all too easy to issue a thank-you letter that is beautifully worded yet fails to contain the "magic words" the IRS requires.**

Over a decade ago, the IRS adopted requirements for documenting tax-deductible charitable contributions. These rules govern the type of documentation an individual or corporation must keep to substantiate a gift to a charitable organization. In fact, if an individual makes a charitable contribution of more than $250 to an organization, that person may not claim a tax deduction for the contribution unless she has the required receipt by the time she files the tax return.

It can be difficult to square IRS rules with your standard donor-recognition practices. It is all too easy to issue a thank-you letter that is beautifully worded yet fails to contain the "magic words" the IRS requires. While the donor may appreciate your eloquence, she is unlikely to make another gift if your oversight means she cannot deduct the charitable contribution.

So what should an individual or corporation use as documentation to prove that a gift is a deductible contribution? If a contribution is $250 or more, the individual or corporation is required to obtain a receipt with these three features:

- A statement that the charity received the contribution
- The amount of the contribution or a description of the property contributed
- A statement whether the donor received any goods or services in exchange for the contribution

Below is an example of language you may use to meet this requirement. You do not have to use these exact words, but each part must appear in your thank-you letter.

Sample Language for Acknowledging a Charitable Gift

Thank you for your contribution processed on *[date]* of *[amount of cash contribution or description of property. If this is a gift of property, do not value the property]*.

[Then insert one of the following statements:]

We estimate that the fair market value of the *[goods or services]* you have received from *[name of the organization that provided a benefit to the donor]* is $*[FMV]*. The amount of your contribution that is deductible as a charitable contribution for federal income-tax purposes is $*[deductible amount]* (the excess of the amount of your contribution over the value of the goods or services we provided to you).

[or]

As no goods or services were provided to you in return for your charitable contribution, the entire amount of your contribution is tax-deductible to the full extent otherwise allowed by law.

Under IRS rules, it is critical that the gift acknowledgment indicate whether the donor received goods or services in return for the gift. An individual authorized by the organization to issue tax receipts should sign the receipt. Donors must have the receipt by the time they file a tax return for the year the gift was made (including any extensions).

If your organization is lucky enough to receive contributions in excess of $10,000 in the form of cash, foreign currency, cashier's checks, money orders, bank drafts, or traveler's checks, you must file IRS Form 8300. This form requires you to report the amount and method of payment, to describe the transaction (an unrestricted charitable contribution or other type of transfer), and to verify the donor's identity. You may verify by examining a document normally accepted for identification, such as a driver's license, passport, or other official document. You must provide the donor with a copy of Form 8300 as filed with the IRS.

Vehicle Donations

New rules became effective January 1, 2005, regarding charitable donations of vehicles.[3] These rules limit the value of the charitable deduction a donor may take for a donated vehicle and place specific receipt requirements on a charity to substantiate the donation of a vehicle. The required content of the receipt depends on the charitable organization's intended use of the vehicle and are outlined in the instructions for new Form 198c. In general, if a charity sells the donated vehicle without "materially improving the vehicle" or putting it to a "significant intervening use," the receipt must include:

- Donor's name and taxpayer identification number
- Vehicle identification number
- Certification that the vehicle was sold in an arm's-length transaction between unrelated parties
- Gross amount received by the charity for the sale of the vehicle
- Statement that the deductible amount may not exceed the gross amount received by the organization for the sale of the vehicle

The nonprofit must give this acknowledgment to the donor no more than 30 days after the vehicle's date of sale.

If, instead, the organization retains the vehicle for its own use, it must give the receipt to the donor within 30 days of the date of the contribution of the vehicle, and it must include:

- Donor's name and taxpayer identification number
- Vehicle identification number
- Certification stating the intended use of the vehicle or any material improvement intended for the vehicle and the intended duration of such use
- Certification stating that the vehicle will not be transferred in exchange for money, property, or services before completion of the intended use or improvement

The IRS has issued extensive guidance on these new rules for vehicle donations, including what is considered a "material improvement" or a "significant intervening use." Consult these resources to determine

[3] *These rules were created under the American Jobs Creation Act of 2004, Pub. L. No. 108-357, 118 Stat. 1418 (2004), and codified at IRC § 170 (f) (12) and 6720.*

which receipt requirements apply and how to satisfy them. The receipt must be submitted to the IRS with the donor's tax return and filed with the IRS by the charity. Specific penalties are imposed on a charity that issues a false gift receipt for a vehicle donation or fails to furnish a gift receipt as the new law requires.

Disclosure

The IRS requires donors to obtain receipts that include the three elements listed above. In the interests of good donor relations, most nonprofits are careful to ensure that their receipts include all the required information.

However, under certain circumstances, the IRS imposes a burden to disclose on the charitable recipient. If a donor pays more than $75 to a charity, and the organization provides any goods or services to the donor in exchange for the gift, it must provide the donor with a written disclosure statement. It should state that the amount of the deductible contribution is limited to the excess of the amount contributed by the donor over the value of the goods or services the organization provided to the donor. Furthermore, the statement must include a good-faith estimate of the fair market value of the goods or services the donor received. The nonprofit is not required to value the donor's contribution.

Substantiation for Foundations

If you are a development officer for a nonprofit, you probably are soliciting gifts from private foundations. A foundation is not required to substantiate gifts to recipient organizations under the rules discussed above. Because a foundation does not pay income tax, it is not required to prove that its contributions are tax-deductible.

Instead, a different set of rules applies. A foundation must prove that any distribution is qualified for purposes of complying with the foundation tax rules. At minimum, the foundation will want to verify that the organization you represent is a 501(c)(3) organization and a public charity. A foundation may ask for a copy of your organization's determination letter from the IRS. In addition, for particularly large grants a foundation may require a signed copy of the grant letter and program information about your organization, such as a copy of your latest budget, annual report, or most recent tax return.

Substantiation of Noncash Gifts

Increasingly, donors are willing to donate property, as opposed to making only cash gifts.

Increasingly, donors are willing to donate property, as opposed to making only cash gifts. Accordingly, it is important to understand how the IRS expects these gifts to be valued and reported. There is potential for abuse by donors who overvalue property to reduce the amount of tax they must pay to the government. To keep track of property donated to nonprofits, the IRS requires the donor, the tax-exempt organization, or both to submit a series of reporting forms. Following is a discussion of the two forms that can affect the charity receiving a noncash donation.

Form 8283

An individual or corporate donor must file Form 8283 if the amount of the donor's deduction for all noncash gifts made to charitable organizations is greater than $500. The primary function of Form 8283 is for the donor to set forth the value of the property for which the deduction is claimed and for the charitable organization to acknowledge receipt of the gift.

If your organization receives property for which the donor is claiming a charitable deduction in excess of $5,000, your organization's name, address, and employer identification number must be included on Form 8283. In addition, an authorized official of your organization must acknowledge the gift and state that it will file Form 8282 in the event the organization sells, exchanges, or otherwise disposes of the donated property within three years after the date your organization received the property. The person acknowledging the gift to the charity must be an official authorized to sign the organization's tax returns or a person specifically designated to sign Form 8283. Note that a person in the organization's development office is not likely to qualify as an authorized individual unless an officer or the board of directors has specifically designated that individual to sign.

By signing the donor's Form 8283, the 501(c)(3) organization is not indicating that it agrees with the claimed fair market value of the donated property. Therefore, simply signing the form should not make your organization liable for overvaluing the property. The donor is required to furnish you with a copy of the signed Form 8283.

Form 8282

If your organization disposes of property for which it signed a Form 8283 within three years after receiving a contribution, you are required to file Form 8282 with the IRS. There are, however, two important exceptions in which Form 8282 does not need to be filed.

1. If the original recipient organization provided on its appraisal summary a statement that the appraised value of a donated item was not more than $500 at the time of the contribution; and
2. If the property the charitable organization received is consumed or distributed without consideration in fulfilling its charitable purpose or function.

In all other cases, Form 8282 must be filed within 125 days after the date your organization disposes of the property, and a copy of the form must be provided to the original donor.

The requirement to file Form 8282 applies to successor organizations if the property is transferred to another charitable organization. If you fail to file Form 8282, fail to include all of the required information, or include incorrect information on the form, you may be subject to IRS penalties.

CHAPTER 12

Corporate Matching Gifts:
Explanations, Essentials, and Ethics

By Amy J. Phillips | Gift Registrar | Smithsonian Institution

Each year corporate enterprises give money to support the missions of nonprofit organizations in a variety of ways. This article takes a close look at one of them: matching gifts.

Although the term "matching gift" might seem self-explanatory, several definitions could be valid. Because it is not an outright or involuntary gift from a corporation to a nonprofit organization, in my view a matching gift is a form of conditional grant. Typically companies use an application and review process to determine whether they will disburse matching contributions to the nonprofit organization requesting them.

Receiving matching gifts is not guaranteed, even if the institution—as well as the individual gift for which a match is requested—is deemed eligible for a matching gifts program. A corporation decides who will receive matching funds and has no obligation to make the match. No federal regulations mandate that corporations provide philanthropic support of nonprofit organizations through matching gifts or other means. Matching gifts programs represent a tremendous potential asset to the nonprofit community, however. Using a few basic methods, a nonprofit organization can reap the benefits of matching gifts to support its charitable mission.

The history of matching gifts dates back to 1954, when General Electric board chair Philip D. Reed started the General Electric Corporate Alumnus Program, the purpose of which was to support educational initiatives at academic institutions. The premise was clear and simple: a corporation and the individuals it employed clearly benefited from the education provided by the many academic institutions in the community. Therefore, it was in the best interest of the corporation not only to provide philanthropic support to these educational institutions, but also to encourage their employees to give back to their alma maters.

There is no standard form of operation for corporate matching gifts programs, but that would certainly make the lives of staff members handling matching gift requests much easier.

Many companies have followed GE's path. There is no exact count of how many companies have matching gifts programs, but directories listing such programs show roughly 9,000 firms, plus a number of subsidiaries. CASE, HEP Development Services and Blackbaud offer these directories. An increasing number have moved toward setting up a corporate foundation or similar charitable entity to manage their matching gifts program. In 2004 the Giving USA Foundation estimated that nonprofit organizations had received more than $1 billion in matching gifts alone.

There is no standard form of operation for corporate matching gifts programs, but that would certainly make the lives of staff members handling matching gift requests much easier. Each corporation establishes:

- Eligibility guidelines, including the type of organizations with which it matches contributions and who is an eligible donor (employees, spouses, retirees, board members, etc.)
- Matching dollar amounts
- Matching ratio
- Time frames for application and gift disbursement

As matching gifts programs have matured and evolved, more detailed program parameters have become the norm rather than the exception. Except in certain circumstances involving smaller companies, it is unusual for anyone submitting a request for a matching gift not to have access to well-iterated and readily accessible eligibility requirements for both employees or other eligible donors and the non-profit recipient.

Higher-education institutions are the focus of many corporate matching gifts programs. Some academic institutions with a religious affiliation have faced a conflict or challenge over matching gift eligibility. It is common for matching gifts programs to exclude religious or religiously affiliated institutions. Frequently athletic programs that are a part of academic institutions are not eligible for corporate matching funds, also.

With the occasional exception, best practices across the country involve applying matching funds to the same purpose as the original individual contribution. Typically, the more restricted the fund to which the donor has directed a gift, the less likely that a company will want to provide matching funds. Unrestricted annual giving is the most common type of institutional support to which corporations are willing to send matching dollars. Gifts in support of building or other capital projects, for example, tend to be eligible for matching funds far less frequently than annual funds or even scholarship programs.

Typically, the more restricted the fund to which the donor has directed a gift, the less likely that a company will want to provide matching funds.

When it comes to actual dollars matched, the common denominator in the vast majority of corporate matching gifts programs is that only the tax-deductible portion of any charitable gift from an individual qualifies for matching funds. In exceedingly rare instances, certain corporations will provide matching funds for memberships at museums, but this is the exception rather than the rule.

More companies now place a value on the volunteer time employees give in support of charitable institutions and provide matching funds for those efforts (this kind of initiative frequently is referred to as "dollars for doers"). Other prevalent standards include the most common matching ratio of 1:1, although some programs set matching ratios from 0.5 up to 3 (or more) for each dollar an individual contributes to a nonprofit organization.

Corporate matching contributions often are disbursed in the form of cash, but some companies (IBM is a prime example) offer matching contributions in the form of equipment. Depending on the philanthropic goals the corporation is trying to advance through matching gifts (or perhaps because of budgetary constraints), many companies impose caps on dollar amounts to be matched, based either on individual requests—per gift or per year—or on total dollars requested by all eligible donors. In addition, they may set minimum amounts per individual gift, with the most prevalent being $15 or $25.

It is common for matching gifts companies to request some form of confirmation of a nonprofit organization's eligibility to receive a charitable contribution. For the very first matching gift requested by a nonprofit—or sometimes even for the first match request of every calendar or fiscal year—many companies ask for a copy of the organization's 501(c)(3) letter to confirm the institution's charitable status. Some companies may request additional information, such as a copy of the organization's mission statement or the most recent annual report.

Even a trial run at starting a matching gifts program by concentrating on major donors is likely to have a big enough impact on your bottom line to convince any skeptics to expand your program.

Claiming a need for adherence to the PATRIOT Act, some companies have begun to request even more information. There is some debate, however, over what companies need to request and what nonprofit organizations are obliged to provide to comply with this law.

Corporations may not request a receipt from the nonprofit organization for every matching gift received, but IRS regulations stipulate that charitable organizations must issue tax receipts for gifts of $250 or more. Nonprofit organizations should send appropriate receipts to corporations providing matching contributions. In the case of corporate foundations, however, receipts are typically unnecessary, since such foundations are nonprofits. Even so, it is considered good and reasonable practice to acknowledge the corporation's contributions on an annual basis and to recognize the matching contributions in any regularly generated, institutional donor rolls or lists.

Essentials

Now are you ready to jump in, get your matching program started, and bring in more money for your nonprofit organization? From here I'll take a closer look at how you can start or improve a matching gifts program for your organization.

Organizations that have not yet pursued the acquisition of matching funds frequently ask whether the resulting revenue stream is worth the time and effort needed to process matching gift requests. Absolutely! Even a trial run at starting a matching gifts program by concentrating on major donors is likely to have a big enough impact on your bottom line to convince any skeptics to expand your program. It provides a positive flow of money to your organization and, provided you play by the rules, is one of the simplest means of bringing more dollars in your doors.

The first step toward building your matching gifts program is to obtain employment and board affiliation information from your donors and their spouses. For academic institutions, this data collection can be incorporated easily in regular processes such as alumni directory surveys. For other nonprofit organizations, it can be a bit more of a challenge, but one of the simplest steps is to start cultivating donors to consider directing matching gifts to your institution. You can educate them about matching gifts programs by dropping a line into all solicitation pieces and gift acknowledgments asking them to check with their employer about the existence of such a program.

I support incorporating matching funds into the calculation of donor recognition societies for any nonprofit organization. Donors with access to matching funds do have a choice as to where they request those dollars to be directed (within the parameters of institutional eligibility, of course). Your donors will choose to request that matching funds be directed to your institution based on the impact they believe those additional funds will have. They also will be influenced by how much appreciation you show of their efforts to request matching funds for your organization.

Acquiring and maintaining employment and board information on your donors is the hard part of the process. Educating and cultivating your donors about the benefits of taking advantage of the opportunities presented by a corporate matching gifts program is the next task. Once the matching gifts requests begin to pour in (as they certainly will if you invest some time and energy in your program), the process becomes a little easier.

Most corporate programs have clear and reasonably concise criteria determining eligibility of the individual donor, the purpose of the gift, and the nonprofit recipient. Simplistic as it sounds, all that remains is to verify that the individual gift (and your organization as the intended recipient) qualifies. Once those details are confirmed, you complete the form in paper or electronic form (and sometimes the donor may bypass forms and let the matcher know of the donation by providing a canceled check or other proof) and submit the request. Now you can sit back and wait for the matching funds to come.

Of course, as may be the case with our individual donors, some matching gifts programs fill a matching gift request more quickly than others. The schedule for distributing matching funds is yet another self-defined parameter for any corporate matching gifts program; some send a check for each match request, while others opt to summarize and fill requests on a quarterly, semiannual, or annual basis. It is reasonable to treat corporate donors in the same manner as your individual donors. That is, if time has elapsed beyond the payment schedule established by the corporation or corporate foundation, and your organization has not yet received the requested matching funds, you might contact them about payment.

Questions occasionally will arise about who gets hard or legal credit for matching gifts. In situations where individual and matching gifts are submitted separately, the individual donor gets legal credit for the gift. The hard credit for a matching gift goes either to the corporation or the corporate foundation, depending on which entity issued the contribution check.

Now there is a twist in processing individual and corporate matching contributions. To cut overhead costs and promote efficiency in handling matching gifts, some companies issue checks to nonprofit organizations in which both a payroll deduction gift from an individual and the subsequent corporate matching gifts have been incorporated. When a single check reflects both an employee's payroll deduction contribution and the corporate matching gift, the charitable organization must determine whether it needs to issue a receipt to both the individual and the company (or corporate foundation), or if the employee has already received tax documentation of the contribution from the employer. In the latter case, the receiving organization should send an acknowledgment thanking the employee for the gift, rather than a tax receipt. (For details on how other nonprofits handle recognition or soft-crediting for matching gifts, see the 2004 Donor Recognition/Soft-Crediting "best practices" survey by John Taylor and Charlie Hunsaker. Go to *www.case.org*, and in the CASE Code box type the term "CreditSurvey" for an analysis and "CreditSurvey2" for results.)

Once you have established a program for soliciting and processing matching gifts for your nonprofit, consider increasing the amount of matching funds you acquire. Establishing a "corporate agent" as the advocate for support of your nonprofit organization within a company might be as easy as approaching an alumnus, board member, or other affluent donor to your institution. Engage this person to play the role of cheerleader on behalf of your organization and—within guidelines of corporate administrative approval and authorization (not to mention ethically appropriate standards)—to prompt other employees to support your institution with individual gifts and matching funds. This could lead to the establishment of a mini-campaign within the matching gifts company.

Aside from working through an individual corporate agent, your institution can cultivate a relationship with a matching gifts company, agreeing on communication and promotional strategies and promoting support of your nonprofit institution. Among the key success factors are appreciating the contributions of individuals and the corporation and celebrating the success of your campaign, even having a party to acknowledge all who played a part in reaching the mini-campaign's goals.

. . . your institution can cultivate a relationship with a matching gifts company, agreeing on communication and promotional strategies and promoting support of your nonprofit institution.

Technology can be a useful tool in starting and maintaining a robust matching gifts program. The database management tools we use have become more sophisticated, enabling copious amounts of information to be stored and accommodating various levels of linkage between constituent records. Although information is not available about every corporate matching gifts program, for the many about which information exists you can enter details in your database reflecting matching ratios, matching fund distribution schedules, and minimum and maximum qualifying individual-gift amounts. It is worth the time you invest to capture all of this information only if you are willing and able to maintain and use it to your best advantage. The more information you capture and continually update, the better you become at targeting matching-gift solicitations, producing reminders, and projecting matching-gift revenue.

Once you have employment information on your donors, you can project matching-gift revenue. But enter projections only after an individual gift has been made and the match request submitted. Anticipating income simply because a donor happens to work for a company with a matching gifts program (possibly basing projected income on the existence of a match "expectancy" in lieu of a match "pledge") is like trying to reap a crop before sowing the seeds. Matching gifts are not guaranteed; corporations and their foundations can and do adjust or even terminate such programs. And the companies are not obligated to inform the nonprofit community of such changes, although most try to do so.

Ethics

Every organization should adhere to eligibility requirements—for both individual donors and recipient organizations—for the benefit of all charitable organizations.

Problems arise when individuals and institutions do not adhere to corporate program eligibility standards when requesting consideration for matching funds.

This cannot be overstated: Every organization should adhere to eligibility requirements—for both individual donors and recipient organizations—for the benefit of all charitable organizations. If there is any question about whether an individual contribution or a potential recipient organization is eligible, the mantra always should be, "When in doubt, check it out." Corporate matching gifts programs do not operate in a vacuum, although it is true that some programs seem challenging to contact for verification of their parameters. No matter what the issues, it is absolutely better to err on the side of caution and ensure that all the right steps are being taken to allow for the best result to all parties: individual donor, recipient institution, and matching gifts program.

Because corporate matching gifts programs have grown and expanded to support a wide spectrum of charitable organizations, those who manage these programs have to become savvy about providing means for individuals to make contributions to nonprofit institutions.

Companies take pains to promote philanthropy through and with their employees when a matching gifts program is implemented. Programs conduct discussions, define eligibility parameters, and clearly indicate which donors are eligible to have charitable gifts matched and what organizations are eligible to request matching funds. Even the type of individual contribution is now being assessed to determine what form of support by an eligible donor will be considered suitable for matching funds.

With the rare exception of certain memberships at museums, etc., the rule of thumb is that only the tax-deductible portion of an individual's charitable contribution is considered eligible for matching funds (and even some portion of membership fees may be tax-deductible; see IRS Publication 526.) Any benefit that meets or exceeds IRS-defined de minimus value to the eligible donor for a charitable contribution to your institution should trigger a downward adjustment equal to the value of that benefit before the matching funds request. (See Chapters 10 and 11 on IRS rules regarding quid pro quo, including the 80/20 rule for athletic event seating.)

Active, full-time employees of a company are the largest and most common pool of donors who qualify to have their charitable contributions matched by their employer. As previously suggested, some programs give matching funds for contributions by employees' spouses, retired employees or their spouses, or perhaps corporate board members. Siblings, cousins, or in-laws of individual donors otherwise deemed qualified rarely if ever are considered eligible for matching funds.

Knowingly facilitating the acceptance of assets through an otherwise ineligible donor to increase the matching gifts revenue for your institution is unethical. Similarly, no nonprofit organization should condone or encourage an eligible donor to pool funds by collecting contributions from otherwise ineligible donors and then cutting an individual check to facilitate a match request. If discovered by the matching gifts company, such activities are grounds for requesting the return of matching funds already disbursed and the termination of any future philanthropic support by the company.

It is neither safe nor wise to request matching funds if program guidelines do not address a specific question you have about the eligibility of a certain gift—a contribution through a donor-advised fund (DAF), for example. More and more corporate matching gifts programs are including specific language in their eligibility requirements to exclude otherwise eligible donors from obtaining matching funds if the donor contributes a gift through a DAF, family fund, or foundation, or even another type of community foundation.

Who Can Make a Pledge—And Who Can Pay It?

In response to growing debate within institutions—and in some cases between institutions and the donors—the following information is provided as a guide. The ultimate determination regarding appropriate actions in an institution always rests with the lawyer and auditor responsible for ensuring compliance with legal and financial regulations for that institution.

For the purposes of this article, a pledge is an obligation by a donor to a donee. The pledge must meet the criteria for "contributions" in the form of unconditional promises to give, as outlined by the Financial Accounting Standards Board (FASB, which first established the standard; the Government Accounting Standards Board, GASB, has set similar criteria).

A promise to give is "a written or oral agreement to contribute cash or other assets to another entity," as outlined in FASB's Statement of Financial Accounting Standards No. 116, p. 30. A promise carries rights and obligations. The recipient of a promise to give has a right to expect that the promised assets will be transferred in the future, and "the maker has a social and moral obligation, and generally a legal obligation, to make a promised transfer." Once such a promise is made, to the extent that the nonprofit may record it as an asset, the maker of the promise assumes an offsetting liability. "Liabilities are probable future sacrifices of economic benefits arising from present obligations of a particular entity to transfer assets or provide services to other entities in the future as a result of past transactions or events," according to Concept Statement 6 of the FASB statement, p. 31.

Thus, a recordable or enforceable pledge or promise to give may be made only by the entity assuming liability and responsibility for satisfaction of that commitment. The maker has no authority to so obligate another entity over whom it has no legal or financial control. It assumes full and total responsibility for satisfaction of the obligation.

Amplifying this, CASE Management and Reporting Standards state: "A pledge can be made only by the entity exercising legal control over the assets to be given. Therefore, an individual cannot make a pledge that includes anticipated matching contributions from an employer or some other source. Nor can an individual commit funds that may be applied for through a donor-advised fund or community foundation. . . . An enforceable, countable pledge includes only those funds that will be given by that legal entity" (*CASE Management and Reporting Standards*, 3rd ed., p. 40).

Auditing firms have widely varying interpretations of the form of documentation necessary to make the pledge "enforceable." Therefore, the auditor typically makes this determination for each individual institution.

Pledges of a donor's assets should be documented, committing to a specific dollar amount that will be paid according to a fixed time schedule. Your institution's auditing firm will suggest what form the written commitment take for booking purposes, including whether e-mail is an acceptable format. It is advisable that the donor stipulate to the amount, purpose, and payment period in a written document to the nonprofit organization. Some auditors, however, will acknowledge a letter from the institution to the donor, outlining the same details based on a conversation held with the donor, as a bona-fide commitment from the donor. It is advisable, however, that such a letter require the signature of the donor with a copy returned to the institution. Again, seek guidance from your auditor.

So an entity may make a binding pledge or promise to give only if it can assume full personal responsibility and liability for the entire amount. It generally cannot encumber another entity; it is "on the hook" for the entire amount. But does this mean that another entity cannot assist the maker of the pledge or promise satisfaction of that commitment? Much depends on the relationship between maker and payer, and also on the legal nature (tax classification) of the entity rendering a payment.

Clearly it is not legally possible for certain categories of foundations or charities, including donor-advised funds, to satisfy another entity's pledge or promise to give. According to Michael D. Finley, IRS Chief of Branch 3, Income Tax and Accounting, in a private letter ruling dated June 21, 2000:

"A charitable pledge is an obligation of the donor to give money or property to a charity at a future time. Where a charity (including a charitable organization of which a donor advised fund is treated as a component part) relieves a donor of a substantial obligation by satisfying the donor's pledge, the charity is providing the donor with an impermissible benefit. Accordingly, a donor's charitable pledge may not be fulfilled by a single payment or a series of payments from the charity."

An attorney for a large private university observes:

"Although I will not provide an opinion regarding this matter, it would appear that if a donor has a pledge on the books, one way to proceed might be for you to voluntarily cancel the pledge before the gift from the conduit Foundation is made [and without any legally binding agreement tying the cancellation to the Foundation gift]. This could be very risky, however, and the donor is assuming all of the risk. The only safe procedure is to make sure donors understand that a pledge may not be satisfied except by a direct gift. The conduit foundations [e.g. Fidelity, Community Foundations] were established as and intended to be the donee charity and therefore there can be no linkage."

Most corporations offering employee matching-gift programs clearly state in their guidelines, and frequently in the match application form, that their contribution may not be used to satisfy a personal obligation of an employee. In fact, many such programs require that their contribution go to a specific fund or program and not necessarily where the employee made the original gift.

In some instances, however, someone other than the maker can pay toward another entity's pledge. A common example is a spouse or other family member. Sometimes the individual owns a business or is one of its principals and causes a gift to be made toward that pledge. However, given some of the potential tax issues in these situations, it is always best for the payer to state clearly in writing that the payment indeed may be applied to the other entity's pledge.

—John Taylor, Principal, Advancement Solutions

Individual pledges are a decidedly controversial topic. The answer that covers the vast majority of such situations is that the individual who makes a pledge to your nonprofit organization has no legal control over the assets the employer might use to fulfill a matching-gifts request. According to guidelines established by the Financial Accounting Standards Board (FASB), "A pledge must meet the criteria for 'contributions' in the form of unconditional promises to give. Thus, a recordable/enforceable pledge or promise to give may only be made by the entity assuming liability and responsibility for satisfaction of that commitment. The maker has no authority to so obligate another entity over whom they have no legal or financial control. They assume full and total responsibility for satisfaction of the obligation." (See *"Who Can Make a Pledge and Who Can Pay on It?"* on page 168 for details.) Increasingly matching gifts parameters address the question of pledges by making ineligible any requests for matching funds to fulfill a personal pledge.

Corporate matching gifts programs exist to cultivate individual philanthropy and encourage a positive impact on society through support of nonprofit organizations. The rules are simple: Follow the program guidelines and your eligible nonprofit organization will receive matching funds in support of your mission. If we all play by the rules, we can ensure that our employer—whether a primary or post-secondary academic institution, museum or cultural organization, healthcare facility or other charitable association—reaps the benefit of corporate philanthropy through matching gifts.

References

Matching Gifts Administration: Examining the Evolving World of Matching Gifts, 3rd edition. Washington, DC: CASE, June 2005, *www.case.org/books.*

Taylor, John H. "Who Can Make a Pledge—And Who Can Pay On It?" February 2005, *www.supportingadvancement.com.*

Advancement SERVICES

Section IV: Donor Relations and Stewardship

CHAPTER 13

Stewardship: An Integral Part of Development

By Kathy Ruvolo | Executive Director, Constituent Relations | University of California, Irvine

Stewardship is an often overlooked—or underappreciated—component of advancement. But the first step toward a successful fundraising program is recognition by your institution that stewardship is an integral part of development or advancement. Stewardship is about meeting and exceeding donor expectations, which can be a huge task.

To do good stewardship, everyone within your institution needs to get on board. Stewardship is a global (or institutional or team) responsibility, not just that of development or advancement staff. At most institutions, especially larger ones, someone in advancement leads stewardship efforts; in the best scenario, a stewardship office will take the lead. Stewardship professionals need to look, act, and be compensated like major gift officers. They need to get involved in cultivation strategy and interact with donors and prospects. Ideally, stewardship is a full-time responsibility, not a task done as time allows. Rather than an afterthought, stewardship should be systematic, strategic, and consistent, with a strong commitment to quality, timeliness, efficiency, and effectiveness.

With the exception of staff salaries, stewardship does not require a substantial outlay. Most efforts can be accomplished with minimal expense. Focus on keeping your activities personal and sincere, and be aware that most donors do not want (or expect) tangible gifts.

Starting or growing your program is not easy. Here are some questions to ask yourself:

- Does your institution, as a whole, understand and embrace donor stewardship?

- Is your board of directors or trustees involved in fundraising and stewardship? And if not, why not?
- Do you have quality, efficient systems in place to manage gifts and track and ensure proper and effective stewardship of donors?
- Are gifts and endowment income being spent on a regulated basis, and are you sure that spending is taking place in line with donor intent?
- Are donors regularly being shown the impact of their giving and how their money is invested and spent?
- Are donor relations and stewardship top priorities of the information technology staff at your institution?
- Has your institution invested the resources necessary for a successful stewardship program? Do you have a stewardship or donor relations office with sufficient staff to manage your organization?

If you answered "no" to any or all of these questions, you have work to do. Understanding these obstacles is the first step toward overcoming them. Tackle them one-by-one, and establish standards and best practices by building relationships with key stakeholders, providing education and training on campus, and implementing new programs.

To ensure your stewardship program is successful, create a program that will be effective, efficient—and most important, one that will withstand personnel changes.

This chapter gives examples of stewardship programs that will assist your advancement program in its overall mission of raising money, creating awareness, and building relationships. Before getting into the details, it helps to be reminded why donors give and what they expect after they make their gift.

Why Donors Give

Here are some of the reasons donors give to charities such as educational institutions:

- They want to make a positive impact by furthering your institution's mission and improving or furthering causes near and dear to them.

- They have confidence, trust, and respect for the institution and its leadership.
- They have confidence that their gift will be managed well and spent as intended (*see Chapter 1 for a discussion of the Donor Bill of Rights*).
- The ask is made by one of their peers.
- They wish to repay a feeling of indebtedness or obligation (by a former student or grateful patient).
- They desire to honor or memorialize others (loved ones, former faculty mentor, etc.).
- They seek the recognition they will receive both internally and publicly; to leave a legacy.
- They hope to develop a partnership that could result in benefits to them or their companies. (Corporations might give if some of their best recruits come from your institution.)
- They seek access to faculty research and the university chancellor or president.
- They contribute for tax-deduction purposes.

Donors need to be reassured that their faith in you is justified.

What Donors Expect

Donor expectations largely determine your success in fundraising, and industrywide standards strongly affect those expectations. Donors need to be reassured that their faith in you is justified. Managing expectations is crucial to meeting or exceeding them; remember to commit to donors only what you know you can deliver.

Because donors compare and measure stewardship activities against those of the best programs they encounter, it is essential that stewardship professionals stay informed about what others are doing. Benchmark against your peers; it will pay off.

Below are examples of donor expectations. Keep in mind that each donor is unique; know your donors and get to know their expectations. There is such a thing as "too much" or "not enough" stewardship:

- Acknowledgment—timely, proper, and personal. This basic tool has the greatest capacity to add value, or do harm if overlooked.

- Accountability—showing donors they have made a wise decision. Donor confidence is reinforced and builds.
- Information—communication about the positive impact of the gift and how it has helped further your mission and improve life.
- Recognition—some expect more than others. And some feel uncomfortable or embarrassed when the subject is addressed. They don't want to look as if they gave just for the recognition. They need to be assured that you genuinely want to recognize them.
- Engagement—creating partnerships or relationships with faculty or others at the institution.
- Wise management of funds—sound investment practices.

To meet the donor's expectations, you should develop a solid stewardship plan, including consistent policies and practices.

Getting Started

Best practices in stewardship programs include:

- Commitment from the top (institution priority)
- Principle-based leadership
- Compelling vision
- Focused mission
- Active strategic plan
- Systematic policies and procedures
- Established program built on basics
- Automated information systems
- Retention of and competition for top personnel
- Open, flexible environment
- Involvement of volunteers
- Commitment to long-term growth

Central Support at UC Irvine

At UC Irvine, the office of stewardship's mission is to develop overarching programs that recognize, inform, and engage donors through acknowledgments, publications, reports, and outreach activities. These programs have been developed (or are being developed) to withstand changes in personnel. Listed below are the central services provided for our schools, units, and central departments. Keep in mind that UCI is a large, public university that raised $102 million in FY 2005-06, with a gift count of nearly 25,000. Large or small institutions can implement many of the programs below. The use of technology and automation allows you to get the job done efficiently and effectively, regardless of the size of your institution. As a point of reference, our stewardship office is composed of 4.5 full-time equivalent (FTE) staff members.

We conduct annual stewardship planning for all donors who have given a total of $100,000 or more to a school or unit.

Building Relationships, Education, and Training

We build relationships and partnerships by meeting and communicating with "centers of influence" on campus (financial aid, academic affairs, deans' offices, accounting, development, among others). We conduct regular meetings with key staff in these areas to define and emphasize the importance of stewardship and their role in the process. When we work with these areas, we use a "partnership," not a "policing," approach. We are there to help them and our institution.

Planning and Checklists

We conduct annual stewardship planning for all donors who have given a total of $100,000 or more to a school or unit. A representative from the office of stewardship schedules these meetings with all school or unit-based development officers. The checklist is a tool to develop, plan, and schedule stewardship activities for each donor for the fiscal year. We use SunGard Higher Education's Advance to enter scheduled activities into the donor database and report to senior university advancement personnel.

Acknowledgment Tracking

Every Monday morning, we send a weekly electronic report of all gifts received the previous week to all schools and units. The report is intended to report gifts received and, more important, to track and ensure that proper and timely acknowledgments are sent to all donors of $250 or more (an IRS requirement, although we think all donors, large and small, should receive similar confirmation). The report includes an indicator for "no acknowledgment received." This prompts the departments to get the letters done. Letters received are flagged on each gift and pledge record in the Advance system.

Endowment Expenditure Tracking

We developed an automated process to track endowment spending. It is intended to notify (and bring into compliance) departments that are not spending or are reinvesting the income into the corpus of the funds. Semi-annual, color-coded reports go to schools and units:

- **Red Form—Alert:** No spending on the fund for one or more years.
- **Yellow Form—Caution:** Records show the income on the endowment is being reinvested into the corpus of the fund. Departments are asked why they are reinvesting, if they wish to continue, and why.
- **Green Form—Thank you for Spending:** Now tell us how you used the funds.

The beneficiary department on campus completes reports and returns them to the office of stewardship. Our office monitors and analyzes the returned forms and produces a report summarizing each school's or unit's funds, including the total of unspent funds. We send this report to all deans and unit heads.

Scholarship and Fellowship Administration

To track students who have received donor-funded scholarships, we developed an automated interface between financial aid's database and our donor database, Advance.

Once a month, we receive a download from financial aid listing students who received a scholarship. The student's Advance ID is included in the download, so we can match records with our database. The information is recorded on both the student's and the donor's record.

As a result, we launched a student thank-you initiative, and students are now writing letters to the donors who support them.

Our office also facilitates setting up donor-student thank-you lunches and dinners and assists financial aid with marketing and awarding of donor-funded scholarships.

Donor Honor Roll

Annual publication of individual and corporate giving is a must. Some sections of the honor roll include individual donor profiles, endowed chairs, endowed scholarships and fellowships, cumulative giving, consecutive giving, and support groups. The publication is distributed each year in November or December. Surveys show that donors like and appreciate receiving this publication.

Reports

During our annual stewardship checklist visits with schools and units, we identify donors to receive stewardship reports custom designed and generated in-house (spiral bound with custom cover and photos).

Reports give recognition to the donor and include our institution's vision and values statement, a financial summary (history of donor's giving), and a report showing the impact of the donor's gift (written in collaboration with the gift beneficiary, such as the chair holder, scholarship recipient, or dean).

The annual fall report goes to donors who have established or contributed to endowed funds. Elements include a letter from the president of the UCI Foundation, a campus update, a statement of the fund's purpose, recipient(s) of fund income, use of funds available for spending, and financial performance and disbursements.

Cards

Under the Chancellor's Parking Card Program, four parking passes are sent to donors of $1500+ annually. The Anniversary of Gift Card Program sends an anniversary card celebrating the date of gift goes to donors who have made significant gifts (naming gifts, establishment of a chair, etc.). Selected donors receive birthday wishes. A card or small gift is personalized, based on the donor's relationship.

Memorial Bench Program

A donor who wishes to memorialize or honor a loved one can purchase a memorial bench. The benches are placed on campus with recognition plaques affixed.

Recognition Gifts

The office of stewardship assists schools and units in obtaining recognition gifts for donors. These gifts (collages, photo albums, and the like) are highly personalized and proportionate to the donor's gift. The requesting school or unit is billed for the cost of the gift.

Faculty and Staff Donor Event

Our goal is to help move these donors from their first-time gift to getting involved with the campus in a more substantive way.

At many institutions, donors on the faculty and staff—especially those who give through payroll deductions—are overlooked. At UCI each year in the spring, all faculty and staff donors are invited to a recognition reception at the chancellor's campus home. This encourages continued and increased giving by current employee donors and encourages giving by other faculty and staff. This event gives us an opportunity to communicate the value of private support to the campus and educate employees about the role of advancement.

New Donors

The office of stewardship sends a welcome packet to all new donors of $250 or more. The purpose is to thank donors for the gift, acknowledge that it is their first gift, reinforce the importance of private support to UCI, offer our service as a liaison to the campus, and encourage them to visit the campus. Included is a voucher for an athletic or arts event, based on the level of the gift. *(When giving benefits, keep in mind the IRS quid pro quo rules, outlined in Chapters 10 and 11.)* The office of stewardship works closely with the annual fund because many of these donors will give to the campus through this method.

Each year, more than 1,000 individuals make first-time gifts of $250 or more to UCI. Our goal is to help move these donors from their first-time gift to getting involved with the campus in a more substantive way. Therefore, we conduct an event to thank our newest donors, reinforce the importance of their support, and encourage them to develop a more personal relationship with the campus and various officials (especially unit development officers.) If you don't have the budget for such an event, consider piggybacking it onto another one that draws a considerable crowd.

Monitoring Inactivity

Our office regularly monitors $100K+ donors who have not had contact reports entered on their records within the past 12 months. *(See Chapter 8, Tracking Prospects, for more information on tracking.)* The office of stewardship works with the managers of these donors to develop a follow-up plan to ensure and maintain continuity of communication over time. In some cases, these donors are reassigned to another development officer.

Events

The office of special events reports to the director of stewardship. Events are carefully planned and executed to steward and cultivate donors.

Finally, one obvious way to do good stewardship, albeit often overlooked, is to ask your donors what they want. Every donor is unique. Some might want reports, but others do not. Some might want to be actively involved with your school, but some might not. Some might want public recognition, but others might want to remain anonymous. A good time to start is when the gift is made; inquire at this time about what donors expect in return for their generosity. Be cautious, and do not make promises that will be hard to fulfill.

Remember, stewardship is an easy and inexpensive step to ensure that your fundraising programs are successful. Don't be shortsighted and only raise money; our best prospects are previous donors.

CHAPTER 14

Successful Gift and Pledge Agreements for Educational Institutions

By Christopher M. Johnston | Assistant Vice President, Constituent Relations & Senior International Officer, International Relations | University of Virginia

Kathy Ruvolo | Executive Director, Constituent Relations | University of California, Irvine

This chapter is a guide to drafting gift or pledge agreements between donors and educational institutions. While written for educational institutions, the concepts are easily transportable to any nonprofit organization. Examples of several of the agreements discussed in this chapter can be found in the appendix of *CASE Management and Reporting Standards*, 3rd edition (CASE, 2004).

Gift and pledge agreements serve several purposes. They:

1. Protect the donor's and the institution's current and future interests
2. Clarify the specific agreement(s) between an institution and the donor concerning the donor's gift or pledge to the institution
3. Ensure that the pledge is binding on the donor's estate
4. Allow for future circumstances that were unforeseeable at the time of the agreement's writing and execution

Successful agreements properly outline and clarify the donor's and the institution's intentions in providing and accepting the gift or pledge. They also clarify the duties and expectations of all the parties. These agreements are highly recommended when a donor is providing support for an endowment, chairs, professorships, faculty fellows, capital projects, institutional namings, planned gifts, and multiyear pledges. In rare cases, these agreements may be used in a legal action pursued by one or both parties to enforce the agreement's terms. Therefore they are and should be legally binding documents.

This chapter provides basic components that institutions may consider when creating their own gift or pledge agreements. Because of the unique circumstances surrounding each gift or pledge at your institution, it is difficult to provide a uniform template for all gifts or pledges. As you create each agreement, it is best to use clear and concise language that all parties can understand, as well as future prospects or donors associated with the gift or pledge (heirs to an estate, for example) and the institution's personnel responsible for administering the gift.

Suggested Gift or Pledge Agreement Components

The following suggested components will be explained in greater detail below:

1. Title
2. Introduction
3. Charitable Tax Information (Nonprofit Exempt Status)
4. Gift Description and Payment Schedule
5. Gift Purpose and Administration
6. Future Considerations
7. Recognition, Publicity and Reporting
8. Binding Obligation
9. Miscellaneous (situs, amendments, effective date)
10. Signatures

Title

Your agreement's title may be as simple as "Gift Agreement" or "Pledge Agreement." You also may wish to include the donor's name and a brief description of the gift or pledge. For example, if it is to establish a scholarship fund in the name of the donor, you might title the agreement:

Gift Agreement
To Establish The Jane and John Doe Endowed Scholarship Fund

Introduction

The introduction includes a list of the parties involved in the agreement. In this paragraph, include the exact legal names of all parties referred to in the agreement—the donor(s), the institution, the donor's or institution's foundation (if applicable), as well as the institution's related parties (school or college, department, center, program, etc.). For future convenience and to avoid having to list each party's full name throughout the agreement, you also may wish to use an abbreviated name for each of the parties. This reference is generally noted in parentheses—for example, "Jane and John Doe (Donors)"; "University of Learning (University)"; and the University's "School of Humanities (School)"; etc. It shows how you will refer to the respective entities throughout the document.

Consult with legal counsel when additional entities—such as an individual wishing to include himself or herself, as well as the donor's family foundation or trust—enter into the agreement. This is because self-dealing and other legal and financial issues may arise in creating the agreement. You also may wish to include a very brief description of the gift's purpose. A sample introduction might state:

> The purpose of this agreement is to summarize the mutual understanding of Jane and John Doe (Donors) and the University of Learning (University) regarding the establishment of an endowed scholarship fund at the University's School of Humanities (School). This agreement will be made a part of the University's permanent records and is intended to serve as a guide to those who administer the fund in the future.

Charitable Tax Information (Nonprofit Exempt Status)

Use this section to refer to your organization's tax status. For example:

The University of Learning represents that it is qualified as a charitable organization and a 501(c)(3) nonprofit, public, benefit organization (federal ID 95-254XXX).

Gift Description and Payment Schedule

This section describes the type of gift or pledge, includes its total value, and outlines how and when the donor intends to satisfy the gift or pledge. Below are some examples to consider for various gift types:

Example A [Pledge]:

The Donors irrevocably pledge $1,000,000 (one million dollars) to establish the Jane and John Doe Endowed Scholarship Fund as described by this document. Pledge payments will be made as follows:

- $500,000 (five-hundred-thousand dollars) on or before (DATE)
- $500,000 (five-hundred-thousand dollars) on or before (DATE)

The Donors may accelerate the completion of this pledge at the Donors' discretion.

Example B [Outright Gift]:

The Donors intend to gift, outright and concurrently with this agreement, to the University $1,000,000 (one million dollars) or the following assets with an (estimated/appraised/established) aggregate fair market value of $1,000,000 (one million dollars):

Asset: ______________________Value: ____________________

Asset: ______________________Value: ____________________

on or before (DATE).

Example C [Charitable Remainder Unitrust]:

The Donor intends to establish a charitable remainder trust, designed to pay ____ percent (__%) to the Donor for his/her lifetime, with _____ percent (___%) of the remainder interest passing irrevocably to the University. The (estimated/appraised/established) fair market value and net present value of the asset to fund the Unitrust are $_________(FMV) and $_______ (NPV).

Example D [Bequest]:

The Donors intend to provide a bequest in their (will/living trust) naming the University as a(n) (irrevocable) beneficiary of ($__________ / ______%) of their estate.

Example E [Insurance or Pension Beneficiary Designation]:

The Donors intend to designate the University as an irrevocable beneficiary of ($__________/___%) in the following (insurance policy/IRA/pension/Keogh/profit sharing/401(k) account):

Name of (Policy / Account):______________________________

(Policy / Account) Number:______________________________

Name of (Agent/Broker):______________________________

Contact Information (Agent/Broker):______________________

Gift Purpose and Administration

This section describes the purpose and use, as well as the administration, of the gift. It also helps ensure that the parties understand and agree upon their intent to provide and receive the gift.

Issues surrounding the gift, such as quid pro quo and others, also may be discussed in this section. You may use language to indicate your campus policy on investments, spending policies, UMIFA, administration fees, etc. For instance:

> The purpose of this gift or pledge is to establish the Jane and John Doe Endowed Scholarship Fund (Fund). The Fund's annual distributions will support undergraduate scholarships for students enrolled in the School of the Arts' Music Program.
>
> The endowed Fund will be managed by the Foundation's board of trustees in accordance with the Foundation's investment and disbursement policies, and in accordance with the terms and conditions of the Uniform Management of Institutional Funds Act (UMIFA). The Fund may be combined with the Foundation's other assets for investment purposes. The total return earned by the Fund, in excess of the payout amount provided for expenditure, will be retained to protect the corpus principal from the effects of inflation. The annual payout portion of the endowed Fund

> will be managed by the Foundation's board of trustees in accordance with the University's policies on current funds.
>
> The Donor is aware that this gift will comply with current policy and administrative guidelines of the University, that the naming is subject to approval by the chancellor or president, and that this gift will be subject to the University's administrative fee policies for gifts to the campus.

Future Considerations

. . . every effort should be made to comply with the terms of the agreement; however, as institutional needs and priorities change, so may a designated gift's purpose.

Gifts made in perpetuity (such as endowed or naming gifts) may undergo changes in certain gift purpose(s). This section provides language to assist the parties in dealing with potential future changes. This language also may serve to protect the university if or when it no longer can fulfill the university's obligations stated in the agreement or the gift's purpose. Of course, every effort should be made to comply with the terms of the agreement; however, as institutional needs and priorities change, so may a designated gift's purpose. It is especially important to include similar language for gifts to establish endowed funds and namings, as well as deferred gifts or bequest expectancies. For instance:

> In the unlikely event that at some future time it becomes impossible for this gift to serve the specific purpose for which it was created, the chancellor and the University Foundation's president shall direct that the gift or pledge be devoted to purposes that they deem to be the most consistent with the wishes of the Donor and, if possible, in consultation with the Donor.

Recognition, Publicity, and Reporting

Use this section to clarify agreements regarding gift or pledge consideration, appreciation or recognition, possible public disclosure options (anonymity or prior approval issues, etc.), and the university's future reporting responsibilities (stewardship). For example:

> In order to honor the Donors for their support of the University, the University's School of Engineering Building shall be named "Jane and John Doe Engineering Hall." The commonly used name will be "Doe Hall." The naming will be handled consistent with University policies, including identification of the building on University maps and through appropriate signage on the

building. The naming will be for the useful life of the structure and is contingent upon fulfillment of this pledge.

The Donors agree to allow the University to publish their names in various University publications, or in recognition areas displayed at the School of Engineering that list other donors to the School of Engineering. For recognition purposes, the Donors shall be identified as "Jane and John Doe" (or as "Anonymous"). (Broad public announcements of the gift or pledge shall be made only as mutually agreed upon in advance by the Donors and the University.)

The University's president or chancellor and the University Foundation's president will consult with the Donors on an annual basis to ensure consistency, continuity, and institutional memory for the gift's purpose. This annual meeting will include a determination and coordination of the endowed Fund's annual distribution purpose(s); progress toward agreed-upon goals; and plans for upcoming academic year(s). The University Foundation also will provide the Donors with an annual stewardship report detailing the Fund's disbursements from the prior academic year.

Binding Obligation Clause

This section may be necessary for pledge agreements (where gift installments may be made over a period) or for an outright gift agreement signed before the transfer of an asset from the donor to the university. For instance:

The Donor intends this gift or pledge agreement to be fully enforceable against the Donor's estate to the extent that the obligation has not been satisfied by gifts completed following the date of this agreement.

Miscellaneous

This section may be used for miscellaneous provisions, such as situs, future amendments, and effective date. For instance:

Situs: This Agreement is executed in and shall be governed by the laws of the state of ______________________.

Amendment: This agreement may be amended at any time by written agreement signed by each party.

Effective date: The effective date of this agreement shall be the date the agreement is fully executed.

Signatures

Provide appropriate spaces for each required signature and signature date. Be sure to include both spouses for married couples, especially for universities located in community-property states. Research and understand your institution's policies on gift acceptance, and be sure to include all required and appropriate signatures.

It is recommended that the institution's parties execute the document(s) before obtaining the donor's signature, to ensure that changes to the agreement will not have to be made after the donor's signature. Also, be sure to properly indicate the exact names and titles of all parties signing the agreement. Other university personnel also may serve as the agreement's signers, especially those who have a relationship with the donor and whose school, college, or program will benefit from the gift or pledge. For example:

For the Donors:

Jane Doe Date

John Doe Date

For the University:

OFFICER'S NAME Date
Chancellor/President

For the Foundation:

NAME Date
President

For the School:

NAME Date
Dean

Successful gift and pledge agreements result from a university's productive relationships with donors. As such, every agreement will contain special language applicable to the agreement's donor(s), the gift's purpose, and the arrangements agreed upon. More important than an agreement's terms are continuing cultivation and stewardship of the donor. If the relationship is successful, so will the agreement—even if its terms change.

CHAPTER 15

Rebuilding a Stewardship Program

By Scott Fendley | Director of Advancement Services | Wabash College

Stewardship programs are an important part of any advancement or development office's plan, yet benign neglect of such programs can lead to myriad problems with donors and potential donors. An advancement office can lose sight of the functions of stewardship and donor relations while it embarks on new strategic plans, fundraising initiatives, and building projects. It also is easy to lose sight of those areas if you have high staff-turnover, especially in middle and senior management.

However, a stewardship program can be rebuilt to become successful for both donors and institutions. Although it may take years to erase the effects of a fallow stewardship program, taking the initiative to reform and reshape stewardship and donor relations can regain credibility with your donors and the fundraising community as a whole. A successful stewardship and donor relations program not only gives your donors peace of mind that their generous gifts are being used for the purposes they intended, those programs ensure ongoing cultivation of your donors that can lead to even more generous gifts in the future.

The 'Good Old Days'

Take a look at some old donor files from the 1980s and earlier. Before the computerization of advancement and development offices, many thank-you letters to major donors were handwritten, copied on carbons, and quite personal in nature. The development office knew the major donors and kept meticulous paper records regarding donor activities, personal history, and personal interests.

With the advent of affordable computers, word processing programs, and mail merges, those letters became progressively less personal and more like form letters from major corporations. Early software did not have the capacity to reflect all the nuances of a donor's relationship to the institution and did not allow the institution to capture much personal information, either.

Also, in early campaigns, once a donor made a gift and received an acknowledgment, the gift officers moved on to the next prospect without conveying the success of the efforts to the donor, much less scheduling a return visit by a gift officer. Donors became restless, and some did speak out about being "forgotten" in the quest for new donors and new money.

Stewardship Plans

To alleviate these problems, advancement and development offices wrote stewardship plans in an attempt to ensure that donors received thanks for gifts and pledges. They also tried to ensure that donors who gave major or special gifts were thanked in more personal and appropriate ways. Many times these programs were implemented with the best of intentions; however, because of management changes, presidential changes, staff turnover, and a lack of buy-in from the staff or the institution as a whole, the programs did not have the desired effect.

So how does one begin to rebuild a stagnant and stale stewardship program? It is not simple, especially if the institution's culture needs to change to embrace stewardship and donor relations. But it can be done. The key is to identify a campus champion for stewardship, involve staff from all areas of advancement and development, achieve small victories, and measure your success. Then a stewardship and donor relations program can become a model for your advancement and development staff, giving donors and your institutional community peace of mind that the gifts are being utilized properly and donors thanked appropriately.

Common Work

Philanthropy is not all about raising dollars, endowing scholarships, or building buildings. Instead, philanthropy concerns "common work." Dr. Paul C. Pribbenow, president of Rockford College, writes about this in his e-mail newsletter, *Notes for the Reflective Practitioner.*

A good stewardship program must involve the entire institution, from president to faculty, staff at all levels, and donors. The notion that stewarding the gifts of our donors is a responsibility for the entire community is vital to the success of any stewardship program. Without this concept, many programs are doomed to fail, even with the best of intentions.

A good stewardship program must involve the entire institution, from president to faculty, staff at all levels, and donors.

Find a Champion

It is important that a senior advancement or development officer become a champion for stewardship at the institution. This champion should be able to carry the message of stewardship and donor relations at all times and introduce it as often as appropriate.

When gearing up for the public phase of capital fundraising campaigns, many institutions lose sight of stewardship and donor relations. Prospects need cultivation plans, events need to be planned and executed, and reports need to be written, so progress of the campaign can be tracked easily for all interested parties.

A champion for stewardship should be able to keep the donors in mind when these plans are being formulated. Asking, "What impact will this have on the donors to our campaign?" will keep stewardship in focus. It could lead to cultivation plans involving stewardship events where donors are thanked publicly, and reports in which donors are thanked and recognized properly, no matter what the level of their gift. If appropriate, donors should be told about their endowment's performance and the recipients of scholarships or prizes during the year.

The champion also should advocate for a budget for stewardship and donor relations. Implementing a good plan requires investment, and the institution should not be reluctant to spend this money, whether for travel for stewardship visits, events for donor recognition, or printing and publishing endowment reports for donors.

Don't allow the stewardship champion to dictate policies and procedures. Involve others in the formulation of these plans to avoid the risk of alienating the staff needed to implement them. If staff members believe their institutional and professional knowledge and insight are being ignored, then they probably will not work hard to ensure the program's success. Revitalizing a stewardship program requires the entire advancement and development staff's buy-in.

Convincing someone to become the champion may not be easy. However, by showing currently successful stewardship and donor relations results and asking peer institutions about their successful programs, you should be able to identify someone who can focus on the program's key objectives.

Form a Committee

The champion should empower advancement and development staff to form a committee to evaluate stewardship and donor relations from top to bottom. Existing stewardship policies and procedures, if any, should be totally and thoroughly re-examined. If no formal policies and procedures exist, the committee should formulate them.

Peer institutions are a great resource for those involved in such a task. Reach out to institutions and organizations of similar size with a similar number of donors. You may end up exchanging ideas about programs and policies. Visit other institutions, too.

This committee should include members from all areas of advancement and development and encompass all levels, from senior management to support staff. The committee approach ensures that ideas from all sectors are brought to the table and carefully considered.

A Plan

The stewardship committee should have a hand in drafting the final stewardship plan. This plan should consider all aspects of stewardship and donor relations, including:

- Gift acknowledgment, including official tax-receipt procedures
- Stewardship of major donors
- Lifetime giving circle stewardship
- Planned giving stewardship
- Endowed fund reporting

- Scholarship recipient letter rules and procedures
- Stewardship of donors to building projects
- Stewardship of donors for named scholarships, fellowships, professorships, and chairs
- Stewardship of donors for programs, internships, and other projects
- Events (scholarship luncheons, awards teas, meetings with the president or chancellor and other top institutional officials, for example)

When the draft is complete, committee members should present this plan to their departments for revision and comment. Then the committee should rework the draft before presenting it to upper management for review and approval.

This will allow all advancement and development staff to buy into the new stewardship plan; it also will demonstrate to upper management that the whole department has carefully considered the plans.

Take care that donors are not deluged with paper in response to the gift.

Gift Acknowledgment Protocol

Any stewardship plan needs a gift acknowledgment protocol. This document should spell out what receipts and thank-you letters a donor should receive, based on the size of the gift or pledge.

The protocol should indicate that donors will receive a simple receipt letter with the appropriate IRS language. However, for donors at leadership levels, the person identified in the plan could send other letters. Many of these should be hand-signed, so staff can add personal notes to the acknowledgment. In fact, many institutions have their receipt letters hand-signed, so that all donors can receive a personal note if warranted for cultivation or stewardship purposes. However, hand-signing should not delay the mailing of the first acknowledgment to the donor. If it cannot be signed within 24-48 hours of processing the gift, use an automated system.

Take care that donors are not deluged with paper in response to the gift. Although it is important that major donors be thanked properly, some donors may not like receiving six or seven pieces of paper acknowledging their pledge or gift. You *can* say "thank you" too many times! The committee should consider this when formulating the acknowledgment plan; only certain staff should disseminate thank-you letters. Knowing who is sending what and when is critical.

Directing Traffic

Start working the plan immediately after it is approved. Use a team approach because all members of advancement and development have a hand in proper stewardship of all donors. A donor relations coordinator should be charged with the day-to-day oversight of the plan. The coordinator is essential to any stewardship plan. This person should manage all aspects of stewardship and donor relations on campus, with special emphasis on:

- Student thank-you letters to donors
- Endowed fund reports
- Special donor events on and off campus
- Creation and execution of donor relation plans for major gift donors
- The honor roll of donors

The champion should advocate for formation of the coordinator position, and it should be part of a permanent advancement effort, if the budget will allow. If funding is insufficient to add a new position, coordination should be included in an existing position. Without proper coordination of all donor relations and stewardship activities, a well-intentioned and thoughtful stewardship plan can be derailed before it starts.

Roadblocks

Roadblocks will stand in the way of any plan's success. Perhaps you cannot get information from financial aid to do the scholarship letters in a timely manner. Or perhaps one department on campus refuses to write a letter to the donors of a departmental chair because it is "not their business."

Also, the culture of the institution may create impediments to the full embracing of a stewardship plan that involves other departments outside advancement and development. Again, advancement is "common work," and that means stewardship stretches across the entire campus.

Working through such roadblocks can be difficult, but none is insurmountable. The best defense is a good offense. Be proactive and show the department some tangible results of good stewardship for the institution. You can do this by giving specific examples ("Gifts to the Biology Department from prior donors increased after the department sent its donors updates on the latest construction project") or by measuring certain key indicators.

Also, work with the various departments to find common ground. If financial aid is reluctant to divulge information before a certain date, try to find out why and compromise on a date that serves both your purposes. While it is important to get the information out in a timely manner, alienating those you need information from can detract from your ultimate goal. All financial aid officers like to give out money; good stewardship can result in a steady stream for the financial aid budget.

Measurement

While stewardship and donor relations can be part of the "softer side" of advancement, measurement is still important. To convince skeptical departments that good work is being done in stewardship and donor relations, to self-assess your program, or to illustrate to donors how you are improving your efforts, good measurement is critical.

You might consider measuring:

- Attendance at events by donors (or by parents, students, and donors at annual scholarship events)
- Number of donor events in a given year (such as scholarship dinners, awards luncheons, building dedications, luncheons given to internship recipients, etc.)
- Number of letters written by students to scholarship donors
- Number of letters written by professors and chairs to their donors
- Number of days to send out endowment funding reports from the time fiscal year ends (or audit is complete)
- Annual gifts given by donors of endowed funds

Measuring these items can allow you to show results. For example, if only 45 percent of your student scholarship recipients wrote thank-you letters to their benefactors before you hired a donor relations coordinator, and within two years that total increased to 70 percent, with a corresponding increase in annual fund donations by the endowed scholarship donors, then that information shows tangible results. Results also provide good talking points for your major gifts staff when they discuss with donors how you will manage and steward their gifts.

Spread Your Plan

In some institutions, advancement and development are looked at as operations solely for collecting gifts to the institution. Presenting your stewardship plan at an all-hands meeting or to select departments may alleviate some of the roadblocks and allow you to go further in creating a culture where stewardship is "common work" for the entire institution.

Bad news travels fast—sadly, much more quickly than good news.

Academic or programmatic areas, the business office, financial aid, athletics, and even admissions and enrollment may be great places to present what your office is doing and show how the work of stewardship and donor relations affects them. Thus you can show how their work affects donor relations.

Listen and Reassess

After you have begun using your new stewardship plan, take time to listen to your donors. Donors will be heard, and they will talk among themselves. So if a donor confronts his major-gifts officer with a perceived gaffe in your stewardship efforts, take time to investigate the problem before it becomes a major issue with other donors. Bad news travels fast—sadly, much more quickly than good news.

After a year, bring the committee back together and reassess your current stewardship plan. Go over what has worked, what has not worked, and what changes can and should be made to the stewardship effort. There should be no sacred cows; reassess everything and change whatever is not working. Taking time to reassess the plan can only improve your efforts and ensures that you stay on top of stewardship initiatives.

Rebuilding a stewardship program can be challenging, but it is vital and crucial that stewardship and donor relations not be overlooked in any modern advancement and development office. Hard work can and will pay off with satisfied donors, a buzz around campus regarding donor relations events, and better relations with the entire institutional community.

Advancement
SERVICES

Section V: Systems and Technology

CHAPTER 16

Building Your Data Warehouse:
The Foundation of All Data-Related Advancement

By Brian Dowling | Assistant Vice President for Development, Development - Information Systems | University of Michigan

Efficiency is crossing the bridge as fast as possible. *Effectiveness* is deciding whether you need to cross the bridge at all. Systems and databases have never been so important for making both possible.

It used to be that very often, new staff members could not use the computer. This is no longer true. Users have gained a substantial degree of expertise, and advancement services offices need to provide better tools. Good, accurate, and readily available information is a hallmark of successful advancement programs. Infrastructure is 50 percent of the battle. If we spend an inordinate amount of time dealing with information inefficiency, the battle will be lost.

You need to cross the bridge, and soon. A data warehouse is one of the most essential and important projects you can undertake.

This is just a "teaspoon sip." The topic is complex, technically difficult, ridden with jargon and can be confusing. It is important not to be overwhelmed. Think big, start small, and deliver quickly. This sip should give you enough of a taste to create your own recipe for success.

History and Perspective

In general, we have much enterprise resource planning software for human resources, finance, and other departments, but little business information. Our systems have focused on capturing and managing transactions rather than turning information into knowledge.

An increasingly sophisticated view of education sees it as a business with more conventional approaches to revenues and expenses. We put greater emphasis on accountability, compliance, and transparency, and our constituents have higher expectations. Budgets continue to decrease, and we need to be more efficient in managing our institutions. We need better technology to analyze information, a better understanding of information, and better ways to collaborate and make decisions.

I once worked at an institution where the president called us into meetings and requested that we provide a fairly comprehensive list of performance indicators. All this data resided in different systems. By the time the information was compiled and put together, several months had elapsed. It was very time-consuming to compile the relevant data. And this was certainly not an optimal way of making timely decisions. Every time the president asked, the process was the same. We had no data warehouse.

We need to understand our constituents' relationships to the enterprise as a whole.

According to a Berkeley study, 10^{18} bytes of data are being created every year. The world's offices consumed 43 percent more paper in 2002 than in 1999. Both these statistics suggest such a degree of information overload that it seems we cannot deal even with simple information anymore unless we first print it out.

User expectations for presentation have progressed far beyond a stack of green bar every month to graphical, real time, 24/7, anytime, anyplace to meet the demands of our global advancement operations.

Our "traditional" advancement systems contained giving and biographical data. In the 1980s we added prospect tracking. Over the next two decades we added telemarketing, events management, and other peripheral systems. Many of these were stand-alone, had separate reporting tools and compounded the difficulty in providing information. We have added thousands of additional data elements, such as solicitation codes, wealth indicators, relationships, and many more. Data models for "add-on" systems often are as complex as our main advancement system.

Data Mining is No Longer Optional

We need to understand our constituents' relationships to the enterprise as a whole. This often requires combining information from multiple systems, such as advancement, research, finance, purchasing, and student or membership information. We need to compare our summary information to external indicators, such as stock markets. How much did a corporation give? This contribution could include gifts, discounts on purchases, event sponsorships, and sponsored research. Did they give because of changes in the capital markets? All this is difficult to compile in a donor profile.

Along came the Web. It is hard to believe that it has existed for less than two decades. We now have e-mail and Web site statistics, mass communications, multiple touch points, behavior analysis, complex reporting, slicing and dicing. All this makes for extremely complicated data models. How can we possibly integrate this information and provide meaningful knowledge?

Reporting Challenges

Advancement reporting is one of our most challenging tasks. We are an opportunity-driven business. Questions can be asked in a wide variety of ways, and we have a high volume of ad-hoc reporting. It is difficult to revise and rewrite structured query language (SQL) queries. We do not have enough staff to do advanced analysis, since we are constantly busy meeting current reporting demands. Here is a list of other problems:

- **Reports are labor-intensive.** We have imbedded calculations and formulas we have to change in all reports. We end up with conflicting versions, high maintenance, and confusion among users.
- **Reporting tools perform relatively poorly** with large sets of data, particularly if there are more than a few simple joins.
- **Deployment is difficult.** We still use paper and run reports one at a time. We are not really automated.
- **Reports are not standard.** We do not have reports that can be reviewed and compared easily.
- **Reports are inflexible.** The more difficult the report is, the more difficult to change or modify it.
- **Databases are built for transactions.** Many of us still are reporting from our transactional databases. The indexes and organization of the tables are designed for efficiently capturing transactions; they are not good for reporting.

Figure 11: Advancement's Complex Data Models

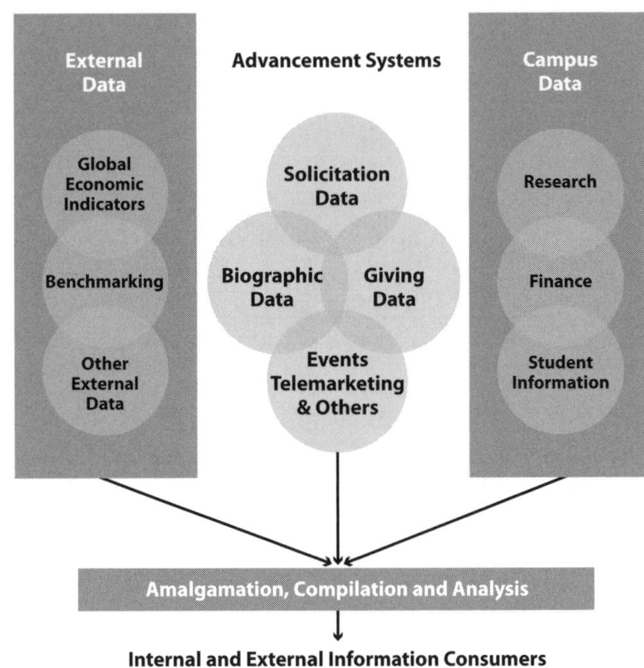

What is a Data Warehouse?

A data warehouse is a reporting database, separate from transactional databases. Your data warehouse will include information from a variety of sources and database formats: your primary advancement system, telemarketing, mass e-mailing, campus systems, and others.

Your data warehouse will facilitate data cleansing, perform transformations (calculations, summaries, etc.), and load data into tables. The tables and indexes will be structured in ways that greatly improve your reporting and analysis capabilities.

It will be the basis of the development of analytical applications. These allow users to look at information and drill down to details to make better business decisions.

Extract, Transform, Load Tool

A data warehouse is usually updated and refreshed from transactional databases on a regular basis, using an ETL tool. I cannot overemphasize the importance of investing in a good ETL tool. If you cannot afford one, you can create and refresh your data warehouse using SQL scripts and batch files. It may not be as elegant or efficient, but it will do the trick.

Figure 12: The Data Warehouse Pyramid

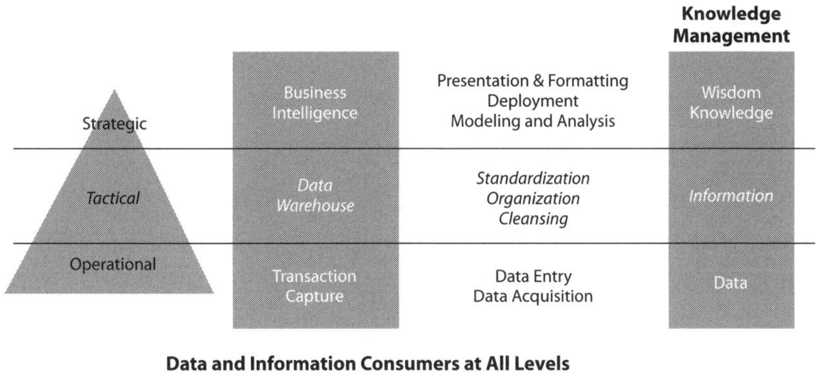

Knowledge Management

Strategic
Business Intelligence
Presentation & Formatting
Deployment
Modeling and Analysis
Wisdom Knowledge

Tactical
Data Warehouse
Standardization
Organization
Cleansing
Information

Operational
Transaction Capture
Data Entry
Data Acquisition
Data

Data and Information Consumers at All Levels

Extract

Data are extracted from transactional tables using multi-threaded, massively parallel, highly efficient processing. The tools allow incremental updates that capture only those records that have been added or changed. So it is not necessary to extract all transactional information in every processing window.

Data can be extracted from diverse data sources: enterprisewide databases, such as human resources, spreadsheets, databases on local computers, Web logs (blogs), or flat files.

Transform

Transformations and calculations, such as identification of outstanding pledge balances, are in ETL language. If you need to change a transformation, you do not have to know a specific database vendor's syntax. If you change your database, you should not have to modify any of the transformations done in your ETL tool. Transformations are independent of the database from which the transactional information is being pulled. Data cleansing, such as calculating the estimated age of individuals whose age is unknown, also may be done during the transformation.

Load

Data are loaded into data warehouse tables and are available to end-users, report writers, and business analysts. ETL tools automate all these processes and calculations. Changes to transformations are automatically propagated. Notifications for job success and failures should be sent out automatically.

ETL tools are an extremely efficient way of creating, updating, and managing your data warehouse. Invest (people and money) in them if you can.

Figure 13: Extract, Transform, Load

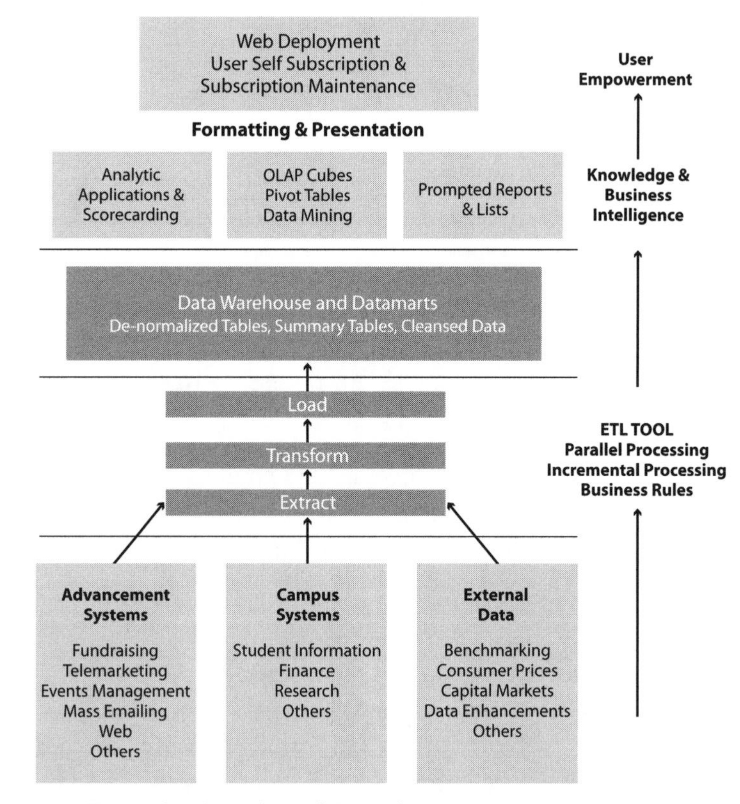

Building Blocks

Ralph Kimball, founder of the Data Warehouse Institute, uses the metaphor of the publisher for a data warehouse. A publisher produces something, distributes it, and updates it at regular intervals. Just like a newspaper or a Web site, it is added to frequently, and information in it must be accurate.

Kimball also uses the metaphor of "the restaurant." The data warehouse is the kitchen, and the dining room is where presentation and consumption take place. Diners stay out of the kitchen because it is full of busy people, sharp knives, and hot liquids. The way in which the meal is prepared is not seen by the consumer. Presentation is important.

Building your data warehouse will involve analysis, interviewing, and understanding your current information environment.

Let's begin...

Figure 14: Data Warehouse Building Blocks

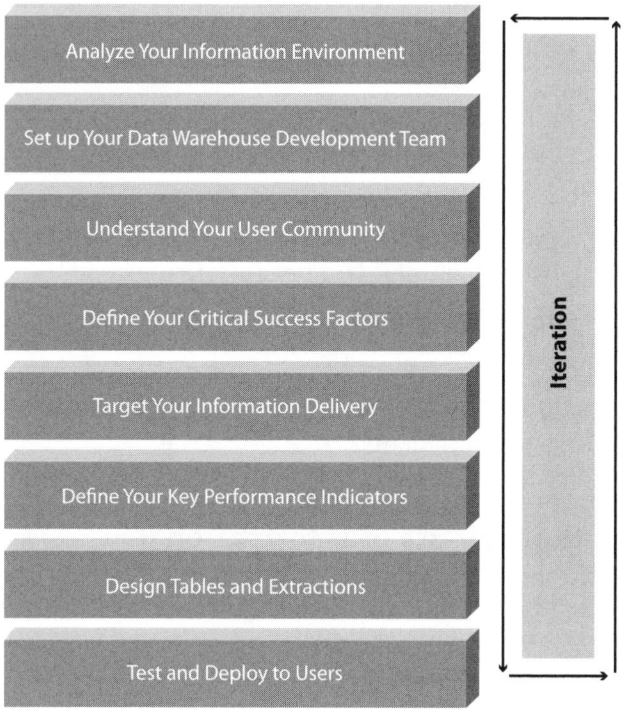

Analyze Your Information Environment
Set up Your Data Warehouse Development Team
Understand Your User Community
Define Your Critical Success Factors
Target Your Information Delivery
Define Your Key Performance Indicators
Design Tables and Extractions
Test and Deploy to Users
Iteration

User Input and Evaluation at All Stages

Analyze Your Information Environment

The first step is to decide exactly what the word "information" means for your organization. You are performing an information audit, and some of these questions can help you:

- Can we show the whole relationship with both individuals and with groups of donors easily? Every time we give out a report, do the major gifts skew the information? What kind of drill-down capabilities will be required?
- Can we measure success and failure using key performance indicators? Do we even know what these indicators should be? We all focus on campaign totals. Do we need to go beyond these? What trend analysis will be required?
- Do we have a common and standardized language to define measures? Annual fund vs. annual giving? Lapsed? Unrealized planned gifts? Overdue pledges?
- Do we have timely and accurate reporting of information? What is our turnaround time on requests? How much of our reporting is ad hoc?
- Are we able to benchmark against other institutions and global indicators?
- Does our information cross organizational boundaries, or does it stand in independent silos?
- Do we know enough in advance to make course corrections when necessary? Monthly? Not until after year's end?
- Does our information include any predictive or forecasting capabilities?
- Is information production aligned with job descriptions and performance measurements?

Some of the Benefits of Information

- Helps to communicate advancement strategy internally and externally
- Helps optimize advancement strategy
- Helps create consistency

- Drives strategic alignment
- Helps development of strategies for directional changes
- Helps focus priorities
- Helps integrate performance analysis and action
- Encourages continuous improvement
- Allows for more rapid deployment of changes
- Allows for rapid deployment when managing issues
- Facilitates integrated continuous cycle of improvement
- Creates a culture of responsibility and accountability
- Helps align people and technology to support advancement and organizational goals
- Codifies our business rules, so we can tell when they are being broken, and when we or the rules need to be adjusted

Sound Familiar?

Here are some characteristics of poor data environments:

- Multiple versions of information and extractions often are inconsistent for use in decision making. Everyone at the meeting has a different piece of paper. You spend most meetings trying to decide whose numbers are correct.
- Efforts are duplicated with multiple presentations of the same or similar information.
- Information extraction is labor-intensive and requires much manual intervention by programmers, business analysts, and end-users to create information.
- Multiple database environments—spreadsheets, flat files, desktop databases and tools—complicate the amalgamation of information.
- Multiple reporting and extraction tools, such as Excel, Crystal, Access, and others, are in use.
- There is a large number of ad-hoc reports.
- Tables and indexes in your reporting environment are a copy of production and do not support reporting well.
- SQL and conventional report-writing tools do not work well for slicing and dicing. Do you have any slice-and-dice tools?

- Libraries of standard reports exist but are difficult to access and utilize. Not everyone has a reporting tool to run the reports.
- Development system reports are inflexible for iterative analysis and do not provide information in a format that is usable as an end product.
- Reports are not well organized or have confusing or conflicting names.
- Multiple reports seem to have a similar purpose.
- Reports are constantly late, with long turnaround.
- There is no real information collaboration strategy between departments or programs.
- Your advancement software has roll-up tables for reporting, but these are relatively inflexible. They may not work at all, depending on how you code your data.
- You run scripts and reports on a one-off basis.
- No automated notification system is in place for job success or failure.
- It is difficult to access information remotely. This is no longer acceptable in the "real-time" world.

Your Data Warehouse Development Team

Your team should be small enough to be manageable, with permanent and rotating members, depending on what data warehouse project you are working on. The team will interview users and design tables. Members possess a combination of technical and business skills. It is important that technical staff do not dominate the process. You will lose participants as they get lost in the jargon. You need members with business process expertise.

Team members should understand that they will be in for the long haul but will rotate in and out of the project. If you are dealing with central information technology, that department must be involved. Members need to understand that the process is iterative. There might not be clear signoff or milestones, which are the norm in most IT projects.

Ultimately the team should be responsible for marketing the data warehouse. It is extremely important to articulate visible successes to get ongoing buy-in and acceptance from senior management.

Understand Your User Community

Every organization is different, and your data warehouse will have unique needs formulated and targeted to your strategies and your user environment. Consider your users' efficiency and ability. You should not have to leave your desk to get information. Web deployment is preferable.

End users are unlikely to develop reports. The more complicated piece is not using the reporting tool but understanding of the underlying data: the joins, indexes and all the other database complexities. Users will run reports in your development system. Even then, they will not always understand which parameters to select. It is a useful strategy to train users to run reports, but do not train them to create reports. Basing reports on the data warehouse will simplify the learning curve for everyone.

Staff turnover in advancement organizations is often high, so institutional knowledge can be lost quickly.

Most users are familiar with spreadsheets, and a limited number of users will be able to understand and use OLAP (online analytical processing) cubes, or Excel pivot tables. Most users will download and manipulate data using spreadsheets to get them into a usable and presentable format.

Staff turnover in advancement organizations is often high, so institutional knowledge can be lost quickly. Typically report training is conducted through folklore, and business rules constantly change. Avoid this by codifying your rules in the data warehouse, which will make interpretation and application consistent.

You will spend considerable time interviewing users. It is important to ask the right questions when building your data warehouse. Do not ask users what they want to see in a data warehouse. They generally will not even understand what a data warehouse is. Instead, ask them what makes them successful in what they do. The answers to this question will be much more relevant and will give you a much greater insight into what their business is and what they need to measure.

Remember this: The average CEO spends about 90 seconds looking at a piece of paper. Understand your target audience and build accordingly.

In many cases, a data warehouse will require a substantial conceptual leap. You will have knowledge gaps among your technical staff. Training is critical in building understanding of new ways to work and the benefits that will accrue. Make sure you have enough staff to handle the task. It is difficult to learn new technology when you are buried in current work. And do not forget to celebrate accomplishments and champions!

Define Critical Success Factors

- Convey the right information to the right people at the right time. This helps motivate sponsors.
- Focus on high-impact processes. Campaign reporting must be completed first. Look at processes through which analysis may increase revenue or lower expenses.
- Create well-designed data models. This is the most critical technical component and the basis of the project. Everything builds on this.
- Make measurable data quality improvements.
- Manage the data warehouse project successfully.
- Ensure that programmers and business analysts can work more effectively.
- Make cost-effective improvements in all aspects of your information strategy.

Other factors will be unique to your organization, such as reduction of outstanding pledge balances, increases in visits to donors, behavior analysis, and more. Your critical success factors also can include the following:

- Provide a single version of the "truth" for all users of advancement information.
- Improve information effectiveness for performance measurement and analysis.
- Align information and reporting with organizational goals.
- Eliminate and reduce work in creating and compiling information.

- Allow drill-down from information to data.
- Record real performance; if a development officer changes schools, or prospects change to a new development officer, how is their performance compared?
- Allow users to collaborate on all aspects of information.
- Focus solicitation and other contact efforts.
- Measure solicitation performance.
- What was the return on solicitation and contact efforts?
- Keep building the relationship for the future.

Target Information Delivery

Target your key sponsors. Once they see the value, you will get ongoing buy-in and funding. Sponsors will give the project visibility. They will want to use the more sophisticated analytical tools. Key sponsors include the vice president, the associate vice president, division and senior development officers, managers of programs such as annual fund, planned giving, and non-philanthropic revenue, programmers and analysts, and other users in advancement and on campus.

Do not target users outside advancement until you have a few projects completed. You want a robust, stable environment with a good selection of reports. By then you will have had time to cleanse and improve your data quality.

Define Key Performance Indicators

It is tough to design performance indicators. We typically focus on campaign totals and snapshots. Many advancement organizations do not do much trend analysis. Some suggested performance indicators include:

- Campaign totals and growth, endowment/expendable growth. GIK, securities and other gift types, revenue mix
- Top projects
- Top donors/major donors: Leadership giving transitions, transformational gifts, board giving, volunteer giving, number of new chairs, successful capital projects

- Pledges; collection and write-off rates
- Personal contacts, mass communications, mass e-mail performance; opt-in, opt-out; contact information accuracy; privacy and compliance
- Moves management, proposal pipeline, clearance and prospect assignment management; performance of development officers
- Processing and database statistics
- Annual fund vs. annual giving; retention; nondonor acquisition; solicitation methods comparison; parents, young alumni and other acquisition groups; faculty, staff, reunion giving
- Telemarketing analysis
- Contact rates: printed mail, e-mail, phone, cell
- Gift and pledge pyramids
- Planned or deferred gift analysis
- Affinity and other non-philanthropic, revenue-generation programs
- Future predicted pledge and cash flow

Design Tables and Extractions

We could go into a great deal of detail here. However, we will describe a few tables to get you started. Many examples are online, and you can post questions to listservs to find out more.

Denormalized Tables

These have considerable information in them, so we can do sorting and grouping easily. These and other data warehouse tables typically combine information from multiple tables to reduce the complexity of your joins.

For example, we can create an entity table with description fields so we do not have to do separate joins to get descriptions. We can then use simple SQL statements to build our queries and reports.

```
SELECT entity_group_description,
COUNT entity_id
FROM entity_fact
GROUP BY entity_group_description.
```

The results:

Alumni:	100,000
Friends:	60,000

There is no need for joins in subsequent queries or reports to get descriptions once the base table has been populated in the data warehouse. This standardizes header column names and facilitates the development of OLAP cubes.

Tables will have calculated information, such as pledge balance outstanding = pledge amount–total payments. When we have these calculations in our data warehouse, we need to change them in only one place. All reports using the calculations will change automatically.

Put calculations and business rules in your data warehouse, as opposed to having complicated formulas in reports.

The following table contains outstanding pledge information. It combines data from the pledge header, pledge schedule, pledge detail, and payments. It is efficient, reduces joins, and standardizes complex calculations and rules. It is easier to maintain this one table than having all these calculations and joins to maintain in 50 separate outstanding pledge reports:

Column	Data Type	Description	Sample Data
id_number	VARCHAR2(10)	Entity id_number.	1000000001
total_pledge	NUMBER(14,2)	Total pledge from pledge header.	1000
total_pmt	NUMBER(14,2)	Total payments from pledge header.	200
total_balance	NUMBER(14,2)	Total pledge—total payment.	800
total_arrears	NUMBER(14,2)	Total arrears from pledge header.	0
total_futamt	NUMBER(14,2)	Total future amount from pledge header.	0
sch_due_in_1_yr	NUMBER(14,2)	Total payments due within 1 year from pledge schedule.	800

Tables to Keep Track of Trends

These tables have fiscal year columns so we do not have to hard-code calculations in our reports: pledges received by fiscal year; contacts by development officer by month across fiscal year.

Tables with Summaries

Summary tables make it easy to deploy on the Web. You do not want to set up a campaign report and have users wait while it cycles through a million-row pledge table to get the campaign total.

Tables to Keep Track of History

If you run regular reports, such as alumni addressable rates, you should create another table to keep a snapshot of the summary information. You can use this to evaluate trends and generate graphs, instead of retyping snapshots into spreadsheets or charting programs.

History tables also may be used to track information, such as development officers' prospect assignments when they move to a different part of the organization. How productive were they with the same pool of prospects over time in each area?

Tables to Help You Work Smarter

All data warehouse tables should save you work, but some examples might not be so obvious. One of my favorites is a fiscal date table:

Column	Data Type	Description	Sample Data
cfy_month_beg	VARCHAR2(8)	Current fiscal year beginning of month.	20050401
cfy_month_end	VARCHAR2(8)	Current fiscal year end of month.	20050430
cfy_prev_month_beg	VARCHAR2(8)	Current fiscal year, previous month to current month beginning.	20050301
cfy_prev_month_end	VARCHAR2(8)	Current fiscal year, previous month to current month end.	20050331
pfy_month_beg	VARCHAR2(8)	Previous fiscal year month beginning.	20040401
pfy_month_end	VARCHAR2(8)	Previous fiscal year month end.	20040430
cfy_beg_minus_1	VARCHAR2(8)	Current fiscal year minus 1 year beginning.	20040401
cfy_beg_minus_2	VARCHAR2(8)	Current fiscal year minus 2 year beginning.	20040401
cfy_memb_start	VARCHAR2(8)	Current membership start year.	20000101

Table to Store Fiscal Dates

This allows you to have "where" clauses in your scripts that use the table to retrieve all the fiscal dates associated with your reporting.

```
SELECT *
FROM gifts
WHERE date_received >= (SELECT cfy_month_beg FROM
a_dw_fiscal_dates).
```

Select all gifts where the gift received date is greater than or equal to the beginning of the current fiscal month.

By including this in all scripts that reference date ranges, you have to change these in only one place to change date ranges in all your tables.

If you include date ranges for previous fiscal periods, you avoid having to calculate or hard-code these date ranges in your scripts or reports. This lowers maintenance in reports and scripts where there may be a different fiscal period, such as an independent alumni association membership year, and it saves you from hard-coding in membership scripts and reports. It also makes it easy to run a large number of reports if you need to backdate. Simply change the current and previous fiscal month dates and run all the extractions and reports again.

I have waxed a little poetic on this last one, but as you can see, the more you think about it, the more exciting it gets. By analyzing your information needs from start to finish and applying a little creativity, you can become extremely effective. Once you build even a few tables you can save yourself tons of work. Report turnaround time will decrease. You will be able to focus on more advanced tasks, such as data mining and analysis.

Where is the End?

Ralph Kimball defines "real time" as anything that is too fast for your extract-transform-load tool. He suggests that "real-time" should drive your data warehouse. What is your turnaround time on report requests? Anything that takes more than an hour should make you begin an investigation into how to change your reporting architecture to serve your customers better.

Increased speeds of data consumption have led to demands by users to "slice and dice" information quickly. They cannot afford to wait for weeks to get a report.

Users have become more accustomed to "information exploring." Spreadsheet proliferation has been a large factor in this democratization of data. Your data warehouse and business intelligence tools will facilitate instantaneous delivery, dramatic new methods of analysis, and measurable improvements in your advancement efforts.

A data warehouse reduces our work, empowers our users, and helps us realize one of the great promises of the information age: knowledge.

Figure 15: Information Optimization

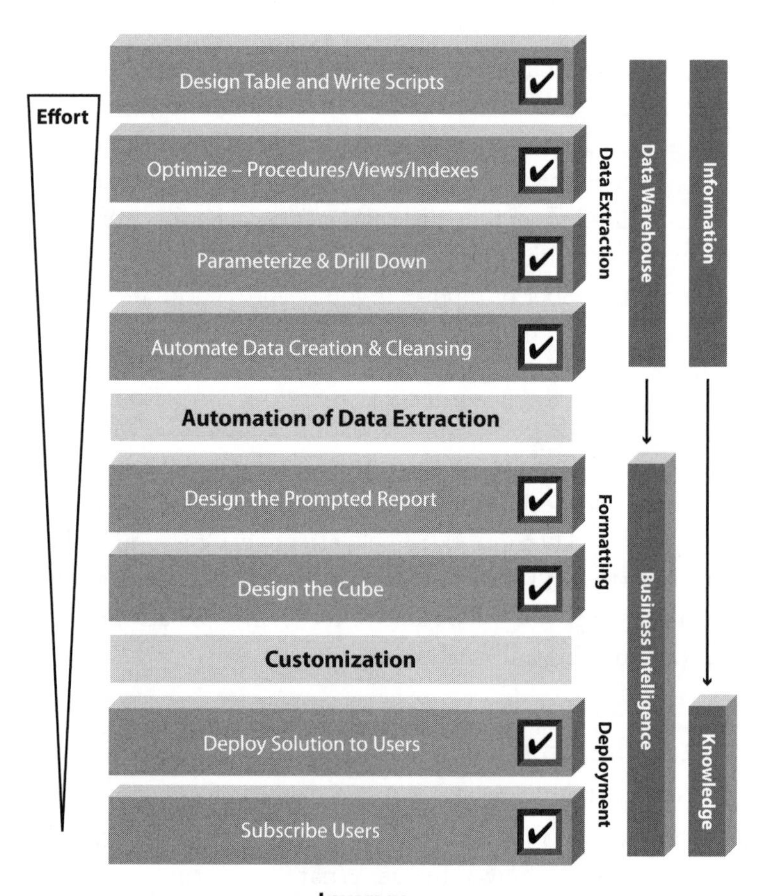

Additional Resources

A wealth of data warehouse information and expertise is available from the Data Warehouse Institute, the Benchmarking and Score Carding Institute, and the Kimball Group. All these organizations have numerous resources, e-mail newsletters, conferences, and books.

Under the reports and systems pages on *www.supportingadvancment.com*, you can find presentations on data warehousing, business intelligence, sample data warehouse tables, sample scripts, and much more. All are geared toward creating an advancement data warehouse.

CHAPTER 17

Evaluating and Selecting Primary Development Software

By Charlie Hunsaker | President | R I Arlington

Jim Williamson | President | Williamson Consulting, Inc.

Having been involved in numerous successful software-selection projects, we believe we have some useful experience to share. (We have learned a thing or two from the less successful projects, too.) Replacing your development office's primary software system is an understandably daunting prospect. Our experience has shown, however, that by following a structured, proven process, you will have a much higher chance of success—and of retaining your sanity. But before we get into the process, let's ask an important question about the decision to acquire a new system.

Are You Crazy?

Identifying and then implementing an information system could take two or three years. The process will be expensive, difficult, and at times frustrating. You will ask yourself numerous times why on earth you got involved in this project. Even so, the potential benefits to your organization could be significant, and who knows? The project might even end up being fun! Before you begin, however, you need to ask yourself a number of questions.

Do You Really Need a New System?

What's wrong with your old one? Can you articulate the enhancements that could benefit your organization? Is there a problem you are trying to solve?

In our experience, a high percentage of the problems staff members perceive as system deficiencies are related to—if not caused by—organizational and human resources issues. Often these supposedly poor systems lack enough trained users, good documentation, effective management, or all three. It certainly would be easier to hire the right staff, develop the documentation, and train the users than to acquire a new system. Are you sure those steps wouldn't go a long way toward solving your problems?

Is Now Really the Right Time?

So you're sure you need a new system. But should you do it now? A basic rule of systems implementation is that the process should be in sync with what is going on in the fundraising program. It always takes longer to convert to a new system than you anticipate. If you have a major campaign planned for the near future, you might want to think about waiting until the campaign is over before moving forward with a system. (We realize that the next campaign may be the reason you are looking at a new system.)

When you are projecting an implementation schedule, don't listen to the vendors.

When you are projecting an implementation schedule, don't listen to the vendors. They often will say it will take six months or so. In reality, experience shows that for most organizations, going from conversion team formation to full implementation takes 18 to 24 months. A complex university with decentralized fundraising but centralized services easily could require 36 months or longer.

Where is Your Organization Heading?

The purpose of a development information system is not to manage information but to implement the fundraising business plan. Managing information—address changes, gift processing, acknowledgments—is easy. Implementing a system to support a comprehensive fundraising program can be very complex.

Does your office have a five-year business plan? If not, stop and develop one before you proceed any further. A realistic plan will prepare you better to select a system appropriate to your needs. Far too many organizations buy systems with complex capabilities no one will use. A plan will help you determine which choice to make: an information system capable of supporting a complex campaign with a regional component; decentralized, constituent-based fundraising; and significant corporation and foundation fundraising—or one that needs to handle only alumni relations and an annual fund.

What Are the Givens?

Is there already a winner? Beware of a rigged process in which you expend considerable resources, only to find out that a preferred (or required) vendor existed all along. Do not waste staff's time if senior management already has chosen a vendor system. But do not expect the staff's buy-in if the decision is made without them.

It is also important to identify, at the beginning, the technical environment in which your new system must work. Does your campus have an information technology plan? Is there a clearly articulated, overarching technology? Does your campus have a "preferred" (or dictated) technology standard? If such a plan exists, stay within it. Do not be the only office on campus with a particular database back-end. Do not buy a system that requires a particular kind of server or network operating system (UNIX, Windows Server 2003), unless such servers already exist on your campus.

From a development office viewpoint, you should lobby for a best-of-breed approach, to give yourself maximum flexibility.

Have you had serious discussions about developing your own fundraising system rather than purchasing a commercial product? If so, update your resume and get off the team. While the topic of "build vs. buy" was worth discussing 10 years ago, today you should see it as a red flag. It will cost more to develop (and document and support) a custom-designed system than to buy one. Experience shows that few in-house projects completely succeed. Although it is true that custom-designed systems generally meet current organizational needs, rarely can they keep pace with changes in technology and regulations and advances in development as well as vendor-supported systems can.

Among other classic discussions is whether a campus should buy a single, integrated system or allow each administrative office to purchase the "best-of-breed." From a development office viewpoint, you should lobby for a best-of-breed approach, to give yourself maximum flexibility. Some excellent single-vendor solutions are available (although few are truly integrated), but chances are that if the campus is looking for a single-vendor solution, your student records or finance office will drive the decision. In development, you will have to take whatever fundraising package comes as part of the package. Lobbying for best-of-breed allows you to look at both the stand-alone and integrated choices and see what fits your needs.

Do procedures, likely prescribed by the IT or purchasing offices, exist for the purchase of systems? Is a formal RFP required? Must you award to the lowest bidder? Must the document be public, or are you free to include information about your fundraising plans? If the latter is the case, you should ask the vendors to sign a nondisclosure agreement. By the way, if the vendor asks you to sign a nondisclosure agreement before you receive the proposal, we recommend that you not sign one. You do not want to assume that liability for your organization. Tell the vendor that you will make your decision based solely on publicly available information.

If you have decided that regardless of this sanity check, you are going to proceed with the project, what's next?

The Selection Process

How you handle your system selection depends on your organization's size and complexity. However, whatever process you use, it must be documented and supported by the senior administration. Seriously flawed implementations almost always are traceable to a flawed process or the lack of true top-level support for the process (or the team).

Before You Start

The following section details the steps in a process we have found to work well for most organizations. If, however, your organization is too small for such a process, remember three basic rules that apply to any organization:

1. Form a committee. Do not try to do it alone!
2. Call the vendors last. Do not start by collecting information from vendors.
3. Never invite the vendors to your organization until you have documented your needs, checked several references, and determined that the vendor might provide an appropriate solution. Far too many people purchase a system because of their relationship with the salesperson rather than the functionality of the software.

What Are the Steps?

The process to identify and acquire a new development system unfolds in four phases:

- Build your team
- Define your needs and communicate them to potential vendors
- Evaluate and select the vendor
- Implement the plan

The last phase is the transition from the selection project to the actual implementation, which also may be a phased project. In the following sections, we outline the steps that we have found useful.

Build Your Team

A critical initial step is creating the project structure, identifying the individuals who will be involved, and defining their respective roles and responsibilities. The lack of such a structure can lead to ambiguous leadership, unclear goals, and missed deadlines. In most cases, the team defined at the beginning of the project will stay in place throughout vendor selection and system implementation. This project structure and overall project management are discussed in more detail later in this section.

A critical initial step is creating the project structure, identifying the individuals who will be involved, and defining their respective roles and responsibilities.

The conversion team will have the following components:

Project sponsor. This individual will be the senior spokesperson for the project, representing it to senior management and the rest of the organization. It is vital that this person be a senior administrator, ideally the chief development officer or someone who reports to the chief development officer, so that he or she can address with authority and on a very timely basis problems that invariably will crop up.

Steering committee. This is a small group of senior staff with ultimate responsibility for the project. They will have overall budget responsibility and responsibility to ensure that sufficient resources are available. The committee will manage any consulting engagements and will make the major decisions based on recommendations from the task force.

This committee makes sure the project stays on track, helps balance project time demands with day-to-day operational priorities, and receives the recommendation about which system to purchase. People from both development and management information systems, with titles like vice president and senior director, will be on the steering committee. The project manager also should be on the committee and keeps committee members apprised of progress, accomplishments, problems, and recommended solutions.

Task force. This is the main working group for the project. It should represent all areas of the organization that will be affected by the new system. Its members will:

- Serve as experts in their respective business area
- Assist in identifying system requirements
- Participate in writing the RFP
- Evaluate proposed solutions
- Recommend the selected vendor to the steering committee

In a large organization, the task force members may head their own subject-matter teams, which will be responsible for gathering requirements for their areas: biographic and demographic information, major prospects, gift processing, alumni relations, technology, etc. The task force member will be responsible for summarizing needs, ideas, feedback, etc., from his or her area. Leaders and other task force members may participate in multiple teams. (See why steering committee members have to balance priorities?) Active participation by task force members is critical in a project of this nature. First, staff members bring to the table important knowledge of your existing procedures and needs. Second, without their participation in and buy-in of the final selection, the implementation is almost guaranteed to fail.

Project manager. In most situations, the project manager should be an experienced member of the development office, rather than someone from IT or an outside consultant. This person should be relieved of other responsibilities so he or she can dedicate full time to the project. The project manager will:

- Coordinate the overall project
- Organize the project with a work plan and reporting assignments

- Manage tasks, timetables, and project reporting
- Manage and motivate the task force
- Communicate regularly with the project sponsor and outside consultants (if any)

The project manager also should establish written project guidelines. We recommend that all contact with potential vendors be made solely through him or her. We also recommend that all communication with vendors be made in writing, not over the telephone. If you find that a particular situation warrants a conference call, then have a "witness," at least one other person from your organization who participates, and document, in writing, the content of the call as soon as it has been completed.

As no project should be conducted in a vacuum, the first activity you should perform is defining needs.

Consultant(s). As implied above, many organizations find it beneficial to have a consultant work with the project leader to organize and manage the project. Consultants can bring experience with the functional areas, with the process, and with the vendors under consideration. Their experience and skill can expedite the process and reduce the risks inherent in major systems projects.

Once you have gotten organized, you are ready to move to Phase II.

Define Your Needs and Communicate Them

As no project should be conducted in a vacuum, the first activity you should perform is defining needs. Gain a clear understanding of the business environment and which systems are being considered. Also determine the benefits management wishes to achieve through automation. Steps in this activity include:

1. Evaluating the present scope of operations
2. Reviewing existing plans for campaigns, technology changes, organization, etc.
3. Documenting management's objectives for undertaking the selection project
4. Identifying criteria for evaluating system selection and installation priorities

Document the present. In certain situations, it is appropriate to identify and quantify the current environment, including hardware, software, people, practices, and associated costs. This is the benchmark for evaluating a new system. Often this can provide the baseline, the proverbial stake in the ground from which to measure future successes. It can also provide vital, existing, cost benchmarks that can feed into a cost/benefit analysis (if the board requires you to do one).

Once you start documenting business processes, you may realize that some things are broken and need to be fixed (the dreaded "re-engineering"). This is frequently true for gift-processing, acknowledgment, or stewardship procedures. If you uncover significant problems, we strongly recommend that you fix them before moving forward. If you have information stored in a shoebox, you will have difficulty implementing a new system—it is very difficult to computerize a shoebox.

Another important aspect of documenting current status is to determine the quality of your existing data. Are they all in one database now, or perhaps spread among two primary databases and a myriad of Excel spreadsheets, Access databases, and paper files? What level of duplication is in your current files? What is your percentage of lost alumni and bad addresses? How much information is in old and undocumented codes? How many data are in free text form that should be codified for easier reporting? The answers to these questions will have a significant impact on both your conversion and the next activity.

Document supporting systems projects. Some organizations pursue this useful activity as part of a selection project. In addition to adding a new software package, you may need to make other changes. Remember the questions we told you to ask before starting the project? Do you have problems with data quality, policies and procedures, organization, staffing, or inadequate training? If so, identify and describe all projects to be considered, to help ensure the success of system selection and implementation efforts. Summarize them in an overall plan with the following steps:

1. Develop an overall systems strategy
2. Prepare project descriptions
3. Summarize costs and benefits
4. Draft plan

Document requirements. Defining and documenting the business requirements may be the most important and lengthy tasks of this phase. Sometimes called a "needs assessment," the process will include significant involvement by the project task force. Working with their individual business teams, members will be the primary collectors of these requirements.

We strongly recommend that the task force focus on documenting uniqueness. Do not spend energy specifying the need for multiple salutations or seasonal address management. If your vendor candidates cannot do those things, you have selected the wrong list of vendors. Focus on your unique requirements (such as the bizarre golf tournament and auction you run every year, the fact that you credit 50 percent of a campaign gift to the alumnus' class totals but not to the annual fund gift total, etc.). Then just presume the vendors can handle the rest.

We have found it useful to distinguish between two types of requirements; what you want the system to do, and how you want it to work. Figure 16 may help you organize the "whats."

Figure 16: Functions Model

Using the schematic, identify what functions you want or need your system to perform. Consider the data, the reports, key processing, etc., that each function must provide for your organization. Consider what interfaces you may require—gift interface with a general accounting system, loading graduates, students, and parents from your student system, connectivity to your Web site, sharing data with your planned giving software, etc. Within each of these functional areas, you also will want to identify how the system needs to work. Do you have special handling of soft credits? Do you have some unusual giving societies? Do you provide special benefits to members of your alumni association? Does your campaign have multiple layers of objectives and goals? Do you have a sophisticated solicitor or volunteer organization? You will want to document all these requirements of your organization. (To jump ahead a bit, the "whats" often get communicated to the vendors in the RFP and the "hows" get documented in the demonstration scenarios.)

Once the requirements have been captured, it is important for the task force to prioritize them.

Once the requirements have been captured, it is important for the task force to prioritize them. You even may want to indicate to the vendors in your RFP which items are critical ("deal breakers"), as well as which ones "would be nice to have." This will allow the vendors to focus their proposed solution on the items most critical to your business.

It is critical at this point that as broad an audience as possible review, and agree to, the articulation of requirements for a new system. This across-the-board buy-in of the requirements is critical to the project's ultimate success.

Develop the Request for Proposal. With this step you pull together all requirements (functional, technical, security, performance, support, cost, contractual, and others) into an RFP to send to prospective vendors.

A variety of formats commonly is used in an RFP for a new system. Your purchasing department may dictate some of the constraints. CASE, EDUCAUSE, other organizations, or your consultant can provide you with examples. As you develop the RFP, it is important to remember to structure it to facilitate evaluation of vendor responses.

Although some vendors develop a proposal claiming they can do everything, others take time to provide an honest indication of their strengths and weaknesses. You probably will find it fairly easy to identify vendors who appear to provide a candid appraisal.

Identify potential vendors. It is important to spend some time developing a list of potential vendors. Do not limit your search to the few vendors who advertise heavily, call you regularly, or make a big splash at a conference. New products are being developed all the time, and many of the older products are constantly being improved, allowing them to serve a broader spectrum of organizations. We recommend that you contact other organizations to learn about their systems and experience in selecting a system.

Probably three tiers of vendors offer different levels of system functionality for different prices. We suggest that you make sure to get a sense of what tier your budget falls into before wasting your or the vendor's time in serious discussion at the wrong level. That is, if you have a $15,000 budget, do not spend time with firms that have systems costing $50,000, $100,000, or more.

Establish evaluation criteria. All participants in the selection process believe their area is the most important part of the development operation. (Don't you want them to believe that?) Without a set of evaluation criteria, your selection decisions will be based on personal preference or perhaps the vote of the person with the most important title. Establishing criteria gives you an objective basis for evaluating vendors and systems. You will be comparing them not only against each other but also against a prioritized list of what is important to your institution.

So what kind of criteria are we talking about? They include functionality, product flexibility, technology compatibility, vendor support and reliability, ease of use, ability to install on a timely basis, etc. You will identify more details for each of these criteria and perhaps additional criteria that may be unique to your institution and situation. We do not typically include cost or price as a criterion; you should look only at vendors you can afford.

It is productive to establish weights for each of these criteria to assist in quantifying your evaluation. You may note that certain criteria are "deal breakers." For example, one client's selection committee members decided that if reference checks pointed up major, unacceptable difficulties in the implementation process, they would discard that vendor system regardless of the weights on other criteria. They said, "If we can't install the system, what is the value of anything else?"

Presumably the vendors you identified to receive the RFP were "viable" and had a track record of working with similar organizations. If, for example, a purchasing department required you to send the RFP to all potential vendors, then your criteria need to include an assessment of the vendor as well as the product. For example, in terms of vendor track record and status in the market, you should consider company size, longevity, financials, stability, etc. What percent of a company's business is in fundraising software? Is it a side venture or the main business? How many clients are similar in size and needs to your organization? If the firm is not a true player, do not even consider it.

Evaluate and Select the Vendor

Develop demonstration scenarios. Because vendors often respond positively to most aspects of an RFP, it is important to lay out a demonstration process that will let users confirm that a vendor's system can meet their needs. This set of activities will structure the demonstration process for the most effective evaluation:

1. Outline the framework of scenarios by functional area
2. Translate requirements into scenarios with detailed scripts
3. Identify selected data for the scripts
4. Publish the scenarios or scripts

Such a process will allow you to control the demonstration and minimize the hype. You might find it helpful to block out a short time, say 30 minutes, for the vendor to pitch the firm and explain why it is the best option for you. But you should dedicate the rest of the time to finding out if the vendor can meet your needs.

Evaluate vendors and systems. You should verify that both vendor and system meet your needs in as many ways as possible: through proposal review, demos, site visits, and calls to other users. Often the selection committee performs these steps in varying order and as part of an iterative process:

1. Review proposals.
2. Identify vendors for further evaluation (two or three semifinalists).
3. Finalize functional evaluation.
4. Contact references (three to five per vendor system).
5. Evaluate technical considerations.
6. Invite vendor finalists to your organization to defend their proposals and perform the scripted demonstrations.

Remember the adage that perfection is the enemy of the good.

You must evaluate functional, technical, security, performance, support, and contractual aspects of the vendor's bid and system. You must understand the installation process, including both your responsibilities and the vendor's. You will have to live and work with the selected system (and vendor) for years; be comfortable with your decision.

Make sure you provide adequate time for the vendor demonstrations using your scenarios. It often takes a two-day-plus exercise to see the full functionality of the vendor's system. Take time over meals to address issues of implementation approach, conversion, training, project organization, staffing, etc.

Some suggest site visits as a means of making a system decision. Recognize that you will learn more about the vendor than the system from a site visit. That can be useful, but is it worth the time when a few phone calls can round up virtually the same information?

Nevertheless, do whatever it takes for your task force to become satisfied with and committed to the selection decision. Remember the adage that perfection is the enemy of the good. Understand that you will not have perfect knowledge of the vendor or system perhaps until years after you have installed it. Get the best information you can and make your decision.

Recommend a vendor. The final step is to make a formal recommendation to the project steering committee. This presentation should include a high-level comparison of the two or three finalist vendors and discussion of the rationale for the decision. Often this is accompanied by a financial analysis showing total project costs, including internal staff resources, required for successful implementation.

Implement the Plan

The key tasks in this phase are contracting with the vendor and organizing for the implementation. These are typically interconnected activities. Part of the contract is the implementation work plan, including arrangements for data conversion, training, development of procedures, system testing and acceptance, etc. For smaller projects, the standard vendor work plan may be adequate; for larger ones, you might consider a separate, intermediate, "discovery" project to just scope the implementation.

A key issue in implementation planning and contracting is recognizing that the vendor sees key deliverables (software delivery, training classes, go-live, etc.) as milestones at which they expect to get paid. The user organization must include all the other activities—setting up the data center and user desktop computers, updating and documenting policies and procedures, system acceptance testing, and other items—in the plan. Note that the vendor may not include all the "user" or "client" activities in its standard work plans.

Successful implementation of a new system is all about project management. This includes management of:

- Your staff
- The vendor
- Vendor contract, costs, timeline
- Staff expectations

From our experience, we know it is important to consider a phased approach to the selection project and use a proven process. You may not follow all the steps above, but ignoring one should be a conscious decision rather than a careless oversight. Murphy's Law has a direct impact on any forgotten steps. By following some of the wisdom of this article, you can select a system successfully. We know. We've done it hundreds of times.

CHAPTER 18

Technical Tools in Support of Advancement

By John Ley | Former Director of Information Services | Southern Methodist University

I recently did a survey in a university advancement office that asked, "As a general rule, my impression of technology is...." The results were:

13%	I'm a total geek...bring it on!
62%	It's a good thing, as it makes my life easier.
16%	It's a good thing, but sometimes it makes my life difficult.
6%	Don't really like it (or it doesn't like me), but I see why it's necessary.
3%	Actually, I don't like it and wish we could do our jobs without it.

How you would answer this question will determine how excited you are about this chapter. Me? I have that "G" emblazoned on my forehead, so I am one of the 13 percent. I hope you, at least, fit into the 62 percent. No matter where you find yourself in this survey, I know you will discover some helpful ways technology can support your advancement office.

But let's not let the tail wag the dog. We do not have technology just because it's there. Technology is designed to make our lives easier, give us ways to do things we were not able to do already, and help us fulfill our mission in a more efficient and effective manner. With that in mind, let's take a quick glance at the missions of our advancement offices.

> "Advancement's mission is to support university goals by focusing on the following areas: reputation, resources, relationships" (Clemson University).
>
> "...preserve and enhance support for the institution among its internal and external constituencies through expert and strategic communications, marketing, relationship building, fundraising, and stewardship" (University of Texas—Medical Branch).

> "University advancement is committed to initiating and providing shared opportunities for our stakeholders that lead to an understanding of, involvement with, and affinity for the University of Saskatchewan."

How can technology help fulfill the mission of these organizations, and yours? How can technology help enhance reputations? Increase resources? Create relationships? Can technology make your fundraising and stewardship efforts more effective? Will technology aid in generating involvement with, and an affinity for, our institutions? Of course, the answer is a resounding "yes." Based on these mission statements, let's break down the areas where technology can boost productivity.

We have come to expect to reach anyone, anywhere, anytime.

Communication is probably the basis of all the ideals mentioned in the mission statements above. Certainly we know of the expectation that everyone has a cell phone and internet access. We have come to expect to reach anyone, anywhere, anytime. Now with cell phones, you can access the internet, receive your e-mail in real time, and have a "text" conversation with someone anywhere in the world. Even our databases have been set up to send e-mail, voicemail or text message based on when an "event" happens. So your business school fundraiser immediately receives a text message on her phone whenever a $10,000 gift from one of her assigned donors is received. Information is provided immediately for her use.

With our alumni, donors, and friends, personalization has always been key. We want—no, we need—to be able to address our constituents in the manner they wish to be addressed. "To the Parents of..." is no longer acceptable coming from an advancement office. Does your director of development address your top donors in the same way your president would? People like to be addressed in so many different ways that we have constructed systems to manage this for us. We have used technology to help us accommodate these needs.

Many institutions are taking the next step in customer relationship management. They are implementing software that will address constituents as they wish. The same software will send them information in which they have shown interest, by request ("Please only send me *this*," or "Send the magazine to my home, but send gift receipts to my business e-mail"), past behavior (they made a gift to the arts last year) or their Web surfing habits (they go to your Web site and click on your athletics links). Using tools like this, we can customize the messages we send to our constituents and still do it en masse. And this is only one part of what CRM entails.

With our constituents we have online communities. These Web sites provide them with a place to go to keep in touch with friends they went to school with, see what is going on at their alma mater, and, if they choose, have "e-mail for life."

Working with volunteers and staff has become easier with portals, where they can log into your organization and receive the information they need, customized for them based on their log-in permissions. These portals can give them access to Web pages with information, services, and documents for their use.

Communication is the foundation of an advancement office. Technology gives us more ways to handle the opportunities we encounter when working with our constituents, both internal and external.

While communication is the foundation, data storage is one of the key resources of an advancement office. We have progressed from mainframe databases to client server and Web server versions of the same thing with much more functionality for the end-user.

Integrated Data System

You have many things to consider when investing in a database, including functionality, support, and ease of conversion, all of which are covered elsewhere in this book. The key point I wish to stress is the relatively new idea of an integrated or enterprisewide system. Using one system across your institution for admissions, student records, advancement, and human resources can have many benefits, including a constituent listed only once in a database on your campus. But with these benefits comes much more coordination and decision making for everyone involved. It can be painful, but in the long run I believe the benefits may outweigh the pain. Others may disagree. It is up to you to decide.

With the complexity of our databases and the need for reporting ever increasing, one option has arisen to make getting the data out much easier. That solution is the data warehouse discussed by Brian Dowling in Chapter 16. A data warehouse is a separate database where information from your main database is transferred in a much flatter or denormalized version. To back up a little, your main database was built (in theory) for optimal performance when you enter and view data. The background structure is usually not optimal for reporting needs, however. The data warehouse combines fields into logical strings that allow you to use reporting tools better. Although good for reporting, the data warehouse structure would not make a good data-entry or viewing database. The two complement each other well, however.

Storing

Another form of data or information that we have not talked about yet is the filing system. Instead of paper files that take up space, eventually disintegrate, and are frankly inefficient, technology has provided us with the ability to electronically image our documents. Document imaging has four basic components, the primary functions you perform when storing and retrieving documents: scanning, coding, archiving, and retrieving.

You might think of scanning as the equivalent of making a photocopy. A scanner is a piece of computer equipment that takes a picture of the document. Generally, as you scan a document, the image appears on your monitor. At this time quality is checked.

Coding

The coding process tells the system where the document is located. This is similar to describing what file cabinet or file folder a document is in. Generally, with the document displayed on your monitor, a separate window displays any number of fields for input. These fields allow you to describe the document.

Once a document is scanned and coded, it is ready for archiving, the process of permanently storing it. At this point you have scanned, coded, and archived your document. In other words, you have filed it for later retrieval and use.

Retrieval

The fourth component of document imaging has nothing to do with putting documents into the system. In fact, it is the opposite. It has to do with retrieving documents. Here the true benefits of a document imaging system may be found: no searching through files, no copying of paper, no sending through interoffice mail. Document imaging saves time, paper, and money.

Now that you know the basics of document imaging, let's come back to what you need to think about before getting your new imaging system. The time spent on planning and designing implementation is critical and cannot be underestimated. Here are some issues you need to consider, along with some suggestions to make it easier for you.

1. What do you do with your old and current files? Do you have the resources to scan and code existing files? Do you store them off-site and begin scanning only new information? Do you pull certain files for scanning? Do you scan only files pulled from the storage facility? Addressing questions like these will save time and financial resources down the road. Be very realistic about your resources and the time it might take to accomplish the goals you have set.

   If you do not have the resources to scan all your files, then you may chose to store off-site what you do not scan. This is what we elected to do at SMU. An inventory was kept of the files sent, and the records manager was responsible for taking requests and ordering the files. Our first idea—having the requester scan the file before it was returned—failed. Over time (three to four years) and many iterations of this plan, we finally hired two part-time students, who began scanning the files before returning them to the storage facility. This was not necessarily an attempt to get ALL the old files scanned but to scan the ones that might be needed again. At this point (six years into the imaging system) we are investigating hiring a vendor to scan ALL our files and eliminate the need for the off-site facility. We have not destroyed any of our old files, even if they were scanned. This will take a culture shift that will be necessary someday.

2. What records will you scan? Is anything too confidential? If so, where are these records stored? Who has access, and how do they know where to find them? Why would the information be considered too confidential? Why would a document that is too confidential be created to start with? Be careful not to fall into the trap of having multiple records management systems to maintain. Remember, sharing information is what enables the advancement office to do its job best.

   The idea of a *paperless office* is a noble one, but it needs much thought. A study of all the types of files and documents you keep should be made so you can be sure to understand the needs of each type. SMU decided that since anything we keep could, technically and legally, be shown to the constituent upon request, we scan everything—that is, everything except employee files (our security is not sufficient to keep these as confidential as we would like). If someone asks about whether a particular document should be stored on the system, we ask whether the document should have been created.

3. What information do you use to code your documents? What fields are required? Which are optional? Could there be too many required fields? Will fewer fields speed data entry but slow retrieval? These are critical issues. Input from the people who perform the coding and scanning, as well as those who will be the primary retrievers of documents, is extremely important.

   One of the more difficult decisions is how to code documents—how you tell the system what *file folder* and *file cabinet* the document is in. It is important to remember that this is a filing system. It does not and cannot replace your donor database. When we designed our coding scheme, it seemed to take forever. Some people wanted upwards of 15-20 attributes per document. The more fields, the longer input takes. Minimally, you will want the constituent's name, the development system ID number, the title and type of document you are coding, and the date of the document. People who will retrieve the documents and those who will do the data entry must reach compromises.

4. What about nondonor files? In most cases, an advancement office might consider scanning only donor files. But what about files related to particular projects, such as scholarship

recognition dinners? How are those files coded? Do you assign a project number rather than a computer ID number? What about standard office files? Do you assign a departmental number? How are those coded for retrieval? A standard format policy is something to think about BEFORE people start using the system.

Certainly, the bulk of our files are those of our donors. It is easy to think of them with their ID numbers, first and last names, etc. But how can you make the coding scheme general enough to accommodate nondonor files? We developed a comprehensive policy that included a range of *project file* numbers and *departmental position* numbers. Project files are about events whose information would not be held in a particular donor's file. Departmental files, like statistics or files related specifically to the department, are stored in a manager's desk.

5. Who scans the documents? Who codes them? Who scans old files? Who scans current files and records? Is this centralized, or does everyone have responsibility in your office? Who does your current filing? Do you hire temporary people to scan old files? Who trains them and monitors their work?

   One of the biggest hurdles we had was determining who was to scan the newly created documents. We took the approach that everyone should use the system. It failed miserably. We expected fundraisers and administrative people alike to scan their documents. Interestingly enough, they never had filed their own documents before. We have been investigating ways to bring the scanning to a central location in our office. In doing this, we would increase the information on the system and the quality control.

6. Who has what access? Do you have various levels of access? Does anyone in the advancement operation have access? Who monitors this access? Who decides who has access? Who will do what training? Do you have a special training group? Is it your computer department? Your records department?

   I guess this begs the question of who is in charge of the system. It is obvious that this is not a one-person or even a one-department show. Your computing area will certainly be involved on the technical side. But this is a very functionally targeted system from your records department and prospect research department. You will need them involved in training and quality control. It should be a truly cross-functional team.

7. What type of quality control will you put in place? Who does it? Who corrects errors that are found? Quality control is very important. It takes valuable time that no one wants to put forth, but in the long run it pays off.

   Quality control is one of the hardest things to maintain. It can be boring and mundane, but it is critical. If you scan or code a document that cannot be read or found, it is worthless. Having someone check 10 percent of all documents scanned is a good way to ensure consistent quality. Poor images can be followed up on with the person who scanned or coded them.

Quality control is one of the hardest things to maintain. It can be boring and mundane, but it is critical.

Now that we have all the data taken care of, what do we do with them? As mentioned above, getting the data out and reporting on them in a meaningful way is imperative to our offices. Analysis of the information allows us to see what strategies have worked, where our giving is coming from, and what we need to do better. Many reporting tools, some very expensive, allow us to do that. Most databases are delivered with a tool that allows you to do some querying on the data and running of lists. Most institutions invest in a high-level solution that can report from your main database or data warehouse, if you have one.

Knowledge Management

An internal tool that can be helpful is knowledge management software. Whether purchased off the shelf or developed internally, it gives you the ability to capture questions, answers, decisions, documentation, policies, training information, procedures, processes, etc., in one place to be queried. This is something that will take your institution a long way. If you ever have gone to "Ask.com," you know what I am referring to. Ask a question and retrieve the information in a meaningful way that will provide you with the answer.

The result is increased meaningful output generated in a more efficient and effective manner. This ability to improve productivity is a constant goal in any office. Technology has proven over and over again that we can do more with less: less error and less manual labor.

Many of these items have become commonplace in our offices, although five years ago they may not have been. Laptops are now provided to development officers to use while on the road. Common network drives are being used to store items for those who need to be able to see them. Wireless connections are available not only at your organization but in many public places. Remote access to your desktop from locations anywhere in the world is now possible. PDAs to help keep you organized hold more information, including names and addresses, maps, and directions, than ever before. They also function as phones, cameras, and e-mail readers.

One of the amazing areas where technology has improved our productivity is data entry. We can load more data faster than ever before. We can submit thousands of names to a service and in the blink of an eye have current addresses or phone numbers returned to us to load back into our system. Our "techies" build online programs for us to link to a spreadsheet and upload our data, rather than having to key it all in by hand. We have online subscriptions to log onto the internet and look up a person's address, phone number, date of death (if, in fact, they are already deceased). Our research offices can look up net worth, assets owned, stocks, and other financial holdings. The amount of information is astounding.

Two other pieces of technology that help increase accuracy and speed data input are barcoding and form scanning. These are useful when dealing with paper sent from and returned to your office. For instance, if you send out a pledge reminder and the recipient would prefer to return the response piece with a check rather than go online and make a credit card payment, you can put a barcode on the piece that contains the person's ID and possibly the pledge number. When the gift is recorded, it calls up the outstanding pledge, saving key strokes and increasing accuracy.

Form scanning, or optical character recognition, is designed to take a form, such as a survey, and capture the data so it can be uploaded into your database. For example, if your graduating seniors choose not to log in to update their biographic information, you can hand them a form during graduation. After they fill it out, the scanner can read that information, which can be uploaded into your database. This saves data entry time, and the information only has to be reviewed for accuracy before uploading.

Self Serve

The last area where technology has proven to be a big help is that of services we offer our constituents to make their lives easier (along with ours). And yes, you guessed it—on the internet. We offer our constituents self-service. They can log into your online giving site and make a pledge, gift, or pledge payment and give a credit card number in a secure location. It is convenient for them, and all you have to do is push a few buttons and the gift appears in your development system just as if you recorded it by hand. While they are making that gift, they can click the matching gift button, check the service you have subscribed to, and see if they work for a company with a matching gift program. They also might notice that their address needs to be updated, so they update it there and click on class notes to let the alumni office know they have had their second child. We are now providing a one-stop shop to help collect the information that makes the advancement office's job so much easier.

As you can see, much of what we use technology for is automation of the processes we do by hand, to allow us to do more skilled tasks. Through the examples discussed here, you can see that many of these features are separate databases or software packages and are even in separate locations. To the end-user or customer, these must all work seamlessly, as if they were one big software package in one location on one machine. They must be user-friendly and intuitive. And of course, they should be online, be accessible anywhere, and increase the amount of self-service. These are important considerations when you prepare to implement technology, whether for internal or external constituents.

Paying the Bill

Now that we have seen all the technology we can use to increase our productivity and service to our constituents, how do we pay for it? In many cases, if not all, the cost of purchasing new technology is offset by the savings incurred or by an increase in revenue. The key is to document your current cost of doing business and compare that with the expected operating costs of the new technology. At some point you would expect to see either an increase in revenue or a decrease in expenses, whereby the system pays for itself over a period of time. This return on investment is what justifies spending the money.

Let's again look at a document imaging system. Using the form below, we estimated all the costs incurred with the current paper filing system, including the number of minutes it took to file and find a document and the average salaries of those doing the work. This calculation even included the costs of trying to find a lost document. We were surprised to find that after just two years, the new system was paying for itself. This is what sold our management on it, and made us realize we are lucky to have it.

Document Imaging Proposal and Cost Justification

	Current	Proposed
Physical:		
# of files cabinets (vertical & lateral)	100	
# of constituent files	100,000	
# of square feet use by files	90	
# of cabinets added annually	10	
Costs (1st year):		
New System Costs	—	189,779
New System Costs	—	23,349
Backlog Input Costs	—	17,418
Annual Cost of New File Cabinets	2,000	—
Input cost- Personnel	136,079	54,431
Retrieve costs - personnel	126,073	8,405
Retrieve cost - misfiled docs	50,429	5,043
Storage Costs	—	—
Photocopies	15,600	3,900
Support/Training/Maintenance	—	47,955
Total (1st year)	330,181	350,280
Growth rate a little over 20% per year		
Estimated expense over 2 years	728,242	537,019
Savings:		191,223

Document Imaging Proposal (continued)

Storage and Retrieval	Current	Proposed
Min per document to index and file	10	2.2
Min/doc to find and retrieve	15	1
Min/doc to find misfiled docs	60	0
% docs retrieved by professionals/exec	60%	60%
% docs misfiled	10%	1%
Labor		
Hourly rate of document filers	9.44	9.44
Hourly rate of document retrievers	19.44	19.44
Hourly rate of execs/professionals	19.44	19.44
Average rate of payroll increases	4%	4%
Photocopies		
Number of photo copies per year	100,000	2,500
Cost per page (including labor)	0.15	0.15
Percent annual growth per year	10%	

For those in the 13 percent and 62 percent brackets (geeks and wannabe geeks) mentioned at the beginning of this chapter, new technology is something to embrace. But for those who are not so ambitious to change the way they do something, it can be frightening. In "Clutter Control," an article in *University Business*, of February 2002, Jennifer Patterson Lorenzetti points out, "Fear can also be a factor at the start of an imaging project.... Overcoming staff uncertainty was as important as choosing the right vendor.... [Some people's] first reaction was, 'I'm gonna lose my job.'" People fear not adapting to the new way of doing things. A critical part of overcoming this fear is to involve them in the decisions, any data cleanup and preparation tasks, the conversion, and the setting of new policies. Buy-in at the beginning of the process saves you a lot of grief at the end. Lorenzetti goes on to say, "Those who were the most fearful are now the biggest proponents." Technology can help people feel better about their job, but they must be involved in bringing it to life.

So what does the future hold for us? Imbedded chips? Mental telepathy? "Built-in" speakers and receivers for true "hands-off" communications for telephone? It is only limited by our imagination and our desire to increase our productivity and service to our constituents. Join me and help expand that 13 percent. Have a "G" emblazoned on your forehead, too.

CHAPTER 19

Project Management for Advancement Services

By Charlie Hunsaker | President | R I Arlington

"Quick, Cheap, Good—Pick Two!"

The project management aphorism above highlights the quandary of a project manager: how to balance the time, the resources, and the work to be done. Organization managers typically want "quick and cheap" and don't realize how much the "good" will suffer with those choices. The project manager must balance all three.

This chapter seeks to address the issues of time, resources, and (quality) work in two situations—first, the implementation of a new system, and second, the ongoing operation of that system. In other words, it looks at both larger projects and ongoing management through a project management lens.

Project management is a process of balancing expectations and reality. It must be iterative, covering planning, organizing, implementing, and controlling. I will outline some of the key project management points applicable to an implementation project in the following paragraphs. (In Chapter 17, Evaluating and Selecting Primary Development Software, we provide a structure for that type of project.) This is typically the largest project that an advancement services operation might undertake. Such protocols are important for both major implementation projects and ongoing task management.

Implementation Project Management

The process first involves planning to define accurately the project scope, resources, time frame, and assumptions; to build a detailed work plan; and to provide a framework to report progress according to the work plan. The scope describes what the users expect to have once the system is operational and what the project team must deliver to meet user expectations. Resources are, of course, staff, hardware, vendor support, etc. The time frame is elapsed time: Can the work be completed and the deliverables produced in that period with the available resources?

Equally important in planning is to recognize the assumptions on which one is basing all decisions. Is it a "vanilla" implementation, or is there significant customization? What resources are available? Does management expect planners to undertake major campaigns, research projects, or other significant tasks in the project time frame? What risks must be addressed in the process? More details on risks later.

Rule #15:
The seeds of problems are laid down early. Initial planning is the most vital part of a project. The review of most failed projects or project problems indicates that disasters were well planned to happen from the start.

Other assumptions address the question of "acceptance criteria," which should cover at least three areas: system usability and operational soundness; installation or conversion success; and user preparedness. I recommend following a work plan with signoffs at key points throughout the project. When acceptance is obtained gradually along the way, the task of finally accepting the entire implementation is far less difficult.

The scope, resources, and time frame should be documented in the form of a detailed work plan. The scope of work should be outlined in logical order, using a "work breakdown structure" and following critical paths. Major segments of work for an implementation should include:

- **Planning and administration.** Establish the framework of people, reporting relationships, and responsibilities for the project. Monitor the project efforts and results to appraise the project steering committee (and management) of status periodically. Obtain timely decisions and approvals to keep the project on schedule. Present final results to management.

- **Facility preparation.** Define and prepare the physical site for software delivery and application building. This includes setting up a data center or network server site, as well as making sure users have the proper equipment. Installation of software will facilitate initial training and prototype testing on-site.
- **Analysis.** Identify and review all activities and tasks required for the institution to understand the system and the installation approach. This also requires all project team personnel (including the vendor) to understand and document the institution's requirements.
- **Specifications.** Carry out activities and tasks associated with finalizing the details (conversion, interfaces, customization, etc.) of the system being installed. This segment should include a major management checkpoint for updating, re-estimating, and approving the revised work plan.
- **Application building.** Program and implement the system according to specifications. These efforts include both programming and tailoring the system using system tools.
- **Procedures and training.** Carry out activities and tasks associated with the development of procedures, along with operational and end-user training, ensuring that the organization is ready to use the system and procedures are in place.
- **Plan and conduct system test.** Test to ensure the hardware and software are ready for use, verifying that organization users are capable and prepared to use them.
- **Conversion.** Carry out activities and tasks associated with the final go/no-go decision, going live, and the transition to routine operations. This includes ensuring that all files are ready for use, all system components and users meet the acceptance criteria, and everything is ready for live operation. Tasks also include conversion and subsequent support, plus a review of the entire project.

Within these work segments, activities, tasks, steps, and, often, substeps should be defined in detail and assigned to individuals and resources responsible for the work units. Assumptions must be similarly documented to keep expectations and reality in balance. A clear plan then allows for effective organization and deployment of resources.

You might find the following guidelines useful in creating your work plans:

- Define the work, deliverables, assignments, dates, and durations at the "task" level. The work breakdown structure might be Segment, Activity, Task, Step, and Substep. You may use other terms, but describe the work detail at this middle level.
- Note that each task should have a work effort not to exceed 40-80 hours; for tasks with repetitive or iterative steps (such as report programming or training sessions), group similar steps into chunks of 40-80 hours or less.

Projects, by definition, have many risks.

Projects, by definition, have many risks. As noted above, another important issue to consider in project planning is addressing these risks. They appear in many areas, including:

- Level of management commitment
- Quality and depth of the systems support organization
- Staff skills and availability
- Quality of vendor support
- Adequacy of system features to support user functions
- Complexities such as interfaces and other custom programming requirements
- Learning curve for new or multiple technologies
- Quality of the project planning and control process

An important part of project planning is identifying in detail the specific risks to the institution and determining how they should and will be addressed. A "risk memo" developed during the planning stages is a vital document for any implementation project. It initially should be used to communicate the risks and build consensus on approaches. Through the project it should be updated as situations change and new risks arise.

Organizing

With the initial plan in place, resources may be organized and prepared to do the work. Project team members, as well as system users and management, must be considered. Personnel must be given work assignments and told what they are responsible for.

My successful clients have found an organization as shown in Figure 17 to be effective.

Figure 17: Project Organization Model

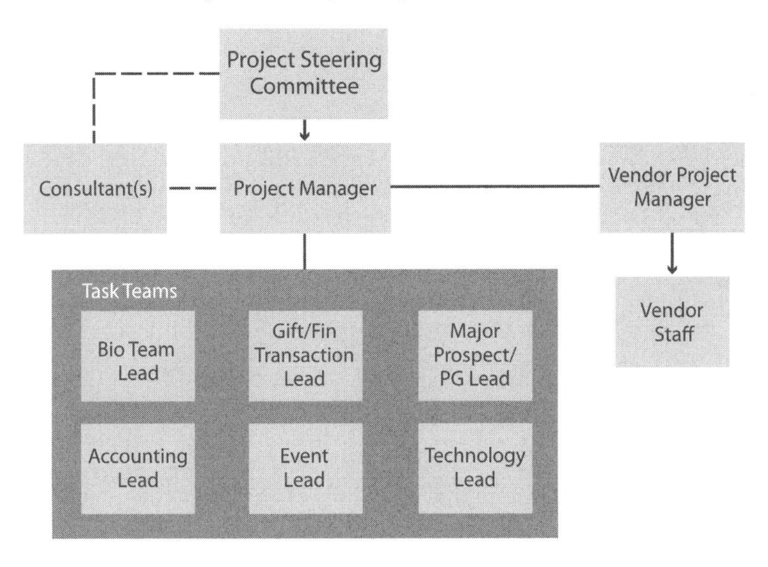

See Chapter 2, The Advancement Services Team and its Role in a Conversion, for discussion of some team-member responsibilities. Now we will explore—or explode—the team further.

The role of the project steering committee is to review and evaluate project progress, monitor resource utilization, and reveal and resolve problems that cannot be dealt with effectively at the project team level. The project team often will make recommendations on organizationwide policies, procedures, and resource allocations. The steering committee has responsibility for reviewing such recommendations for approval in the context of overall organization directions and projects.

This committee typically comprises three to five top managers. The project manager is a member and presents project issues and reports back to the team.

Someone on the committee of project sponsor or champion. The project sponsor should promote the project; this person should assist in balancing project work with other day-to-day responsibilities. The project sponsor also must review the financial and business case for the project as it proceeds.

The project manager is generally an experienced member, either from the information systems department who possesses sound technical and information systems management skills or from the functional area sponsoring the project. On some very large projects, it is helpful to have an application lead as well; this allows the project manager to balance functional and technical requirements. The project manager plays an important role in selecting project team members, completing activities and tasks, and resolving problems related to both the project and the system being implemented.

Rule #5:
Vicious, despicable, or thoroughly disliked persons, ladies, and gentlemen can be project managers. Lost souls, procrastinators and wishy-washies cannot.

The project manager should have overall responsibility for monitoring project progress, reporting project status to the steering committee, and being a focal point for all project communications. He or she also will coordinate consultant and vendor participation in the project. Specifically, the project manager is responsible for:

- Setting up the project team and obtaining the commitment of members to the team. He or she will work with user management to help identify the right team members and will work with application or task team leaders in the detail organization.
- Establishing the priorities that will govern the project. He or she ensures that the schedules for each segment reflect those priorities and the project team understands the project's objectives and priorities.
- Assigning specific work to team members in conjunction with the consultant and vendor to accomplish the project goals. The project manager will be responsible for assigning and explaining specific tasks to team members and working with the team leaders to accomplish these efforts.
- Conducting project team meetings, keeping discussion to the point, and allowing all team members to contribute to the meetings. The meetings, by the way, should have a finite ending time—your team members have other work to do and need to plan accordingly.

- Monitoring project progress, making sure each segment activity is completed in accordance with the plan and priorities of the project. He or she also must address and resolve any problems that deal with the project team. This involves discussions with users and steering committee management in areas related to the project.
- Approving all work done on the project, and overseeing the quality of the work accomplished. It is also appropriate and important to get user signoff on the quality delivery of results throughout the project.

Key to the project manager's success is recognizing that relationships must be built with team members, peer managers, and system users, employing every strategy in the project manager's interpersonal skills arsenal. Relationships must motivate, persuade, pacify, and generally be a foundation for project success. Project managers must develop relationships based on mutual trust, respect, risk taking, and willingness to listen to others. They must work with others to develop solutions that go beyond the project. The project manager must build the team's and the customer's commitment, confidence, and competence.

Relationships must motivate, persuade, pacify, and generally be a foundation for project success.

As shown in Figure 17, I suggest the following application/task teams for a major implementation project:

- The biographic/demographic data team should identify the core information to be tracked on all individuals in the database. This includes name, address, phone, salutations, gender, age, employment, attributes, etc. This team probably will take the lead in mapping the data conversion from any old system to the new system.
- The gifts/financial data team should handle all the details of gifts, pledges, and other financial transactions, including outright gifts, pledges and pledge payments, planned gifts, gifts-in-kind, matching gifts, etc. They also should consider interfaces with banks for cash coming in and with the general ledger. This team should look at the policies, procedures, and training needed to take advantage of the new system functionality for gift transactions.
- The major prospect team should consider both the data and the functionality for fundraising and major prospect management (including planned gift prospects). It should look at the policies,

procedures, and training required to take advantage of the new system functionality for fundraising.

- The information technology team will be responsible for establishing the technology infrastructure to support systems operations. New database, internet/intranet, networking, and other technologies must be tested for effective implementation of the system.
- The general accounting team should consider data and functionality for investment management, scholarship tracking, fund expenditures, and other accounting and financial reporting. This team should look at policies, procedures, and training required to take advantage of the new system functionality for financial transaction purposes.
- The events team (if applicable) or other teams should evaluate volunteer management, campaign reporting, online fundraising, or other functions your organization is including in the implementation project.

Rule #20:
You cannot watch everything. What you can watch is the people. They have to know you will not accept a poor job.

Each team will have a leader responsible for overseeing day-to-day project workload and activities. The leader assigns and reviews work tasks, provides supervision, answers project team questions, and ensures that all major project questions and discussions are communicated up and down the project's organizational structure. Specific responsibilities include:

- Participating as a project team member
- Working with the project manager in assigning tasks to team members and assisting in completing those tasks on time
- Maintaining an overall project perspective while assuming responsibility for a portion of the overall project
- Communicating questions to the project manager and answers to the team members
- Conducting regular team meetings as necessary

- Providing executive summaries of meetings, team progress, and results

Application/task team members will typically be from user departments and will be responsible for providing departmental liaison to the project. A very important aspect of their participation is providing overall user input during the project and then, through their familiarity with the project and the system, supplementing system support to users after implementation. Specific responsibilities on the project include:

- Gathering information about inputs, processes, and outputs of the current system
- Assisting vendor and other project team members in documenting an understanding of the department's needs
- Attending project team meetings to ensure that user interests are being represented
- Assisting vendor and other project team members in developing procedures and training for all users in implementing the system and using it on a daily basis
- Helping obtain approval of results of each segment of work

The consultants' role(s) will vary, depending on the needs of the organization.

The consultants' role(s) will vary, depending on the needs of the organization. They may focus on project organization and management, detailed product support, policy and procedures implementation, training, or any of a number of other areas where the organization feels it lacks the necessary talent. Their role will depend on the organization's needs and the consultants' specific skills.

In general, vendor personnel are responsible for installing their software, programming interfaces and custom programs, converting data, and key aspects of training. Institution staff typically will have more responsibilities for implementing policies and procedures, converting reports from existing formats to the new systems format, system testing, and other aspects of end-user training.

The project manager, consultant, and vendor project manager will come to an understanding about splitting responsibilities among all team members.

Rule #82:
Wrong decisions made early can be recovered from. Right decisions made late cannot correct them.

Adding staff to a late software project makes it later.

Implementation is the execution of the plan by the project team and users. Following a plan, the actual work will be done in the most effective way possible—assuming they planned correctly. Through the project control process, the team can keep the project on course or adjust to a new course. And management, being regularly informed of progress and status, is reassured that its objectives are being met. If situations change or the project gets significantly off-course, adjust the plan and reorganize.

As you proceed with the implementation—the execution of your plan—keep in mind two "laws" that govern projects:

- The 90-90 law of project scheduling suggests that the first 90 percent of the work will take the first 90 percent of the time; the remaining 10 percent of the work will take the remaining 90 percent of the time. The point here is that you need to break your work down into small units so you can clearly identify when it is done or not done; but never try to argue that it is 90 percent complete.
- Brooks' Law says that adding staff to a late software project makes it later. The added people will add complexity and communications time beyond what their work will accomplish. (Fredrick Brooks was the manager of IBM's OS/360 project and author of *The Mythical Man Month: Essays on Software Engineering, 20th Anniversary edition,* which he self-published in 1995, a very good read.)

The last key management concept of project control covers both adherence to standards and routine reporting. Standards should be in place for approaches to key activities, documentation of the project process, and signoffs and approvals. The reporting aspect of project control dictates a project steering committee and formal reporting arrangements, as well as formal reporting of progress according to the work plan.

Assuming you have management approval for the project, organizational and vendor or consultant personnel will begin meeting to outline the implementation, develop a project work plan, and begin identifying responsibilities. The work plan for the whole project and timelines for specific software components should be drafted and entered into a tried and tested, PC-based tool. As mentioned above, although scheduling tools such as MS-Project are available, a simple project control system may be maintained in Excel. It is important to note that institution personnel will have to do work above and beyond that defined by vendors (systems testing, procedures writing, etc.).

I emphasize to the organizations I work with the importance of communication between advancement services and end-users for the success of these projects. A communication channel must be established and continue through the implementation phase, and, I might add, during ongoing operations.

Rule #100:
Never make excuses; instead, present plans of action to be taken.

In the long run, advancement services must understand what users do and how the system can support them. Advancement services should take a proactive role in teaching system capabilities to users. By the same token, users must understand how the system operates, so they can make clear requests to the system up front. The meetings of your project steering committee should succinctly define responsibilities and lines of communication.

System Operations (Maintenance)

After you spend all the time and effort described above to implement your system, a project management environment must survive to track the inevitable requests for system changes, training, bug fixes, hardware problems, and the like. Many effective shops use help desk software like HEAT, Remedy, Magic, Track-IT, and other packages to track and report on these requests; other efficient shops build their own tracking tools. Ineffective shops do not use such tools. I guess you can see my bias here.

With a large project, the issue remains to balance the work, resources, and time to get the work done. You want to be able to identify, categorize, and prioritize your work. Is a work request

The tracking system should allow technicians and users alike to see the status of any request.

- A bug fix?
- An enhancement request?
- A report request?
- A training issue?
- A hardware problem?

The tracking system should capture a name, description, and category for the problem or request, as well as the name of the person submitting it and the date and time of the request. The advancement services group then should assign the problem to the right person to do the work. The tracking system should allow technicians and users alike to see the status of any request (unassigned, assigned, needing additional information, completed, etc.). If the list in any area gets too long, the director should work with the users and advancement management to prioritize the requests; otherwise, they are typically addressed on a FIFO (first in, first out) basis.

I have seen these types of tracking systems used for backlog management as well. That is, if you have three tubs of mail returns from your fall mailing or alumni magazine, use the tracking system to keep track of that backlog. And keep track of it by tub, not wasting time counting each individual piece. Who cares if you have 257 or 263 pieces in backlog? Two tubs of about 130 pieces is accurate enough. If you have an NCOA or Alumni Finder project, or you are planning to implement a new module of your advancement software package, you can use the tracking system to keep it in view and the steps prioritized.

Both IT and advancement services do not keep management informed of the backlogs we face and the work we do. Using this type of tracking tool can show we are getting work done (and at what pace). Over time, these data can be quite useful in helping justify additional staff. If the work is increasing—as recorded in the tracking system—then perhaps we need more staff to handle it.

Remember "Quick, Cheap, and Good—Pick Two." The work, the resources, and the time all have to balance. Using the right tools and disciplines can help communicate this to management. But also remember Cohen's Law: "Work stops when you spend more time reporting on it than doing it." Keep it all in balance.

Rule #93:
Things that fail are lessons learned for the future. Occasionally things go right; these are also lessons learned. Try to duplicate what works.

Installing a new advancement system is not rocket science, but it follows similar project management guidelines. Good luck!

Chapter Endnote:

The various "rules" included in boxes throughout the text are from "One Hundred Rules of Project Management," lessons learned as compiled by Jerry Madden, associate director of flight projects directorate at NASA's Goddard Space Flight Center.

For more information, visit the Project Management Institute at *www.pmi.org* and the Help Desk Institute at *www.helpdeskinst.com.*

CHAPTER 20

Leveraging All Your Advancement Operations on the Web

By Brian Dowling | Assistant Vice President for Development, Development-Information Systems | University of Michigan

Even with all the problems of security, spam, and changing technology, the Web is where business is done. Growth in traffic from 2000 to 2005 was approximately 146 percent, with penetration of 67.6 percent of North American households. Broadband was at 57 percent in the United States and 77 percent in Canada. Internet 2, a much faster version of the current internet, has expanded to more than 150 higher education institutions (but no, we regular people cannot get on it—yet).

Spam and security problems will be solved. The stakes are too high for it not to happen.

Search engines continue to improve, scanning billions of pages and providing us with answers in seconds. When have research tools been more powerful?

Organizations such as Amazon produce a terabyte of data every day. Every time you visit a page, a record of presented links is stored in a database. When you make a purchase, a record of presented links is stored. Consumer behavior is tracked with powerful tools. Our ability to understand our target markets never has been better.

Online images and mapping software will give us three-dimensional, virtual communities we can view from our desktops—have you seen *maps.google.com*? Satellite radio and podcasts are the new radio. Video on demand served through fast bandwidth will change our communication strategies radically. We never have been able to message to so many people at such an attractive cost.

Even now, the Web still is exciting. The 1970s were fun, but the 2010s and the 2020s will bring a virtual community like no other. Unless your organization was around when the printing press was developed, the advent of the internet has been the most radical change in communications in history. And this is just the beginning.

The internet is our primary method of communication to and from our advancement constituents and partners. It is impossible to imagine the world without it.

If you do not have a comprehensive and well-articulated strategy to take extreme advantage of the internet, you need to. There is no better time to redefine how you can leverage all your advancement operations. We need to be at the forefront of using the Web effectively.

Rethink, re-engineer, re-enable.

History of Web Use by Alumni and Advancement

According to Google, the Web has approximately 8 billion pages today. These pages are served by about 50 million different Web sites—an average of 160 Web pages per site.

Now consider only higher-education sites. According to Google, "There are about 200 million Web pages representing approximately 5,000 higher-education Web sites. That's an astonishing 40,000 Web pages on average, per higher-education site, or approximately 250 times more pages than the average site on the World Wide Web."[1]

Web development in advancement generally has followed what happened on campus. There was typically no budget or staff. Whoever could code HTML and post it to a server assumed Web responsibilities. Students often did this or someone took it on as an additional job duty. In a survey run on Advancement-Resources in 1998, out of 58 schools responding, 50 had fewer than one full-time staff member devoted to their alumni and friends Web presence.

Anything was fair game for content. Experimentation was considerable. Examples included a site whose Webmaster contributed movie reviews, the first virtual reunion, an online art exhibition, a junior qualifying exam, trivia, and much more.

Early sites were less concerned with targeted messages and structure and more concerned with just getting something up. The Web was

[1]*Heroes of the Web, by Lance Merker, president and CEO, WebsiteASP, Inc., April 2005.*

a novelty relegated to the "backroom" in our planning. We barely understood the medium, let alone used it to message effectively.

We added online giving and interactive features such as information update forms, guest books, and e-commerce for our merchandise.

Development shops often had larger budgets than alumni associations, so campaign sites often developed separately. Many organizations ended up with a silo approach that reflected their organizational structure. We had separate sites for alumni, the foundation, development, and the campaign.

With the advent of online communities, we built the first data-driven sites that leveraged the use of our advancement databases. Automated interaction between constituents began with features such as "Find a Friend" and online class notes. During the internet bubble of the 1990s, we began to utilize portals. A number of portal vendors went out of business and left us hanging.

Considering that we started with nothing, on a brand-new technology platform and with a completely new messaging environment, we have accomplished a great deal in a short period.

Back to the Future

We have come a long way. We now have Web strategy committees, ongoing budget line items for both creative and content, and we recognize the strategic importance of the Web and other electronic communications. We have servers and technical infrastructure to back everything up, 24/7, real-time, anywhere. Most of us have Web responsibilities in our portfolios. Our sites have been through a few redesigns, and many of us have intranets for policies, procedures, and internal documents. E-mail is the king of push communication and a dominant way of conversing. Multimedia and e-solicitations are becoming commonplace. We can compose our own music (all digitally) and create our own video productions on our desktop. Our messaging is becoming more interesting and exciting.

Leveraging everything that advancement does on the Web is a pretty tall order. It is everything we have dreamed of as a technological enabler, but many of our sites and business processes are fragmented and rooted in the past. We need to move them into the future.

The Web is everything that will be. All applications and business processes are becoming Web-enabled. It is the most cost-efficient way to communicate and enable transactions—ubiquitous, real-time, anywhere. What could be more ideal for outreach?

Guiding Principles

The old maxim is, "The more you give, the more you will get." But "giving more" does not have to mean "spending more." It does mean creating offers and promotions that are useful or interesting to prospects.[2]

No matter how you slice it, content is king on the Web. Giving more will get you more visitors.

We should evaluate how much we are giving out versus how much we should expect to receive. No matter how you slice it, content is king on the Web. Giving more will get you more visitors. More visitors will increase opportunities for interaction and investment.

Web visitors expect robust, well-designed and easily navigable sites with rich, in-depth, compelling, and interesting content. We are competing with everyone out there for that moment of time, and we need to compete with the best. Our competitors include MSNBC, CNN, *Weather.com*, Mapquest, Orbitz, movie sites, and more. How can we provide similarly valuable content?

University traditions and values specific to the institution and to higher education in general should be represented. Relate your site to the "business" of higher education. It should communicate a sense of history and continuity within the framework of the institution and the world and the ways the institution makes the world a better place.

Stale content reduces repeat visits and turns off visitors on their first visit to your site. You have only one chance to make a first impression. The site's "What's New" area needs to be updated regularly—ideally at least daily. No links in this area should be more than a month old, and an archive should store older items. This creates a sense of urgency, so visitors will not want to miss anything. Although this seems like an onerous task, updating can be simple, using a link to an upcoming campus event, for example. To quote a local grocery chain, be "fresh-obsessed."

[2] *Putting Spring in Your Ka-Ching: 10 Direct Mail Tips, by Steve McNamara, MarketingProfs.com.*

An extensive photo gallery should focus on contests for submitting information, trivia quizzes, surveys, games, fun stuff and interactivity. The video game is the most profitable segment of the entertainment industry. Video games have interactivity, intellectual challenge, elements of randomness, and community. This is a useful metaphor to consider when creating content.

Interesting articles from old magazines, yearbooks and other publications also should appear on the site. Articles can be scanned using OCR (optical character recognition) software and converted to HTML pages with very little work. Interactive content, using a variety of online forms for data collection, networking, volunteering, and other activities, helps solicit visitor input in a variety of ways. It gives viewers an action to do and a means to accomplish it.

Options, mission statements, and similar content are necessary for educating visitors. This content loses its impact quickly, even if well designed. Another example is an alumni association constitution. Do not make these pages the focus of your site. You can only tell these stories once. If you have a campaign site, make sure it is updated regularly as well.

Ensure your content considers both external and internal audiences, so you do not duplicate efforts. A staff contact list can be driven from your database and displayed on both the public site and your intranet. If you have to include a description of an area such as advancement services, build it as a component. Think of components as reusable pieces that you can paste into multiple sites.

Giving more than you get reinforces the idea that your organization is providing for the public good. A perception exists that many who work in nonprofits are not as motivated or energetic as those in the private sector. Your site's energy is a good counter.

Design is important, but design without content is beauty without soul. Beauty is transitory. If you plan to spend on design, do a content audit first. You may find you need to invest in the basics first.

Content does not need to be expensive. By training clerical staff in scanning and image editing, you can create a comprehensive and interesting photo gallery quickly. Scan old yearbook photos. Start with the years whose donors are most likely to give. Every time you put up a new year, feature it on the main page of the site, in the "What's New" area. What better way to create a bond with past, present, and future and get a big boost in traffic? We did this on the Colorado School of Mines alumni and friends site, *www.oia.mines.edu*. The resulting increases in traffic were remarkable, and traffic on the photo gallery exceeded that of all other content by several orders of magnitude.

Finally, send a staff member out once a week to take current photos of the campus or organization properties. This is inexpensive, easy, and free content that gets visitors interested in the site. Every time someone sees her picture, she tells someone, who tells someone else. This is called viral marketing. Web cams also work wonders for building traffic.

Transfer of Ownership

A successful identity-oriented strategy for visitors to your site involves including the individual in the identity and the brand. We all look in the mirror on a daily basis, and the mirror image in your site needs to reflect your target audience and markets.

Visitors do not care how we are organized internally.

Visitors do not care how we are organized internally. It is surprising how many sites continue to be set up like our organizational charts. In a random survey of 50 sites, giving was integrated with alumni in only 24. Make your site belong to external visitors rather than the internal advancement staff. Design the site and content from your visitors' viewpoint. Organize the site to reflect your visitors' preferences and behaviors. Make the site about them.

Use testimonials and notable alumni lists, and discuss what value has been provided by giving. Include stories on major donors and some of the smaller donors, where philanthropic spirit is exemplified by actions. If you have a contest, publish a winners' list. Everyone loves a winner.

Allow visitors to add content to the site either directly or though volunteering. Within reason, content should reflect the contributors' viewpoints. Allow some "edge," and don't edit to the point where content becomes "institution speak." A good statement of use goes a long way to mitigate content that varies too much from the acceptable norms of the site. You will need to balance participative democracy with marketing messages. Additional content can include uploaded photos, class notes, branch reports, and other information. Again, this transfers site ownership to participants.

Self-identification holds true for an intranet. Use content-management software and add content maintenance to job responsibilities. This gives ownership to users and makes them familiar with creating and managing Web pages, levels knowledge, and transfers expertise. Publish a list of who uses the intranet the most. Use your intranet to celebrate heroes and good deeds. This leads to behavior reinforcement and ownership.

Ownership Transferred = Acquisition = Relationship Building = Investment.

Power of the Internet

Links are free. Make your site more than just a repository of information by effectively using links to other campus and Web sites.

Give intellectual depth to content. An alumni page for your engineering school's site can have a link to sites on slide rules. Trivial? Possibly, but it adds interest and conveys a message that you have thought about who visits the site and where their interests might lie. Links also should be used for your intranet. If you have a section on ethics and accountability, link to sites that deal with these topics.

RSS feeds are very popular and are a great source of "free" content. Embed news feeds from your news site, online events calendar, and other sites to provide current and updated content automatically.

Cathleen Parsons-Nikolic, author of "Special Delivery" (CURRENTS, May/June 2005), talks about how prospect researchers can use push technologies to identify additional funding sources. A sidebar describes blogs and how advancement officers can use them. (CURRENTS is a magazine published by CASE.)

Service-based Architecture

A generation is growing up that might never write a check, fill in and submit a paper form, purchase music in a store, or read a newspaper. In the next few years, most annual fund gifts probably will be received online. The world is changing and services are being provided in new ways.

Online banking, investment management, travel booking, and exploding e-commerce have resulted in fundamental changes in business processes. You need a strategy to improve your service offerings. Here are some of the many processes that visitors might carry out on your site:

- Address and information updating
- Finding and locating a friend
- Online giving
- Online event registration
- Affinity services purchases
- Merchandise and memorabilia purchases
- Alumni trips and travel registration
- Requesting a transcript
- Career services and job posting
- Networking with classmates with similar interests
- Online classes and education
- Volunteer management and interaction
- Alumni branch management and reporting

You should have a portal strategy to manage personalization and individual preferences. This may not be why the majority of your users visit your site, but it might be one reason they stay on the site.

Service-based architecture is about tracking behavior. *MSNBC.com* recommends articles based on what you have viewed. *Amazon.com* recommends items based on what you have purchased. We all have received follow-up sales and marketing calls after visiting a site, downloading a white paper, or signing up for a service. We also need to deploy Web services and track for harvesting data, profiling our visitors, and making contact.

Services can be targeted at internal users. Your policies and procedures, forms, online reports, and other operations should be available via the Web. Queens University in Ontario, Canada, designed a site for information requests, task assignments, events management, mass e-mailing, and many other aspects of their advancement operations. This kind of site saves time and effort, helps coordination, and is far more efficient than paper-based systems.

When you send out a mass e-mail, make sure you have someone available to respond to inquiries.

Service-based architecture builds in response. When you get a submission, respond quickly. Twenty-four hours should be the absolute acceptable upper limit. Devote staff and resources to make this happen. When you send out a mass e-mail, make sure you have someone available to respond to inquiries. You are probably getting more people asking questions via your Web site than at your front counter. Service-based architecture is about finding what you need easily. It is surprising how many sites do not have adequate staff contacts, addresses, and similar information. Can you get back to the main institutional home page with one click?

Service-based architecture features choice and customization. You should have subscription options for all messaging, such as:

- Do you want to receive the magazine in hard copy or in electronic format? And if electronic, do you want the whole magazine, or just stories tailored to your particular area of interest and in HTML, MIME, or plain text?
- Do you want to receive any information on giving?
- When are the best times to contact you?
- What is the best way to contact you?

Opt-outs and preferences are getting more complex. They should be offered in a menu of choices. Try to limit the "Don't contact me ever" options. Include positive, yes-oriented answers:

- I want to be invited to all campus events.
- I want to be invited to events for my college only.
- I would like information and updates on alumni association benefits.

How many clicks do users have to make to perform critical actions? From a survey of 50 sites:

Number of clicks to online giving form	Number of sites
1	2
2	16
3	10
4	2
0 (no form online)	2

Number of clicks to information update form	Number of sites
1	1
2	6
3	13
4	2
5	3
0 (No online updating)	25

Both giving and information update forms should be one click away from the main institutional page.

When you employ services, you may not see the use that you initially expected. Remember when we debated online giving? Is it really worth setting up, given the small number of transactions? Does our alumni community have the level of registrations that we would like? In some cases, we want to provide services to show we can. This reinforces the idea that our institutions are at the forefront of research and education.

A comprehensive service approach is one of the greatest reinforcements a brand can have. It demonstrates hard work, attention, and orientation to constituents. Well-conceived services convey our organization's ability and attitude.

Serve your visitors well and reap the rewards.

Passive Recall to Accomplish

A local Canadian television station advertises, "Too many Web sites. Avoid the confusion and go to www.ourstation.com to get a list of sites, you can use." With 8 billion-plus Web pages, 50 million sites, and an average of 160 pages per site, all with unique photos, colors, fonts, and navigation structures, it is not surprising that we might become confused.

Remember John Taylor's Introduction: We are in competition. Ease of use (passive recall to accomplish), is critical to encourage visitors to visit the site and return. How many times have you gone to a site to research something, make a purchase, find a place, and left immediately because of confusing navigation, colors, or other elements that made it difficult to use? Did you ever return?

Design your site so it is easy to locate and perform specific tasks and find specific content on repeat visits. Invest in up-front planning so your site will work for the longer term. Once initial content is added, URLs should remain constant. Sites should have these characteristics:

- Single-entry point and clear navigation structure
- Basic structure that does not change too often or too radically
- New features emulate the basic site design and fit in the menu structure
- Comprehensive site map
- Specific alumni and friends search function
- Print-friendly versions of pages

Passive recall is about look and feel. Every time we look at a page and interpret it, it re-identifies the brand. Brand your design to the institutional brand by using the same colors and the same style. Brand your intranet the same way. In the 50-site survey, 40 sites were branded the same as the institutional home page. We serve the institution. Advancement should not be a silo unto itself.

When testing technology, we tend to test what we are familiar with, rather than what needs to be tested. As you work on your site, get those who are unfamiliar with it to test. They quickly will let you know what is wrong. I once designed a login screen that did not accept numbers. I logged on for months. But the first user who tried to access the system had a number in the password.

Leverage the Database

The advancement database is one of your most strategic and valuable assets. It is seldom leveraged to the degree it can be on the Web site to provide interactive, up-to-date, interesting content. It should have the following:

- Alumni directory and related interactive activities, such as networking and community building
- The ability to edit and update class notes and accomplishments
- Giving history, current address, event attendance history, and other information. Maintenance of your own pledge schedule and capacity for pledge payments
- The ability to view who is attending the event or an alumni excursion you have registered for
- Lists of "lost" alumni
- Statistics and reports for class years, reunion, gender, geographic, and other demographic data
- A list of all the alums and/or donors having birthdays today
- A list of the largest gifts by caller on your call center Web site
- A contact list for staff generated from your database, so you have to go to only one place to update contact information

Leveraging the database should go far beyond what you do within your alumni community. You can have a list of lost alumni and offer a prize to those who locate the most lost classmates. You can put together a "living" report from your database to show how many publications, events, and other activities might have been missed. This may be a little controversial if some do not want to be found, but at least you'll find that out, too.

The foundation of leveraging your database is to build a good data warehouse with summary tables and other specialty information from the Web. The list of potential ways to leverage your database on the site is almost limitless and is constrained only by your imagination.

Smoothing Transitions

Smoothing transitions means integrating your Web properties. This is also tied to passive recall to accomplish, since integration makes passive recall easy.

Integration of all alumni and friends-related sites is important. It demands common interface, common metaphors, colors, fonts, navigation system, and one common URL entry point for all sites. School, college, or organization content should be created and maintained using site templates that can be branded to individual units but dovetail into the overall, common look and feel.

Print standards and practices do not work equally well on the Web. Move away from brochure and magazine design concepts to a more interactive Web design. Your pages should not need to use scroll bars. Do not use Times New Roman and other print-friendly fonts that do not translate well to the Web. Your style guide needs a separate section for the Web.

Move away from brochure and magazine design concepts to a more interactive Web design.

If you have an alumni community, it should not be a distinct and separate piece, but completely transparent to the user. In the 50-site survey, 40 sites had communities that were integrated, and 10 were separate and distinct. Do not have your community branded to the vendor. We know these companies but our constituents do not.

Many online gift forms have a different header, footer, and setup from the rest of the pages on the site because the form is hosted on a different server for security and processing. This needs to change. Your online giving form should have the same style as other pages in your site.

Recognize Opportunity Costs

Plan for change and prioritize projects. Assign budgetary responsibility and costs for Web-related projects. Differentiate Web costs from other media, so clear cost/benefit analysis can be done. Separate the direction and determination of strategy from implementation costs.

Ongoing maintenance for technology projects is typically 25-50 percent of the initial investment. Budget adequately for items such as security certificates, server upgrades, and acquisition of new technology. These need to be permanent line items.

Balance Web investment with other media and evaluate the Web as a replacement for traditional media where appropriate. Use modeling to evaluate projects and project outcomes. If we allow users to choose PDF magazine delivery, how many will be likely to do this, given our analysis of click-throughs on our e-solicitations?

Use risk analysis to determine the costs of not moving forward. If 50 percent of gifts are going to be received online within a few years as is predicted, how many gifts will be lost if we do not have an online form?

Opportunity costs can mean not doing something on the Web if it supersedes another overarching priority. If you are missing leadership gift staff because you are redesigning your site, you need to reassess priorities. Leverage your budget effectively.

Manage With Statistics

Insight = Opportunity

Commercial packages for managing Web statistics are very sophisticated, but you should manipulate, massage, and cleanse raw logs before doing your analysis; otherwise, you will make poor decisions based on erroneous information.

Break your target audience into external, internal, staff, technical support, and other groups to provide a clear picture. Remove statistics created by robots. The purer the statistics, the more useful they will be.

- Focus on trends by topical content area and less on overall totals
- Do extensive analysis of click-through behavior throughout the site
- Review behavior of repeat visitors

Adjust your content and navigation based on your analysis. Make popular areas more prominent foci of your content creation. Use statistics to exploit opportunities.

Web statistics should be circulated monthly as part of your regular management reporting. Web work should be part of annual accountability, goal setting, and performance management. Statistics should be used to manage outbound communications such as mass e-mailing. All your electronic media interactions should be recorded. Data mining can be used to help you profile and target more precisely.

Become the organization of the future today so you can handle tomorrow and all that tomorrow will bring.

Know what statistics do not measure. The "hits" number is always higher, but include each item accessed on a site. If you have a graphics-intensive site, hits are higher because each graphic on a page will count as a hit. Some consumer internet service providers refresh a visitor's address. Your distinct visitor count could be overstated. Popular pages may be cached, and hits on these may not always be counted.

Benchmark your site against overall internet traffic growth. If your traffic increased by a lesser amount, you are losing mind-share. This seems obvious, but often we look at our statistics in isolation. Draw inferences, not absolutes.

Become a Web-centric Organization

Becoming a Web-centric organization is how to get from now to tomorrow. It represents a philosophical change in your organization's mind-set. It is coordination, not control—energy through strategies. Become the organization of the future today so you can handle tomorrow and all that tomorrow will bring.

More than 300,000 nonprofits were created in a 10-year period in the United States alone, and many of these organizations are now in the major-gift fundraising game. Tsunami relief and other cause-based fundraising have instigated the transfer of huge dollar amounts to causes other than higher education, and we no longer enjoy the catbird seat.

Baby boom, echo and bust population demographics will lead to enrollments leveling off and more competition for students. Capital markets have been flat, and we continue to struggle for budget. We need to leverage the Web to help offset these problems.

In "Present and Accounted For," (CURRENTS, April 2005) Frank D. Schubert describes the University of Texas at Austin's stewardship system, which facilitates interaction of financial reporting for endowments, students, and donors. All of this is automated through the Web. Students are reminded by e-mail that a stewardship thank-you letter is due. The students write a letter and post to the system, and it is forwarded to development staff and donors. Students can include photos. Imagine a whole community developed around stewardship, philanthropy, acknowledgment, and training future philanthropists. According to the article, this project took a couple of years to complete, but how visionary and very representative it is of the kind of organization we all need to become.

One of the first steps to Web-centricity is to set up a steering committee. Call it something like, "The Emerging Technologies Group." Make sure the committee's membership and mandate cross organizational boundaries. Focus on coordination and synergy.

Institutions should adopt the philosophical stance that they should consider using the Web for everything they do:

- Formulate and design all publications for inclusion in sites, including internal sites. All articles for print always should have your site's URL referenced on each page of the publication.
- Design invitation cards, business cards, stationery, letterhead, and all other print-based forms of communication with the Web in mind.
- Put all processes online, including giving, information updating, registration, and all service requests.
- Allow subscribers to publications to choose electronic-based, as opposed to print-based. Allow donors to choose online receipts as opposed to paper. Make available comprehensive online subscription and opt-out mechanisms.
- Ensure that all software applications and software acquisitions use Web-based technology.
- Do more work on the Web internally to globalize understanding of working with the medium.
- Add Web responsibilities for content, technology, and strategy to job descriptions.

- Make Web strategies an integral part of the annual planning and budget processes.
- Use content management software to make new content easy to deploy by a variety of staff at different organizational levels.
- Ensure ongoing and regular photography of campus people and events.
- Create a common technological framework for Web services.
- Develop portal strategies.
- Develop outbound push-technology strategies.

Web-centricity means looking for integrated solutions for your business processes. Your alumni community vendor may have a content management module. You can use it to manage both your alumni community and your intranet. Integration needs to include ownership, since ownership, responsibility for messaging, content creation, and maintenance all need to be clearly defined and assigned.

Do not forget about training and professional development. Send staff to a Web conference so they can understand trends, techniques, and potential. We tend to limit professional development opportunities to a person's field. The best professional development can be to attend a conference outside your area of responsibility.

You will need policies and procedures such as a mass e-mailing protocol, statements of appropriate use, and more. Many of these will be new to your organization. I am not suggesting that we waste time and lower productivity, but systematically "surfing" Web sites is very valuable. Spend time doing this every day. Do a Google search of university sites, start at the top of the list and review one after the other. Record your comments. After a week or so, you will recognize trends and consistencies. You will be able to evaluate more clearly how your institution compares, and you will be amazed at what you find: a wealth of ideas.

It is important not to clone a site. You will have common elements, such as a staff contact page, but your site will be based on your strategic plan, your target audience, your communication strategy, your budget, and your ability to pull it off. Take what you see, add value, make it your own.

And in the End ...

In 1972, a science fiction author named John Brunner talked about the Home Pape. The Home Pape was a sheet of current news stories. As you read, you could make comments. You could see how many other people were reading and read their comments. We have not even talked about blogs, Wikis, portals, podcasts, feeds, security, privacy, transparency, or any of the societal changes the Web will bring. It is still exciting after all these years, and still just a little crazy.

Do not let all this be overwhelming and cause paralysis and endless discussion. Remember when we used to do data modeling? Sometimes we data-modeled so much that the system never got built. Pick projects that give you immediate and quick return so you can demonstrate success quickly.

And do not forget the human component. Leveraging everything on the Web is like building a highway around a town: good for the traveler, but maybe not as good for the town. When human contact makes more sense, make it a priority. Balance your Web efforts with the need for personal and direct interactions. These are always the most important and effective ways of communicating. Tell people in the next office not to send you e-mails, but to come in and speak with you directly.

Competition among nonprofits has not reached the point where we cannot share our success and network with our peers. Give back. Write articles for your umbrella organizations, contribute articles and presentations to volunteer-run sites, speak at conferences, and teach about what you have learned. We all work for good causes. Making our industry more effective on the Web will increase involvement and investment and improve the world we live in.

Advancement
SERVICES

Section VI: Appendix

A

accountability: The recipient organization's responsibility to keep a donor informed about how it uses the donor's gift.

accounting policy: A policy made by a gift-supported organization that specifies which types of gifts will be counted toward a campaign goal and which types will be excluded.

acknowledgment form: An impersonal printed card used to acknowledge relatively small gifts. (See receipt.)

acknowledgment letter: A letter sent by the recipient organization, or on its behalf, to the donor to express appreciation for a gift and identify how it will be used. An acknowledgment may be a form letter but is usually personalized. (See receipt.)

acquisition mailing: A mailing sent to prospects to attract new members or donors.

actual value: The price that property commands when sold on the open market.

advance gifts: Gifts solicited and given (or pledged) in advance of a campaign's public announcement. Such gifts are necessary to give a campaign momentum and show the organizers the likelihood of success or failure. (See campaign.)

advancement: A term used to define the total process of advancing the mission, goals, and objectives of an organization or institution. The process includes development, marketing, communications, (in educational institutions) alumni or alumnae affairs, and advancement services. (See development.)

advancement services: A specialty that addresses the "back office" aspects of advancement, such as computer systems, gift regulations and compliance, policies, and procedures. (See support services.)

AFP: The acronym for the Association of Fundraising Professionals. Based in Alexandria, Virginia, it's a professional association for individuals responsible for generating philanthropic support for a wide variety of nonprofit charitable organizations.

AICPA: The acronym of the American Institute of Certified Public Accountants, a national professional organization for CPAs. Its mission is to provide members with the resources, information, and leadership to provide services in a professional manner for the benefit of the public, employers, and clients. It is based in New York City.

alumni/alumnae affairs/relations: In an educational institution, the advancement area responsible for serving as a liaison between the institution and its former students and for promoting the institution to that constituency.

annual fund: An annually occurring fundraising program that seeks unrestricted gifts for current-year operations.

annual giving: The yearly act of providing either a restricted or unrestricted gift to the institution, usually in response to an organized appeal. Synonym: annual fund.

annual report: A yearly account of financial and organizational conditions prepared by the management of an organization.

appraisal: Valuation of a gift by an external source. An appraisal is usually arranged by a donor who is claiming charitable income tax deductions for gifts-in-kind (other than gifts of stock traded on a national exchange) if the total of such gifts is over $500. If the total of such gifts exceeds $5,000 ($10,000 for gifts of closely held stock), the donor should obtain a qualified appraisal with a summary on IRS Form 8283. (See valuation.)

appreciated securities gift: A gift of securities with a market value greater than the donor's cost or basis. The increase in value generally represents a potential capital gain, which will incur capital gains taxes unless the property is given to a charitable organization. The value of such a gift is established by calculating the mean between the high and low prices on the date it is transferred to the organization.

appreciation: (1) The increase in property's market value over its original cost or tax basis; (2) gratitude for a gift.

APRA: The acronym for the Association of Professional Researchers for Advancement, formerly the Association of Professional Researchers in America. Based in Westmont, Illinois, it is an organization to foster professional development and promote standards that enhance the expertise and status of development research and information service professionals worldwide.

automated telemarketing: Use of a computerized dialing system that manages phonathon prospects on screen, either automatically (so that the technology essentially manages the prospect pool) or manually (so that it responds to the caller's determination of the pool). Organizations that use automated telemarketing do not use phonathon cards. (See phonathon card.)

automation: A highly technical implementation that usually involves electronic hardware; automatic, as opposed to human, operation or control of a process, equipment, or a system; or the techniques and equipment used to achieve this.

B

basis: The purchase price of an item of property, minus depreciation allowed or allowable as a tax deduction, plus improvements.

batch processing: A system that takes a set (a "batch") of commands or jobs, executes them, and returns the results, all without human intervention. This is in contrast to an interactive system in which the user's commands and the computer's responses are interleaved during a single run.

benchmark: A standard by which something can be measured or judged. The most useful kind of benchmark is one tailored to a user's own typical tasks.

bequest: Assets of personal property such as cash, securities, or other tangible property that a donor leaves to a charity in his or her will and for which the donor's estate will receive a charitable estate tax deduction at the time of death. A testamentary gift. (See testamentary.)

biodemographic information: Data about constituents that provide biographical or individual preferences that are useful in creating a prospect or development profile. (See donor profile and prospect profile.)

book value: The amount of an asset stated in a company's records, not necessarily the amount that it could bring on the open market. (See fair market value and market value.)

C

CAE: The acronym for the Council for Aid to Education, formerly the Council for Financial Aid to Education Inc. Based in New York City, it is a nonprofit national organization dedicated both to enhancing the effectiveness of corporate and other private-sector support in improving education and to helping education institutions acquire private support more effectively. (See VSE Survey.)

campaign: An organized effort to raise funds for a nonprofit organization through solicitation by volunteers, by direct mail, by phone, or all three. (See advance gifts.)

capital campaign: A campaign to raise substantial funds for a nonprofit organization to finance major building projects, supplement endowment funds, and meet other needs that demand extensive outlays of capital.

capital gift: A gift earmarked for endowment; building construction, renovation, or remodeling; equipment; or books and other non-disposable items.

Carnegie Classification of Higher Education: Groupings of American colleges and universities according to their missions. As devised by the Carnegie Foundation for the Advancement of Teaching, the categories are meant primarily to improve the precision of the Foundation's research by clustering institutions with similar programs and purposes, not to establish a hierarchy among campuses.

CASE: The acronym for the Council for Advancement and Support of Education, the publisher of this book. Based in Washington, DC, it is an international association of institutional advancement officers who include alumni administrators, fundraisers, communications and marketing professionals, advancement services professionals, and government relations officers. CASE's mission is to help these professionals advance the cause of education and enhance their institutions by bringing in support, be it in the form of money, alumni loyalty, public esteem, or new students.

CFAE: See CAE.

charitable institution/charity: Any private institution or agency that operates on a nonprofit basis for the public good and therefore is exempt from taxation (though it must pay taxes on income from any commercial operations in which it's involved).

charitable lead trust: A trust that makes payments, either a fixed amount (annuity trust) or a percentage of trust principal (unitrust), to a charity during its term. At the end of the trust term, the principal of the trust can either go back to the donor or to heirs named by the donor. (See planned gift.)

charitable remainder trust: A trust that makes payments, either a fixed amount (annuity trust) or a percentage of trust principal (unitrust), to whomever the donor chooses to receive income. (See planned gift.)

CID: Constituent identification number.

closely held stock: privately owned corporate stock that is not publicly traded on an exchange or in the over-the-counter market. (See securities.)

COD: Computer-originated document, a feature that comes with a document-imaging system. (See document imaging.)

comprehensive campaign: A campaign in which all funds, whether designated for unrestricted, restricted, capital, or endowed purposes, are counted toward the goal.

constituency: A category of donors and prospective donors. A constituency could be made up of alumni, parents, members, staff members, or, in a broader sense, individuals, corporations, or foundations.

contact report/call report: A document filed after any contact with a prospect that outlines the content of the visit or phone call and indicates appropriate follow-up.

conversion: Changing computer programs and data from one language or software system to another.

corporate foundation: The philanthropic organization established to coordinate, over a period of time, the philanthropic interests of a corporation. Such a foundation can be very specific about its field of interest, often limiting grants to causes related to corporate profits. (See private foundation.)

cost basis: The value of an item based on its original cost.

cost/benefit analysis: A financial determination of a program's effectiveness in terms of expenses incurred to produce revenue. In its simplest form, this is sometimes referred to as cost per dollar raised.

cultivation: The process of exposing prospective donors to institutional activities, people, needs, and plans to the point where they're interested enough to be considered ready to give at acceptable levels.

D

database: A collection of information kept in one place and accessible by many users through the same server. A database is one component of a database management system.

database integrity: How complete, and thus reliable, information in a database is. (See data cleanup.)

data cleanup: Removal and/or compression of information in a database to improve its reliability and integrity. (See database integrity.)

decentralized development office: A fundraising department with staff members who are physically located throughout an institution (for example, in undergraduate and graduate schools) rather than in one main office.

deferred gift: A donation that is arranged now and fulfilled later, usually a planned gift. An example would be when donors leave a provision in their wills to make a bequest to a charitable organization. (See planned gift.)

deferred giving: Methods of donating that require nonprofits to wait a year or more before being able to use the gift assets. Deferred giving is now generally considered to be only part of planned giving. (See planned gift.)

development: A term used to define the total process of organizational or institutional fundraising. (See advancement).

development/advancement profile: See donor profile.

direct mail campaign: A fund drive conducted by mail, often for annual giving purposes. Such campaigns are frequently broad-based, with several mailings going out over a specified period. (See segmentation.)

document imaging: Storing records or graphic images in an electronic format. (See COD.)

donor profile: A description of basic information about an individual contributor that's based on research and personally provided information. (See biodemographic information and prospect profile.)

donor recognition: The policy and practice of thanking contributors for gifts, first through immediate acknowledgment by card or letter and subsequently through personalized notes, personal expressions of appreciation directly to donors, published lists of contributors, and other appropriate ways.

donor relations: An area of development that works with both contributors and prospects and oversees cultivation, recognition, and stewardship.

DTC account: An account with the Depository Trust Co., a clearinghouse for electronic transactions of securities.

E

EDUCAUSE: An association formed from the merger of CAUSE and Educom to encourage the introduction, use, and management of information resources and technologies in teaching, learning, scholarship, research, and institutional management. It's based in Washington DC, and Boulder, CO.

electronic screening: A computer process used to determine the giving potential of a wide range of prospective donors. The process, which helps identify top prospects who are loyal and have a propensity to give, provides prospect management and tracking guidance for your development staff. The research is done in online databases and on the Internet. (See prospect screening.)

endowment: Funds that are kept intact and invested. The earnings or a portion thereof are applied to purposes the donor designates.

F

fair market value: The amount for which an item or property can be sold in the marketplace. (See book value and market value.)

FASB: The acronym of the Financial Accounting Standards Board of the Financial Accounting Foundation. Based in Norwalk, Connecticut, FASB sets the standards for financial accounting and reporting for nonprofits as well as the business world. The standards are used by corporations, charities, and other organizations that issue financial statements; by auditors; and by users of financial information.

field: An area on a data record in which specific information about a constituent is located. Examples of fields include first name, salutation, and type of gift.

file management: A method used to organize records, either on a database or in a physical location.

fund account: A category for each type of restriction. Organizations keep such categories separate in order to keep track of a donor's wishes; accounts are later grouped for presentation in the financial statements.

G

GASB: The acronym of the Governmental Accounting Standards Board of the Financial Accounting Foundation.

gift: A voluntary transfer of things of value, usually in the form of cash, checks, securities, real property, or personal property. Gifts may come from individuals, industry, foundations, and other sources; recipients can use them for unrestricted or restricted purposes. Charities make no commitment of resources or services in return for gifts, other than possibly agreeing to put the gift to use as the donor designates. (See personal property and securities.)

gift annuity: A contract between a nonprofit and a donor in which, in return for a donation of cash or other assets, the organization agrees to pay the donor or the donor's designee a fixed payment for life, for which the donor can also claim a charitable tax deduction. (See planned gift.)

gift-in-kind: A donation other than cash. (See in-kind contribution.)

gift processing: The procedure of entering contributions into a database, thereby crediting the donor.

H

hardware: The physical, touchable, material parts of a computer or other system. The term is used to distinguish these fixed parts of a system from the more changeable software or data components that it executes, stores, or carries. (See software.)

I

import/export capability: Ability of a software program to bring in or transmit data from or to other programs.

independent auxiliary: A company that is a subsidiary of another company but has its own executive officers.

infrastructure: Basic support services for computing, particularly national networks.

in-honor-of gift: A donation that's generally a tribute to a living individual and occasionally designated by the donor for a specific purpose. (See memorial gift.)

in-kind contribution: A gift of equipment, supplies, or other property instead of money. The donor may place a monetary value on the gift for tax purposes. (See appraisal, gift-in-kind, and valuation.)

integrated software: A computer program that offers components that can be used in tandem with other programs.

interface: A boundary across which two systems communicate; a hardware connector used to link to other devices or a convention used to allow communication between two software systems.

irrevocable: Incapable of being recalled or revoked; unchangeable; irreversible; unalterable; impossible to retract. The term usually pertains to pledges or planned gifts.

L

legacy: A gift of property by will, especially of money or personal property; a bequest.

letter of intent: A statement of a prospect's intention to make a specified gift or legacy; used when a prospect prefers to avoid making a pledge. Because it could constitute a binding obligation under some circumstances, the prospective donor should seek legal counsel before executing such a letter. (See pledge.)

life income gift: See planned gift.

LYBUNT: An acronym that identifies donors who gave Last Year But Unfortunately Not This year. (See SYBUNT.)

M

mail campaign: See direct mail campaign.

mainframe: A term originally referring to the cabinet containing the central processor unit or "main frame" of a room-filling batch machine. The word was later applied to big iron machines after the emergence of smaller "minicomputer" designs in the early 1970s.

major gift: A large gift, probably of $10,000 or greater, usually meant for capital purposes.

market value: As pertaining to endowment, the book value plus undistributed yield. (See book value and fair market value.)

matching gift: An eligible contribution by an eligible corporation on behalf of an eligible employee whose eligible gift to an eligible institution starts the process.

memorial gift: A contribution generally commemorating a deceased individual and occasionally designated by the donor for a specific purpose. (See in-honor-of gift.)

merge/purge: A computer operation that combines two or more files of names by using a matching process to produce one file that's free of duplicates.

MIS: Management Information System. A computer system, usually based on a mainframe or minicomputer, designed to provide managers with up-to-date information on an organization's performance, such as fundraising totals.

mission statement: A concise description of the purpose of an organization.

moves management: A method of organizing donor cultivation that focuses on maintaining a strong, orderly relationship between donor and institution.

Murphy's law: If anything can go wrong, it will.

N

NACUBO: The acronym for the National Association of College and University Business Officers. It's a Washington, DC-based nonprofit professional organization representing chief administrative and financial officers at colleges and universities. NACUBO's mission is to promote sound management and financial practices.

NAIS: The acronym for the National Association of Independent Schools. It's a Washington, DC-based voluntary membership organization that represents private pre-collegiate schools and associations in the United States and abroad.

network server: A computer, or a software package, that provides a specific kind of service to client software running on other computers.

NIMCRUT: A planned giving term meaning net income with make-up charitable remainder unitrust.

nonprofit organization: A group that qualifies for federal income-tax exemption under Section 501(c)(3) of the Internal Revenue Code or under other 501 classifications. (See Section 501(c)(3).)

O

OCR: Optical Character Recognition. It's a mechanism through which a computer identifies printed or written characters.

P

participation: Percentage of solicited constituents who make gifts. Participation is calculated by dividing the number of donors by the number of constituents solicited.

personal property: Cash, stocks, bonds, notes, paintings, furniture, jewelry, and possessions other than real estate. (See gift and securities.)

phonathon: A fundraising effort in which either volunteers or paid callers solicit gifts or pledges by telephone. Employed especially in annual fund campaigns.

phonathon card: A form that provides the phone solicitor with biodemographic information and a giving history for the prospective donor. (See automated telemarketing.)

planned gift/planned giving: A type of charitable donation, requiring some planning, that's popular because it can provide valuable tax benefits and/or income for life. The terms often refer to the process of making a charitable gift of estate assets to one or more nonprofit organizations; a donation that requires consideration and planning in light of the donor's overall estate plan; or part of an individual's major gift strategy, generally involving a bequest or trust. (See charitable lead trust, charitable remainder trust, deferred gift, deferred giving, gift annuity, and pooled income fund.)

pledge: A verbal or written commitment by a constituent to make a gift within a specific time frame. (See letter of intent.)

pledge card: A printed form used by solicitors in seeking what is most often a legally binding commitment from a prospect.

pledge reminder: A printed form that the charity sends on regular schedule to a constituent who has made a pledge but has not completed full payment.

pooled income fund: A planned gift in which a charity accepts contributions from many donors into a fund, the charity keeps the principal, and the charity distributes the income from the fund to each donor or recipient of the donor's choosing. Each income recipient then receives income in proportion to his or her share of the fund, and the donor receives a charitable income tax deduction. This form of trust is described in paragraph (5) of Internal Revenue Code Subsection 642(c). (See planned gift)

PPA 2006: Pension Protection Act of 2006. Enacted in the fall of 2006, this act, among other things, established parameters for allowing certain withdraws from Individual Retirement Accounts as "contributions" to some nonprofit organizations, as well as added, tightened, or changed regulations pertaining to the donation of specified in-kind property.

premium: A tangible item or benefit that an institution gives in exchange for a contribution, such as a tie with the school logo or free tickets to attend an event. Depending on both its cost and fair market value, a premium could affect the tax deductibility of the original gift. (See quid pro quo, tax deductibility.)

private foundation: An organization established to coordinate, over a period of time, the philanthropic interests of a private entity such as an individual or family. Such a foundation can be very specific as to its field of interest, often limiting grants to causes related solely to the entity's interests. (See corporate foundation.)

private support: Philanthropic support from sources other than the government.

profile: See donor profile and prospect profile.

proposal: A written request or application for a gift or grant that includes why the project or program is needed, who will carry it out, and how much it will cost. (See RFP.)

prospect list: A roster of potential donors maintained by a development or campaign office.

prospect mailing: See acquisition mailing.

prospect management: See moves management.

prospect profile: A research report detailing all of the pertinent facts about a potential donor, including resources, relationships, and past giving. (See biodemographic information and donor profile.)

prospect rating: A procedure for evaluating the giving potential of various potential donors. The ratings depend on the judgments of knowledgeable people who are functioning as a special campaign committee or on assessments made on the basis of specific criteria.

prospect research: A development office's use of numerous reference sources to search for pertinent information about potential donors of all types. (See electronic screening.)

prospect screening: Identifying potential donors and assessing their ability and inclination to give through information gleaned from their peers. (See electronic screening.)

Q

quasi-endowment: Funds that are retained and invested and are either unrestricted or restricted. (See restricted gift and unrestricted gift.)

query function: A user's (or an agent's) request for information, generally as a formal request to a database or search engine.

quid pro quo: A contribution in return for which the donor receives something back, such as a premium, which could affect the tax deductibility of the donor's gift. In the original Latin, the term means "something for something." (See tax deductibility.)

R

receipt: An impersonal printed form sent to the donor that confirms a gift has been received and put toward its designation. (See acknowledgment form and acknowledgment letter.)

research: See prospect research.

restricted gift: A donation for a specified purpose as clearly stated by the donor, for example, for academic divisions, athletics, or research.

RFP: Request for proposal. A written notice listing the requirements for submitting an proposal for a gift or grant. (See proposal.)

S

sabbatical: A leave of absence from the institution, usually given to academicians, but occasionally to administrators. The leave is generally devoted to research and ultimately the production of a paper, proposal, or publication.

Section 501(c)(3): The section of the Internal Revenue Code under which charitable, religious, educational, scientific, literary, and other organizations that meet the requirements are exempt from federal income tax.

securities: Evidence of property, such as a bond or a certificate of stock. (See closely held stock, gift, and personal property.)

segmentation: The process of dividing a constituency into groups to personalize the solicitation material as much as possible, usually for a direct mail campaign. (See direct mail campaign.)

software: The instructions executed by a computer, as opposed to the physical device on which they run. (See hardware.)

solicitation mailing: See direct mail campaign.

source: Origin of the gift, such as an individual, corporation, or foundation.

steering committee: A group of leaders that bears overall responsibility for establishing a campaign or development program until a permanent campaign committee assumes this responsibility.

stewardship: A program of annual reporting to donors that tells how their gifts were used and often inspires repeat giving. (See donor relations.)

stock power: A written form giving the charitable organization the power to liquidate a gift of securities. (See securities.)

strategic plan/vision: A concise written statement of an institution's future direction.

support services: Technical areas of a development program or fundraising campaign that deal with prospect research, mailings of appeal letters, gift processing, list preparation, clerical operations, and so on. (See advancement services.)

SYBUNT: An acronym that identifies donors who gave Some Year But Unfortunately Not This. (See LYBUNT.)

T

tax deductibility: That portion of a gift that donors can deduct from their taxes, depending on their tax bracket and whether the charitable institution provided any quid pro quo services. (See quid pro quo.)

technology compatible: The ability of different systems, such as programs, file formats, protocols, and even programming languages, to work together or exchange data.

telethon: See phonathon.

testamentary: Of or pertaining to a will; bequeathed by will; done, appointed by, or founded on a testament or will. (See bequest.)

token value: A nominal price placed on a gift as a matter of form. The IRS publishes token values in its final bulletin of the year—for example, for 2007 you would check Rev. Proc. 2006-53.

U

unrestricted gift: A donation made unconditionally and without any restriction; the reverse of a restricted gift. (See restricted gift.)

user: Someone doing "real work" with the computer, operating it as a means rather than an end; or someone who applies a program, however skillfully, without getting into the internals of the program.

V

valuation: The act of estimating value or worth; setting a price; an appraisal of the value of something. (See appraisal.)

vendor: A seller; someone who exchanges goods or services for money.

VSE Survey: The Voluntary Support of Education survey published annually by the Council for Aid to Education. The survey includes detailed information on gift income, enrollment, endowment market value, and educational and general expenditures from colleges, universities, and private elementary and secondary schools. The figures are on private gifts and grants received from alumni, parents, other individuals, foundations, corporations, and other organizations. (See CAE.)

Page references in italics indicate illustrative material.

W

Y

ABOUT THE EDITOR

John H. Taylor is a leader in the field of advancement services, and has helped organizations effectively manage relationships with constituents for more than 20 years. He has worked in a variety of roles, including as editor of the first edition of *Advancement Services: Research and Technology Support for Fund Raising* (CASE, 1999), as well as consulting editor of *CASE Management and Reporting Standards* (CASE, 2004). Mr. Taylor has shared applications of advancement strategies as an instructor for Duke University, faculty for CASE conferences and symposiums, and through frequent speaking opportunities at numerous other software user, corporate, and nonprofit organization conferences.

For 14 years, Mr. Taylor led gift processing and reconciliation efforts, managed the maintenance of an accurate database of more than 400,000 records, and assumed responsibility for all aspects of security donations at Duke University. Through his guidance as director of alumni and development records, the institutional advancement staff at Duke improved gift processing productivity by more than 100 percent, developed procedures to reduce its lost alumni rate to less than 4 percent, and created an award-winning alumni website.

While serving as vice president for research and data services for CASE, Mr. Taylor managed research efforts and helped develop the CASE Matching Gifts Clearinghouse.

Mr. Taylor assists nonprofit organizations with strategic plan development and execution. His work involves auditing advancement operations, determining preparedness for comprehensive campaigns, and assessing procedures. He helps organizations design, implement and maintain effective database management policies, including pre-conversion systems assessments and post-implementation analysis. He began consulting in 1992, and serves clients through Advancement Solutions Consulting.

He manages FundSvcs.org, an online community (listserv) and information exchange site he created for advancement services. Mr. Taylor resides outside of Atlanta, Georgia.

You can reach Mr. Taylor at *john@advancement-solutions.com.*